The Politics of Job Creation
in Economic Crisis

The Politics of Job Creation in Economic Crisis

Copyright ⓒ 2023 Jong Sun Lee
Printed in Seoul, Republic of Korea

All rights reserved. No part of this volume may be reproduced in any form or by any means, except for brief quotations, without written permission from BAIKSAN Publishing House

BAIKSAN Publishing House
885 Tongil-ro, Eunpyong-gu, Seoul 03329, Republic of Korea

E-mail:bshj@chol.com

First Printing:September 5, 2023
ISBN   978-89-7327-850-3 93330

The Politics of Job Creation
in Economic Crisis

by

Jong Sun Lee

BAIKSAN Publishing House

Contents

PREFACE · 13

ACKNOWLEDGEMENTS · 22

CHAPTER 1 INTRODUCTION · 25

CHAPTER 2 REVIEW OF LITERATURE ON ALMPs · 31

2.1 Concepts of ALMPs ·· 31
    2.1.1 The Origin and Concepts of ALMPs ································ 31
    2.1.2 Measures and Scope of ALMPs ···································· 32
    2.1.3 Two Pathways of ALMPs: High Road or Low Road? ·············· 34

2.2 Theoretical Approaches to ALMPs ··· 37
    2.2.1 Interest-Based Approaches ··· 38
    2.2.2 Institutionalist Approaches ·· 40
    2.2.3 Idea-Oriented Approaches: Coordination & Diffusion Theory ······ 43
    2.2.4 Analytic Framework ·· 45

CHAPTER 3 RESEARCH DESIGN · 49

3.1 Hypotheses and Method ·· 51
    3.1.1 Hypotheses ··· 51
    3.1.2 Method ·· 56

3.1.3 Datasets ·· 60

3.2 Case Study ·· 63

CHAPTER 4   TRENDS AND CHANGES OF EXPENDITURE OF ALMPs - 67

4.1 Trends and Changes in Expenditure of ALMPs ·· 67

    4.1.1 Welfare Regimes and Expenditures of ALMPs ································· 67

    4.1.2 Expenditure of Training ·· 71

    4.1.3 Public Employment Services and Employment Incentives ················ 73

    4.1.4 Direct job creation and Start-up incentives ··································· 76

    4.1.5 Trends of ALMPs within Welfare Regimes ·································· 80

4.2 Determinants of ALMPs ·· 84

4.3 Summary ·· 91

CHAPTER 5   SWEDEN: ECONOMIC CRISIS AND ALMPs - 97

5.1 Introduction ··· 97

5.2 Economic Crisis in Sweden ·· 99

    5.2.1 Pre-2008 Economic Crisis: Formation and Change of The Sweden model · 99

    5.2.2 2008 Economic Crisis ··· 109

5.3 Responses to the Economic Crisis ·· 112

    5.3.1 Political Responses ·· 112

    5.3.2 Economic Responses ·· 115

    5.3.3 Labor Responses ··· 120

5.4 Labor Market Policies for Job Creation ·· 128

    5.4.1 ALMPs in the 2008 global economic crisis ································ 128

    5.4.2 Main Measures of ALMPs ·· 133

5.4.3	Labor Market Policies on Youth Unemployment	140
5.4.4	Job Policies for Immigrants	144
5.4.5	Trends and Changes of ALMPs	148

5.5 Summary ·········· 152

CHAPTER 6   GERMANY: ECONOMIC CRISIS AND HARTZ REFORMS - 155

6.1 Introduction ·········· 155

6.2 Economic Crisis in Germany ·········· 156

6.2.1	Pre-2008 Economic Crisis	156
6.2.2	The Great Recession and the 2008 Economic Crisis	159

6.3 Responses to the 2008 Economic Crisis ·········· 162

6.3.1	Political Responses	162
6.3.2	Economic Responses	166
6.3.3	Labor Responses	167

6.4 Labor Policy for Job Creation ·········· 170

6.4.1	Policies for youth Job Creation	170
6.4.2	Hartz Reforms: Welfare-to-Work Reforms in Germany	173
6.4.3	Youth Guarantee and Job Training System	188
6.4.4	Evaluations of the Hartz Reforms	192
6.4.5	Trends and Changes of ALMPs	196

6.5 Summary ·········· 200

CHAPTER 7   KOREA: ECONOMIC CRISIS AND JOB CREATION POLICIES - 205

7.1 Introduction ·········· 205

7.2 Economic Crises in Korea: Causes and Progress ·········· 207

7.2.1　The 1997 IMF Economic Crisis ·· 207

7.2.2　The 2008 Global Economic Crisis ·· 209

7.3 Responses to the Economic Crisis ··· 212

7.3.1　Political Responses ·· 212

7.3.2　Economic Responses ··· 218

7.3.3　Labor Responses ·· 221

7.4 Labor Policies for Job Creation ·· 225

7.4.1　IMF Economic Crisis and Expansion of Employment Insurance System ·· 225

7.4.2　The 2008 Global Economic Crisis and Changes in Job Policy ······ 230

7.4.3　Trends and Changes of ALMPs ·· 248

7.5 Summary ·· 251

CHAPTER 8　CONCLUSION · 255

8.1 Analytic Results of Trends and Changes on ALMPs ························· 256

8.2 Findings of Case Studies on the Research Puzzle ···························· 259

8.3 Comparing Analysis of Job Policies in the 2008 Economic Crisis ·········· 263

8.4 Politics of Job Creation and Policymaking ·· 268

8.5 Theoretical Implications ··· 271

APPENDIX A　*Summary of Variables* · 278

APPENDIX B　*OECD Classification of Labor Market Programs* · 279

REFERENCES · 281

INDEX · 293

LIST OF FIGURES

Figure 2.1	Types of Active Labor Market Policy	35
Figure 2.2	The Process of Policy Choices & Key Factors	46
Figure 4.1.	Expenditures of ALMP in OECD countries: 1985-2017	68
Figure 4.2.	Comparing ALMP Expenditures by Welfare Regime: 1985-2017	69
Figure 4.3.	Comparing ALMP Expenditure in OECD countries: 1985-2017	70
Figure 4.4.	Comparing the Expenditure of Training in OECD countries: 1985-2017	71
Figure 4.5.	Comparing Training Expenditure in Case Countries: 1985-2017	72
Figure 4.6.	Comparing the Expenditure of PES in Case countries: 1985-2017	74
Figure 4.7.	Comparing the Expenditure of PES by Welfare Regime: 1985-2017	74
Figure 4.8.	Comparing the Expenditure of Employment Incentives: 1985-2017	75
Figure 4.9.	Comparing Employment Incentives in Case countries: 1985-2017	76
Figure 4.10.	Comparing Direct Job Creation by Welfare Regimes: 1985-2017	77
Figure 4.11.	Comparing Direct Job Creation in Case countries: 1985-2017	78
Figure 4.12.	Comparing Start-up Incentives by Welfare Regimes: 1985-2017	79
Figure 4.13.	Comparing Start-up Incentives in Case countries: 1985-2017	79
Figure 4.14.	Trends of ALMPs by types in SMCs: 1985-2017	81
Figure 4.15.	Trends of ALMPs by types in CMCs: 1985-2017	82
Figure 4.16.	Trends of ALMPs by types in LMCs: 1985-2017	83
Figure 5.1.	The Swedish Model	100
Figure 5.2.	Change of Swedish Industrial Structure	105
Figure 5.3.	Changes in Real GDP Growth and Unemployment Rates	107
Figure 5.4.	Changes in GDP Growth and Unemployment Rates	110
Figure 5.5.	Industrial conflicts, Sweden, 1985–2014	121
Figure 5.6.	Organization rates and Coverage ratio	122
Figure 5.7.	Unemployment Rate, 16-64 Years of Age	144
Figure 5.8.	Comparing Expenditure of Unemployment support and ALMPs in Sweden: 1985-2017	149
Figure 5.9.	Trends in Expenditure of ALMPs in Sweden: 1985-2017	150
Figure 6.1.	Growth and Unemployment rate in Germany: 2000 - 2018	157

Figure 6.2.	Comparison of Employment Rate Changes in Major OECD Countries	161
Figure 6.3.	Comparing Expenditure of Unemployment Support and ALMPs in Germany: 1985-2016	197
Figure 6.4.	Trends in Expenditure of ALMPs in Germany: 1985-2017	199
Figure 7.1	Real Growth & Unemployment rate in Korea: 1970 – 2012	208
Figure 7.2.	Trends of Unemployment Benefits and Support for Employment stability & Vocational competency development	228
Figure 7.3.	Expenditure of ALMPs in Korea: 2000-2012	249

LIST OF TABLES

Table 3.1	Datasets	61
Table 3.2	Classification of Welfare Regimes	62
Table 3.3	Comparing Institutions and Organizational Structures of Three Countries	64
Table 4.1	Results of Regression of Panel Data: Determinants of ALMPs	88
Table 5.1.	Trends in union density by industries, Sweden: 1990 - 2014	123
Table 5.2.	ALMP Programs in Sweden: 2008 – 2013	129
Table 5.3.	Participants in ALMP programs: 2008 – 2013 (percent)	130
Table 6.1.	Comparison of Unemployment Rates in Major EU Countries: 2006-2012	160
Table 6.2.	Policies of Agenda 2010	173
Table 6.3.	The Hartz Reforms	175
Table 6.4.	Reform of the Unemployment Benefit System	182
Table 6.5.	Unemployment Benefits System Reform and Change	186
Table 6.6.	Percentage of part-time workers in Germany (%)	195
Table 7.1.	Comparing the 2008 Economic Crisis with 1997 IMF Economic Crisis	213
Table 7.10.	State of Youth Internship at SMEs: 2009 ~ 2015	243
Table 7.11.	Process of Social Service Job Projects: 2003-2009	245
Table 7.12.	Status of Participation in Job Sharing (as of October 31, 2009)	247
Table 7.13.	Budget for Job Policies for 2008-2010	250
Table 7.2.	Structural Reforms of Four Sectors after IMF Economic Crisis	214
Table 7.3.	Liquidation Plan of Insolvent Large Enterprises in June 1999	219
Table 7.4.	Status and System of Employment Security Project: 2014	226
Table 7.5.	Types and Causes of Blind Spots in Employment Insurance	229
Table 7.6.	Comparing the Job Policies in the Economic Crises	231
Table 7.7.	Employment Services with Activation Programs	236
Table 7.8.	The Number of Participants and Employment Success Rate by Employment Success Package	239
Table 7.9.	Types of Youth Internship	242
Table 8.1.	Job Policies and Comparison of Three Countries (Summary)	264

PREFACE

Recent periodic economic crises and unemployment have raised awareness of the importance of better jobs and related policies. Job creation in times of economic crisis becomes even more pressing and politically charged. When faced with economic recessions, governments and politicians are tasked with the formidable challenge of stimulating their economies and ensuring the creation of sustainable employment opportunities. The rapid digital transformation following the global financial crisis in 2008 and the spread of the COVID-19 pandemic in 2019 have brought about new waves of job crises. OECD countries are making efforts to achieve sustainable economic growth and create new jobs. Active labor market policies (ALMPs) are identified as key strategies for increasing employment in most OECD countries. ALMPs have broadly been accepted by politicians and economists across the ideological spectrum, from liberalism and conservatism to social democracy. However, ALMPs in these OECD countries are different and more specific, and conditional based on the politics and institutions for job creation in each country.

The main puzzle in this book is about the different pathways of job creation before and after the 2008 economic crisis. This book aims to examine how and why countries chose ALMPs in response to the 2008 economic crisis and explain the politics of job creation in which the political dynamics among social stakeholders influence or structure the policy-making process on employment and job creation during times of economic crisis. This book tries to use both quantitative and qualitative analysis (case studies) by focusing on the process of policy choices and expenditure data analysis. This book quantitatively explores cross-national variations in total expenditures and changes in the distribution of spending on several types of ALMPs over time. It also tries to analyze causal factors that have resulted in differences in expenditures on ALMPs, including partisan control, bargaining system, union density, and neoliberal influence.

For this, the book consists of two parts. In the first part, this study analyzes the expenditures and trends of ALMPs in the OECD countries based on the updated pooling of OECD datasets (1985-2018). While quantitative analyses can reveal forces that have led to the adoption and changes in labor market policies, there is still insufficient understanding of how domestic politics has influenced the adoption of various ALMPs. Therefore, the second part seeks to provide an in-depth understanding of how and why the domestic policy process has shaped the adoption of ALMPs, given the economic situations, state structure, and institutions.

The case studies focus on the policy choices of three OECD countries: Sweden, Germany, and Korea. These countries belong to different welfare regime types in Esping-Anderson's classification (1990). However, they have in common succeeded in rapid economic development based on an export-oriented economy. Also, these countries have quickly recovered from the shock of the 2008 global economic crisis. As the background of economic success, these countries' labor market policies and job strategies are pointed out. Nevertheless, the types of ALMPs among these countries are somewhat different. Therefore, it is necessary to look at where differences in ALMPs come from.

Based on the research findings, this book presents theoretical implications regarding job expenditures and policies related to these countries. In general, the ALMP expenditures of Social Democratic Market Countries (SMCs) as a percentage of GDP are generally higher than those of Conservative Market Countries (CMCs) or Liberal Market Countries (LMCs), while the spending of ALMPs has a relationship with economic downturns and crises. Interestingly, the expenditure on training has gradually decreased except for the recent economic crisis among OECD countries. Although the spending on training in CMCs does not reach the level of SMCs, it has remained constant. While the overall expenditures on training have decreased, the spending on Public Employment System (PES) and subsidies such as employment incentives and subsidized employment have been growing. However, in the period of economic crisis, particularly, the Korean government has considerably relied on direct job creation, unlike countries in SMCs and CMCs.

The left party or left-wing government has positively affected the expenditure of ALMPs. Also, institutional factors such as union density rate and wage-setting coordination system have a positive relationship with ALMPs' expenditure in SMCs. Expenditures on Training in SMCs are still higher than in other types of welfare states. Sweden was similar until the early 2000s, but after the mid-2000s, training spending fell significantly, while employment incentive spending increased. In Sweden, the decline in spending on vocational training has to do with the emergence of a right-wing coalition government in 2006. The Swedish government emphasized the supply side of the labor market based on neoliberal policies and cut off the 'Plus Job' policy, some employment subsidies, and unemployment benefits. The recent increase in employment incentives spending in Sweden is also a strategic choice in terms of responding to neoliberal influences. Even after the Social Democratic Party's government took power in 2014, the budget for vocational training has not increased. It is analyzed that the changes in the industrial structure according to the 4th Industrial Revolution make the existing vocational training not valid.

In Germany, training spending occupied the highest proportion among the types of ALMPs. However, the expenditure on public employment services (PES) has recently outpaced the spending on vocational training. Especially, the expenditures of PES since the mid-2000s have been higher than spending on vocational training in Germany, which has a strong vocational training system traditionally. The Hartz reforms resulted in the radical change of labor market policy, including the reorganization of the Federal Labor Office (Federal Labor Agency), installation of Job Centers, amendment of the Dispatch Worker Act, and tax benefits for low-wage work (Mini-job, Midi-job), based on the idea of 'Welfare to Work' reforms (Agenda 2010). In 2008, the Merkel government strengthened the job placement function of the Federal Labor Agency, provided subsidies for curtailing working hours, and extended worker support programs with an emphasis on employment. The tradition of labor management and co-determination at the corporate level worked positively to overcome the unemployment crisis caused by the 2008 global economic crisis, keeping cooperative labor-management relations over the reduction of working hours, the system of working hours account, and the introduction of short-time work allowances. The mini-jobs and mid-jobs have made achievements in improving the quantitative indicators of the labor market through the flexibilization of the labor market and the creation of jobs, but they have problems in terms of job quality, such as the expansion of low-wage workers and exclusion from social security systems. In short, the evaluation of the Hartz reform can be summarized by the quantitative improvement of the employment indicators and the qualitative deterioration of employment. In particular, the expansion of part-time employment contributed to reducing the unemployment rate by promoting low-wage work. However, the growth in non-regular workers has been evaluated to have a negligible effect on the reentry of the unemployed into the regular labor market. Recently, the German government has introduced measures, including the introduction of the statutory minimum wage system and strengthened regulations on dispatch work. Therefore, ALMPs in Germany have focused on strategies for activating the unemployed, including job placement and matching services. The expenditure of PES has rapidly increased after the 2008 economic crisis.

Korea relied on direct job creation in the 1997 IMF and 2008 global economic crises. Korea's active labor market policy has been pursuing only short-term, temporary policy effects rather than long-term plans. The reasons the Korean government has relied on direct job creation are twofold. First, these policy measures have functioned as a kind of social safety net in Korea, where the social welfare system was not properly set up, and they have contributed to protecting the livelihoods of low-income people. Second, public work programs have stabilized employment indicators by lowering the unemployment rate through the creation of short-term jobs in the public sector. However, these programs were temporary measures to cope with economic crises, and the issue of job sustainability remained unresolved.

In response to the 2008 economic crisis, OECD countries have recently increased expenditures on PES and employment incentives rather than spending on job training. Most countries have preferred short-term job creation measures over long-term human resource development policies. The case study also shows differences in the expenditures and types of ALMPs that the three countries adopted in response to the economic crisis. Variations in ALMPs' spending in these OECD countries were specific and conditional based on the politics of job creation in each country.

Based on the results, OECD countries may be more likely to take the low road instead of the high road. If the 'high road' is a pathway that generates high-skilled workers and well-paying jobs, the 'low road' is a pathway that primarily generates low-skilled workers, low-wage, and temporary jobs. High-skilled jobs require workers to perform analytical and cognitively demanding tasks, while low-skilled jobs demand workers to perform routine and simple tasks. Therefore, countries heading toward the high road are more likely to adopt ALMPs directed toward skill upgrading and human capital development through lifetime training (or retraining) and higher education. Jobs on the low road are mainly replaced through short-term training provided by the employer for specific tasks in that firm. In this case, OECD countries are more likely to rely on short-term and temporary ALMPs, such as job-matching services and job creation policies through public work.

The results in this book show that in OECD countries, spending on short-term and pro-market-based policies such as PES and employment incentives has increased, rather than increasing spending on traditional vocational training. There are two possibilities why this has happened. First, in the face of economic crises, each government is more likely to prefer job matching or incentives to maintain employment due to the short-term policy effects. Second, the need for traditional manufacturing-oriented vocational training has been relatively reduced due to the recent digital transformation and the transition to the knowledge service industry. As Bengtsson argues, "Up-skilling might not have the same effect today as it did in the mid-20th century" (Bengtsson 2014, 67). Up-skilling in knowledge-based economies requires more cost and time than job training during the post-war industrial development period. In short, traditional vocational training requires significant budgets and training hours. Extreme changes in the labor market structure favor short-term job placement and job matching over longer-term vocational training, which requires more policy attention and spending. The main reason the proportion of vocational training spending in ALMPs has significantly decreased seems to be a change in the industrial structure and the deepening effect of neoliberalism in the 2000s. The transition from manufacturing to service economies has largely affected the expenditure on training in OECD countries. Jobs in service economies are typically organized around quite simple and/or narrow tasks, often highly routinized. In this case, countries are more likely to rely on short-term and temporary ALMPs, such as job-matching services and public work, rather than vocational training, which requires more time and resources. Most countries are seeing a gradual increase in spending on government subsidies, such as short-term, pro-market-based PES and employment incentives and subsidies, instead of financial spending on vocational training. This clearly shows that neoliberal economic ideology has a major impact on ALMPs in OECD countries. Under the neoliberal economic system, governments and corporations tend to emphasize flexibility and efficiency within the labor market. Therefore, they prefer short-term education and job matching rather than vocational training, which requires a certain amount of time and social cost. As the industrial structure changes from traditional manufacturing to the service industry, the type of ALMP is also shifting to financial spending on short-term employment services and employment incentives rather than financial expenditure on vocational training.

However, short-term, and pro-market-oriented policy measures such as job matching and employment incentives have produced negative consequences such as low-wage job creation, job instability, and social inequality. This book critically examines such neoliberal tendencies (low road) in recent active labor market policies and emphasizes the importance of social investment policies for the high road. In short, current trends in ALMPs are more likely to exacerbate job insecurity and income inequality in OECD countries. Therefore, ALMPs need to be supported by social investment policies targeting higher education, the amelioration of social inequality, and the protection of increasing atypical labor.

As highlighted in the ILO's report on job creation for a brighter future, commemorating its 100th anniversary, efforts to solve job problems and address social inequality issues in times of economic crises require social dialogue among key social stakeholders. With the recent digital transformation, the advent of the Fourth Industrial Revolution, and the normalization of remote work after the COVID-19 pandemic, the possibility of job crises looms larger. However, even the crisis of jobs due to such digital transformation and the Fourth Industrial Revolution can have both positive and negative effects on human labor, depending on how we respond to these changes. If we can reduce working hours and share jobs despite economic and job crises, human life has been improved.

In the current capitalist economy, digital transformation and Artificial Intelligence (AI) can significantly reduce the number of jobs. However, if we can find policy solutions that allow for reduced working hours and job sharing, we can sufficiently overcome the problem of job crises. Therefore, the problem of job crises in times of economic crises depends on how we create institutional frameworks in the political realm to confront them, which can be referred to as the "politics of job creation."

Ultimately, responding to job crises in times of economic crises and creating new jobs can be seen as issues of policy matters in the economic domain and simultaneously as political choices for major social stakeholders. In short, the question of whether to take the high-road or low-road path concerning job policies depends on the policy choices of social stakeholders in the politics of job creation.

Finally, I sincerely hope that this book will contribute to the formulation of better job creation policies in the future.

Jong Sun Lee
Korea University, Seoul

ACKNOWLEDGEMENTS

This book is an outcome of my long research journey on labor and job creation policies. It would have been impossible without the personal and practical support from numerous people. My sincere gratitude goes to my family, friends, and research colleagues for their support and patience over the last few years.

I am deeply thankful for my esteemed adviser, Professor Michael Ensley at Kent State University. I could not have succeeded without his invaluable support and guidance. Besides my advisor, I would like to thank the members of my thesis committee, Professors Andrew Barnes, Casey Boyd-Swan, and Dong Hun Kwak. Their critical analyses and warmhearted advice are greatly appreciated. I am also incredibly grateful to Professor Mark Cassell and Terri Murphy in the department of politics at Kent State University. They helped me in various ways during my course of studies.

My gratitude is also extended to all the research fellows and friends for their help, support, and interest. In particular, I would also like to express my deepest gratitude to Professor Gil-sung Park, Dae-yop Cho of the Department of Sociology at Korea University, and Professor Seung-rok Park of the Department of Economics at Hansung University. I would also like to thank Mr. Sung-yun Hwang for reading the thesis draft and offering suggestions for improvement.

My indescribable thanks go to my parents and family. In particular, I thankfully acknowledge the supports from my wife and son, Ae ran Choi and Taehan. Through their love, patience, supports, and unwavering belief in me, I've been able to complete this work.

Lastly, until the publication of this book, I deeply appreciate their efforts and contributions, Kim Chul-Mi, the president of BAIKSAN Publishing House, and the editorial team.

Chapter 1

INTRODUCTION

Sustainable employment and new job creation are significant policy issues in the age of globalization, especially in hard times of economic crisis. Severe economic shocks may generate substantial social problems, including high unemployment and fiscal crises, and undermine the established institutions and rules of the welfare state. Economic crisis may also provide the necessary political and economic conditions for radical welfare state reforms (Taylor-Gooby 2013; Vis 2009; Shahidi, 2015). The reason that this study focuses on the Great Recession of 2008-2010 is that unemployment reactions to economic variations were greater than the other economic crises that occurred after the Great Depression (Erhel and Levionnois 2013). Previous economic crises were mainly regional and local crises in semi-peripheral countries, including Mexico in 1994-95, Asian countries in 1997-1998, Russia in 1998, and Argentina in 2001. The effects of the economic crisis could be contained without causing a major impact on the core states. However, the 2008 economic crisis originated in the United States (US), one of the core countries. It has affected all countries, as well as all of the stock markets, banks, and financial institutions in the world. The global banking system and financial markets normalized with international cooperation and the bailout of the US, which has the dollar as the key currency. However, unemployment in OECD countries has not improved in a while or until now in some countries.

Since the 2008 economic crisis, most OECD countries have experienced reducing manufacturing jobs and jobless growth in the domestic economy (Summers 2015). The technology (computer-based automation) and structural changes in the labor market have been the main reasons for joblessness growth. In particular, the changes from manufacturing to service economies and deepening economic competition in the global market bring new challenges for welfare regimes in employment growth, wage equality, and budgetary constraint (Iversen and Wren 1998; Scharpf 1997). Facing these challenges, EU members and OECD countries have tried to reform their welfare system and labor market. The reforms have proceeded in two different directions. While passive welfare budgets, such as unemployment benefits, have been shrinking, active labor market policies to help the unemployed get back to work have been prioritized (Hemerijck 2013; Becker 2011; Bonoli and Natali 2012; Morel, Palier, and Palme 2012; OECD 1994). During the 1990s, the OECD and European Union (EU) spurred the adoption of reforms in OECD countries (Armingeon 2007) based on the Jobs Study (1994; 2006) and the European Employment Strategy (EES 1997).

Nowadays, active labor market policies (ALMPs) are identified as key strategies for increasing employment in most OECD countries (OECD 2006; Bonoli 2010). ALMPs have broadly been accepted by liberal and conservative politicians as well as liberal economists because they can provide social security "without necessarily resorting to redistributive measures and without changing established social hierarchies" (Armingeon 2007, 907). However, a comprehensive study of the trends and changes of ALMPs is relatively rare in political science and public policy, except for the studies evaluating the effectiveness of each of the individual ALMPs (Hetschko et al. 2020; Kluve and Schmit 2002; Card et al. 2010; Boone and Van Ours 2009; Layard and Nickell 2011; and van Vliet 2010, 2011).

This study is designed to compare and analyze the changes and recent trends of ALMPs in OECD countries and explain the role of domestic partisan politics in shaping those changes. There are several reasons a systematic analysis and update of the research on ALMPs is needed. First, the overall level of spending on ALMPs is not converging between welfare regimes, as neoliberal reasoning would predict (OECD 1994; 2006). Why has this prediction of convergence not happened? Although ALMP is favored by both social democratic and liberal politicians, there are still significant cross-national differences and domestic political conflicts regarding the scope and appropriate mix of ALMPs (Armingeon 2007). If the spending on ALMPs varies between the OECD countries, how can these variations be accounted for? In other words, if there is a similarity or difference in the expenditure and/or type of ALMPs between welfare regimes or among countries within them, how can we explain it? What are the determinant factors that resulted in such similarity or difference?

Second, the 2008 Great Recession has brought new challenges to labor markets in OECD countries. Thus, understanding how OECD countries have attempted to address unemployment and whether recent global economic pressures have pushed governments to adopt similar policy responses are pertinent questions. The main puzzle this study addresses is to explain the different pathways of job creation before and after the 2008 economic crisis in terms of the mix of high-road and low-road ALMPs. If the 'high road' is a pathway that generates a large number of high-skilled workers, well-paying jobs, the 'low road' is another pathway that primarily generates low-skilled workers, low-wage jobs, and gig jobs (Milberg and Houston 2005, Wright and Rogers 2010). High-skilled jobs require workers to perform analytical and cognitively demanding tasks, while low-skilled jobs demand workers to perform routine and simple tasks. Therefore, the countries headed to the 'high road' are more likely to adopt ALMPs directed towards skill-upgrading and human capital development through lifetime training (or retraining) and higher education. Jobs on the 'low road' are mainly replaced through short-term training provided by the employer for the narrow tasks in that specific firm. In this case, the countries are more likely to rely on short-term and temporary ALMPs, such as job-matching services and job creation policy through public work.

The third reason to revisit the scholarship on ALMPs is that, while quantitative analysis have and can reveal forces that have led to adoption and changes in labor market policies, there is still insufficient understanding of how domestic politics has influenced that adoption of various ALMPs. This study seeks to provide an in-depth understanding of how and why the domestic policy process has shaped the adoption of ALMPs, given the economic situations and state structure and institutions (Gourevitch 1986; Glassner and Keune 2010). In particular, there has been inadequate attention on the role of political parties and social interest groups(i.e., workers' and employers' organizations) in explaining the response to the economic crisis of 2008 and why OECD countries have adopted different types of ALMPs.

To answer these research questions, this study will quantitatively explore cross-national variations in total expenditures and changes in the distribution of spending on the different types of ALMPs over time. To assess the factors that resulted in differences in the expenditures on ALMPs, this study examines several potential causal factors including neoliberal influence, changes in industrial structure, partisan control, bargaining system, and union density. This study will analyze how the expenditures and trends of ALMPs have changed in the period before and after the 2008 economic crisis.

While this study focuses on the trends and changes in ALMPs using quantitative data and methods, these analyses of the changes in ALMPs will be supplemented by case studies of Sweden, Germany, and Korea. According to Esping-Anderson's classification (1990), these countries belong to different welfare state types. However, they have succeeded in rapid economic development based on an export-oriented economy. Also, these countries have quickly recovered from the shock of the 2008 global economic crisis. In the background of economic success, the labor market policies and job strategies adopted by these countries are pointed out. Nevertheless, the types of ALMPs among these countries are somewhat different. Therefore, it is necessary to look at where differences in ALMPs come from. The case studies on the policy choices that these countries have made in response to the economic crisis of 2008 will demonstrate how and why domestic partisan politics shaped the type of ALMPs adopted.

In short, this study will explore the politics of job creation in OECD countries in response to the 2008 economic crisis. The politics of job creation are defined as the political dynamics of social actors and their social consequences in the process of policymaking over job creation in times of economic crisis. This study will argue that variations on the expenditures of ALMPs in OECD countries will be more specific and conditional per the politics of job creation in each country. However, this study will also argue that although the total expenditure for ALMPs is still not converging among OECD countries, the recent trend of types of ALMP has been partly similar in these countries.

This study will show that in response to the economic crisis, many OECD countries have recently increased expenditures on employment incentives and public employment services (PES) rather than spending on the job training for human capital development. In other words, they have recently preferred short-term job creation measures instead of long-term based human resource development policies. Therefore, this study will argue that the OECD countries may be more likely to enter the pathway of low-road policies of short-term job creation instead of the high-road policies of human resource development. At the same time, this study will argue that recent trends in ALMPs will likely increase and reproduce job insecurity and income inequality in OECD countries. This study will suggest that ALMP needs to be supported by social investment policies such as high education, early childcare, amelioration of social inequality, and protection of increasing atypical labor.

The next chapter will review theories and research on ALMPs. Chapter Three will present the research design, including the hypothesis and analytic method. Chapter Four will discuss the trends and changes in the expenditure of ALMPs, based on the general analytic results and findings on ALMPs in the OECD countries. Chapter Five will examine the responses to the 2008 economic crisis and job creation policies in Sweden. Chapter Six will analyze the Hartz reforms and policies for job creation in Germany. Chapter Seven will examine the economic crisis and job creation policies in Korea. Chapter Eight will conclude with a discussion of theoretical implications and lessons concerning ALMPs in OECD countries.

Chapter 2

REVIEW OF LITERATURE ON ALMPs

This study aims to analyze the politics of job creation and its policies in times of economic crisis. In this study, the term "politics of job creation" refers to the political dynamics between social actors that influence or structure the policymaking process regarding employment and job creation during times of economic crisis. The policies can be seen as social and political consequences of this process. A key strategy in the politics of job creation is the active labor market policy(ALMP). ALMP is recognized as the crucial policy for unemployment and new job creation in most OECD countries. This chapter will review the concepts and measures of ALMPs. Next, the theoretical approaches for analyzing ALMPs are examined.

2.1 Concepts of ALMPs

2.1.1 The Origin and Concepts of ALMPs

The basic rationale for ALMP is to help the unemployed get back to work rather than provide them with income support and thereby risk prolonging unemployment (OECD 1994, Armingeon 2007). However, ALMPs have different origins and take different shapes in OECD countries (Bonoli 2010). ALMPs have developed in Sweden as an essential part of the social-democratic strategy, consisting of three policy pillars with the solidarity wage policy and social security system. Though it started as a genuinely social democratic policy, it has been accepted by liberal and conservative politicians as well as liberal economists, as it also fits into a liberal ideology (Amingeon 2007).

Therefore, the concept of ALMP also varies according to scholars (Swenson 2002, King 1995, Torfing 1999, Taylor-Gooby 2004, Barbier 2004, and Bonoli 2010). For instance, Swenson (2002) focuses on ALMPs developed in Sweden by financing extensive vocational training programs. However, King (1995) used the term "active" to describe the workfare approach in the liberal market countries (LMCs), which combines placement services with stronger work incentives, time limits on recipiency, benefit reductions, and the use of sanctions. Torfing (1999) distinguishes between "offensive" and "defensive" workfare to describe the Danish variant of activation. Unlike in the United States, in Denmark, offensive workfare relies on improving skills and empowerment rather than on sanctions and benefit reduction. Instead of these terms, Taylor-Gooby (2004) uses the terms "positive" and "negative" activation. In addition to the two types of "liberal and universal activation," Barbier (2004) also recognizes that the third type of activation might exist in continental Europe, one that puts more emphasis on social inclusion and less on actual labor market participation.

2.1.2 Measures and Scope of ALMPs

ALMP aims at helping unemployed people through "enhancing labor market mobility and adjustment, facilitating the redeployment of workers to productive activities, and generally enabling people to seize new job opportunities" (Armingeon 2007, 905).

The OECD 1994 Jobs Study suggests two key recommendations to resolve a high and persistent unemployment problem: addressing unemployment and related benefits and promoting active labor market programs. ALMP consists of the public employment services and benefits administration, training, job rotation and job sharing, employment incentives, supported employment and rehabilitation, direct job creation, and start-up incentives (OECD 2013). In short, ALMP is based on the activation strategy to promote (more or less obligatory) the participation of people dependent on unemployment benefits or social assistance in work (van Berkel and Borghi 2008).

In response to the economic crises, the OECD countries have tried to promote employment in many ways, such as providing tax breaks, subsidizing companies or industries, investing in vocational education and job training, etc. It can be defined these measures as a labor market policy. Therefore, the labor market policy consists of active labor market policies(ALMPs) and passive measures such as unemployment benefits and early retirement allowance. At the same time, the labor market policies are supported by fiscal policy in the states.

This study will specifically focus on the expenditure of ALMPs rather than the general labor market policies. ALMPs focus on the long-term unemployed who lost their jobs and/or will lose them shortly or who find it difficult to gain employment given their current conditions. In general, ALMPs have focused on two labor market transitions from (1) unemployment to employment; and (2) inactivity to employment for the disabled, inactive spouses, and individuals with family responsibilities. According to the OECD classification of labor market programs, ALMPs consist of several programs as follows: Public employment services and administration, training, job rotation and job sharing, employment incentives, supported employment and rehabilitation, direct job creation, and start-up incentives (See Appendix 1).

Due to the diversity and complexity of policy measures, it is not easy to figure out the characteristics of ALMPs in the OECD countries. Therefore, this study will analyze the trends in ALMPs based on the OECD classification and official expenditure data, as the OECD datasets for ALMPs since the 1980s are the most reliable and accurate encapsulation of ALMPs. At the same time, to analyze where differences in ALMPs come from, it will explore how and why the politics of job creation shaped the type of ALMPs adopted.

2.1.3 Two Pathways of ALMPs: High Road or Low Road?

Regarding analyzing ALMPs, this study will utilize Bonoli's typology (Bonoli 2010) and the concept of two pathways of capitalism (Milberg and Houston 2005; Wright and Rogers 2010): "high road" or "low road." Based on the pro-market employment orientation of policy and its emphasis on human capital investment, Bonoli (2010) suggests a new typology of ALMPs: incentive reinforcement, employment assistance, occupation, and human capital investment or up-skilling (See Table 2.1).

According to Bonoli, the first type of ALMP, "incentive reinforcement," refers to measures that aim to strengthen work incentives for benefit recipients. The second type, "employment assistance," includes placement services or job search programs that increase the likelihood of a jobless person establishing contact with a potential employer. The third type of ALMP, "occupation," consists of job creation and work experience programs in the public or non-profit sector. Finally, ALMPs can rely on "up-skilling" or providing vocational training to jobless people (Bonoli 2010). This typology is very useful to understand the development of ALMPs.

Figure 2.1 Types of Active Labor Market Policy

		Investment in human capital		
		None	**Weak**	**Strong**
Promarket employment orientation	**Weak**	(Passive benefits)	**Occupation** Job creation schemes in the public sector Non-employment related training programs	(Basic education)
	Strong	**Incentive reinforcement** Tax credits in-work benefits Time limits on recipiency Benefit reductions Benefit conditionality	**Employment assistance** Placement services Job subsidies Counseling Job search programs	**Upskilling** Job-related vocational training

Source: Bonoli (2010). p.441

According to Bonoli, ALMPs have different origins and take different shapes across time and countries. For instance, the key type of ALMP was up-skilling in the 1950s and 1960s, direct occupation in the oil shocks of 1973 to 1975, and mixes of incentive reinforcement and employment assistance since the mid-1990s. In particular, the mid-1990s signaled a new reorientation of ALMP in OECD counties. Since the 1990s, unemployment was essentially the result of economic globalization and an excess supply of low-skill labor. Low-skilled workers have faced substantial work disincentives due to jobless growth, a lower earning potential, and unemployment benefit or other welfare subsidies. Therefore, new emphases of ALMPs have put on the work incentives and employment assistance for encouraging and facilitating reentry of unemployed workers into work (Bonoli 2010).

Since the 2008 Great Recession, the OECD countries have been faced with high unemployment rates again. There is also much greater importance for the ALMPs. Today, ALMPs include several policy measures to bring the unemployed workers back to work by providing various mixed types of labor market programs: public employment services (PES), job training, job rotation and job sharing, employment incentives, supported employment and rehabilitation, direct job creation, and start-up incentives (OECD 2011). As Bonoli (2010) argues, ALMPs have developed in the interaction between the changing economic context and existing labor market policies.

In explaining the changes in the trend of ALMPs before and after the 2008 economic crisis, the concept of two pathways of job creation is considered in this study (Milberg and Houston 2005; Wright and Rogers 2010). If 'high road' is a pathway of job creation, in which it generates many high-skills, well-paying jobs, "low road" is another pathway of job creation that primarily generates low-skills, low-wages, and temporary jobs (Wright and Rogers 2010). The jobs in high road require high levels of skills that workers perform analytical and cognitively demanding tasks. Therefore, the 'high road' is directed towards skill-upgrading and human capital development through lifetime training (or retraining) and higher education. Instead, low-skilled jobs demand workers to perform routine and cognitively undemanding tasks. The jobs on the low road are mainly replaced through short-term training provided by the employer for the narrow specific tasks in that particular firm. Therefore, the 'low road' capitalism is directed towards wage moderation, less training, and stronger work incentives. Indeed, in this case, the expanding of ALMPs would be allocated more for public employment services, employment incentives, or public work than for vocational training and life-long education. As a result, it is likely to create low-skilled workers, which leads to a dual labor market, divided into a small number of regular workers and many non-regular workers. These typologies and two concepts would be useful to explain the changes in the trend of ALMP and differences in the OECD countries.

2.2 Theoretical Approaches to ALMPs

Economic crisis leads to policy debate and political controversy over solutions to unemployment and job creation. As Gourevitch argues, out of conflict over unemployment, job creation policies emerge. Policies require politics because, as the responses to the economic crisis, policies require political support (Gourevitch 1986, 19). To understand the variation and change of policy choices, it needs to understand the politics that produces them. Understanding the politics of job creation as a policy choice is possible by looking at the politics of support for different economic policies in response to the economic crisis. By examining what countries do, by looking at how their responses vary, we can learn something about factors that lead them to choose particular policies.

Recent ALMP studies are based on several theoretical perspectives, including interest-based approaches such as the power resource theory (Esping-Anderson 1985, 1990, Korpi 1983, 1989, and Stephens 1979), institutionalist approaches (Hall and Soskice 2001, Estevez-Abe, Iversen, and Soskice 2001, Huber and Stephens 2001, 2005, Iversen 2005, and Bradley and Stephens 2007), and idea-oriented approaches with policy diffusion theory (Armingeon 2007, Seeleib-Kaiser and Fleckenstein 2007, von Vliet 2010, Vliet and Koster 2011, and Obinger *et al.* 2013). This section will review these theoretical approaches that help explain the existence of ALMP and studies of political economy perspective on how and why countries chose particular policies in response to economic crises.

2.2.1 Interest-Based Approaches

Interest-based approaches to ALMPs focus on the interests of the principal actors, whether conceived as individuals or as groups (Hall 1997). In an economic crisis, social actors, affected by their situation, evaluate alternative policies in relation to the likely benefits or costs. Interest-based approaches, therefore, examine policy support by examining the placement of social actors in the economy itself. They generally concentrate on explaining variation over time and across nations in patterns of policies (Gourevitch 1986).

The power resource theory is the central theory of interest-based approaches that can explain the characteristics and differences of ALMPs within OECD countries. The power resource theory assumes that the distribution of power within prominent social actors is related to the success and failure of policies (O'Connor and Olsen 1998). The power resources approach also admits that the distribution of power resources varies, shifting over time and between countries (Korpi 1998). Based on the power resource approach, scholars analyzed the diversity and characteristics of social policies and distributions in European countries in the 1970s and 80s. Power resource theorists mainly focused on the role of labor unions and left parties, explaining the different levels of development and efficiencies of social policies in the welfare states (Esping-Anderson 1985, 1990, Korpi 1983, 1989, and Stephens 1979).

Esping-Andersen (1990), in *The Three Worlds of Welfare Capitalism*, defines

ALMP as one of the characteristics of the "social-democratic" welfare regime. Katzenstein (1985) also assumes ALMPs are a product of corporatist arrangements that economic openness and vulnerability have made possible in the small European states. As Katzenstein argues, ALMP in Sweden can be a kind of a major cross-class compromise, allowing social democrats to pursue their political objectives without endangering the profitability of capital. In the context of economic growth and labor market shortages of the 1950 - 60s, the Swedish social democratic party developed ALMPs to provide skilled workers for expanding industrial economies (Swenson 2002). The Swedish model, or the so-called Rehn-Meidner model, had several characteristics: equality in the wage distribution, sustainable full employment, and Swedish industrial modernization (Bonoli 2010). Instead of income policy through wage increases, the social democratic party made a compromise of the solidarity wage policy with labor unions that traded off wage restraint for full employment and job security. ALMP in the Swedish model had a role in retraining unemployed workers and connecting them with expanding high productivity industries.

However, Pierson (2000) argues that the power resource theory (PRT), focusing on relationships between unions, social democratic parties, and the state, has difficulty explaining previously unrecognized issues according to changing structures of economic production, especially in a service-based economy. Radical changes from industrial to postindustrial employment structures have created new challenges for welfare regimes in employment growth, wage equality, and budgetary constraint (Esping-Andersen 1999, Iversen and Wren 1998, Scharpf 1997).

For instance, the development of information technology and consequent changes in the industrial structure may have affected the expenditure or type of ALMPs. In general, traditional job training has a relationship with manufacturing economies (Bonoli 2010). As Bengtsson (2014, 67) argues, however, "up-skilling might not have the same effect today as it did in the mid-20th century." Upskilling in the knowledge-based economies needs more cost and time consuming than job training in the period of post-war industrial development. In the transition from manufacturing to service economies, OECD countries have been faced with a choice between two types of job creation pathways: the high road and low road (Milberg and Houston 2005). In the low road, jobs are typically organized around very simple and/or narrow sets of tasks, often highly routinized. Therefore, countries on the low road are likely to choose measures of ALMP, including short time-based employment incentives or job matching services, rather than upskilling through life-long education and higher education.

In short, interest-based approaches such as the power resource theory help explain the variations and differences of ALMPs in OCED countries. It highlights the degree to which policies tend to benefit some groups and disadvantage others. At the same time, it provides us with a useful way for understanding how changes in the international political economy can affect the domestic politics and policies of a nation (Hall 1986, Armingeon 2007).

2.2.2 Institutionalist Approaches

Institutionalist approaches locate the primary causal factors behind policies and their performance in the organizational structures and institutions. Institutionalist scholars who take this approach emphasize institutional differences across nations and their persistence over time (Hall 1997). They suppose that the specific policy variations are closely linked to the ways in which countries differ in institutions

(Gourevitch 1986). Therefore, institutionalist researchers have focused on quite different politico-economic configurations within the welfare regimes (Hall, 1998, 1999, Soskice 1999, and Hall and Soskice 2001). They argue that welfare regimes are strongly associated with distinct systems of economic production and organization.

The 'Varieties of Capitalism' (VOC) approaches are largely categorized into at least two capitalist political economies: coordinated market economies (CMEs) and liberal market economies (LMEs) (Hall and Soskice 2001). The coordinated market economies are again divided into Northern European social democratic market countries (SMCs) and continental European market countries (CMCs) based on Christian conservatism (Esping-Andersen 1990, Estevez-Abe, Iversen, and Soskice 2001, Huber and Stephens 2001, and Iversen 2005). As Armingeon (2007) argues, ALMPs have become an integral part of the welfare state in the Nordic countries in the 1960s and 1970s. For instance, Sweden's coordinated bargaining systems and ALMPs have been working as the most efficient way to deliver real wage constraints and thus job creation in highly unionized countries (Huber and Stephens 2001, 2005).

The corporatist structure and bargaining system may have affected the level of expenditure of ALMPs (Schmitter 1974, Lehmbruch 1979, and Bradley and Stephens 2007).[1] The corporatist political economies in the Nordic countries have developed a distinctive ALMP in their models of economic growth and employment creation (Huo and Stephens 2015). For example, in Sweden, ALMP would further facilitate wage restraint and thus reduce the tradeoff between unemployment and inflation (Huo

---

[1] Lehmbruch defines the corporatism as an "institutionalized pattern of policy formation in which large interest organizations co-operate with each other and with public authorities, in the implementation of such policies" (Lehmbruch 1979, p. 150).

and Stephens 2015, 413). In general, studies on corporatism suggest that the more centralized collective bargaining systems are, the more effective real wage constraints work, resulting in positive employment (Schmitter 1974, Esping-Andersen 1990, Hicks and Kenworthy 1998, and Bradley and Stephens 2007). Armingeon also assumes that the relationship of employers to the state may be of crucial importance. As he argues, in countries where employers are coordinated by their organizations and have a cooperative relationship with the state and trade unions, they will support ALMP more strongly, and this support will make ALMP more effective (Armingeon 2007, 913)

Continental European countries did not favor redistributive strategies between social groups to the extent seen in the Nordic countries. Under the fiscal pressures, which have been high since the mid-1980s or early 1990s, the introduction of a new program such as AMLPs was difficult since it may require resource redistribution from the traditional schemes (Armingeon 2007, 914). In these continental European countries, therefore, the development of ALMPs was also delayed. Above all, the social insurance system and its governance structure have acted as an obstacle to the development of ALMPs in Germany and France (Clasen 2000, Eichhorst et al. 2008).

The liberal market countries (LMCs), in where union organization rates and the collective bargaining system are relatively weak but influences of employers' associations are very strong in influencing policy choices, are more likely to use the short period-job creation programs such as start-up incentives or employment incentives for employers and employees (e.g., USA). Also, countries where unions and employers' associations are traditionally weak, but the bureaucratic autonomy of the state is relatively strong in effecting policy choices are more likely to approve direct job creation programs in hard times (e.g., Korea).

2.2.3 Idea-Oriented Approaches: Coordination & Diffusion Theory

Another theoretical approach to ALMPs emphasizes the role of ideas or the importance of cultural variables such as economic ideology and culturally specific orientations deeply rooted in national history. The idea-based approaches assume that the policies chosen by governments are strongly influenced by the ideas about appropriate policy or best practice dominant within the relevant professional community (Hall 1997, 184). Since the mid-1990s, ALMPs have rapidly spread across OECD countries. Then, the open method of coordination (OMC) in the European Union can be pointed as one of the reasons why ALMPs have rapidly spread.[2] The OMC, as a new framework for cooperation between the EU countries, takes place in areas that fall within the competence of EU countries, such as employment, social protection, education, youth, and vocational training. In this case, the OMC is principally based on benchmarking, i.e., the comparison of EU countries' performance and the exchange of best practices monitored by the Commission (EUR-Lex).

Recent studies on ALMPs that have focused on the role of the OECD and the EU are based on the diffusion theory (Armingeon 2007, Vliet and Koster 2011, Obinger *et al.* 2013). While previous studies on ALMPs in PRT and institutionalist approaches have mainly focused on domestic factors such as political interests and institutions, the diffusion theory considers state adoptions of new policies as emulations of previous ones by other countries. State policymakers faced with complex problems such as high unemployment seek decision-making shortcuts and choose policy ideas

---

[2] The OMC, originally created in the 1990s as part of employment policy and the Luxembourg process, was defined as an instrument of the Lisbon strategy (2000). It is a form of intergovernmental policy-making that does not result in binding EU legislative measures and it does not require EU countries to introduce or amend their laws (EUR Lex homepage)

that have been successfully implemented in other countries (Armingeon 2007). In analyzing international impacts on ALMP, however, Armingeon concludes that the impacts of international organizations such as OECD and EU are conditional on domestic politics, institutions, and extant policies. If policy recommendations are compatible with national institutions and political goals, they are more likely to be implemented at the national level (Armingeon 2007, 911).

Van Vliet (2011) also analyzes how European integration influences social and labor market policy reforms in the EU member countries. As a result, he argues that the social expenditures of EU member states have converged and increased on average since 1995, and social protection levels have also been increased in most of the countries, whereas those of non-EU countries have diverged. However, he argues that although there has been an EU-specific trend of shifting resources from passive to active labor market policies, ALMPs have not converged much in the period 1995-2002, showing that countries opted for different configurations of ALMPs. Van Vliet and Koster (2011) argue that shifts from passive policies to ALMPs have been made by the process of mutual learning through peer review programs rather than vertical peer pressure from the European Commission and the Council.

Seeleib-Kaiser and Fleckenstein (2007) assert that the German unemployment policy adopted in 2002 emulated the UK approach to activation through government-commissioned studies. In this regard, the influence of neoliberalism ideology as another backdrop to this diffusion theory should not be overlooked. The unemployment and job crisis due to neoliberalism has played a role in promoting the spread of ALMP and partly policy convergence among EU and OECD countries. Due to economic ideology, globalization (market openness), and influences of global economic governance such as OECD and EU, labor market policies in the OECD countries have changed from passive to active measures. Even though there are differences in the expenditure and policy choices among these countries, the greater influences of neo-liberalism and global economic governance, the more activation paradigm these countries have adopted (Hemerijck 2013).

On the other hand, Eighhorst and Konle-Seidl (2008) argue that despite considerable initial variation across national models with respect to the scope and intensity of activation, a contingent convergence of instruments, target groups, governance modes, and outcomes can be observed. Bengtsson and Berglund (2012) also argue that in Sweden and Denmark, public policies are reoriented towards two types of ALMPs, including "employment assistance" (e.g., job subsidies, counseling, job search programs) and "incentive reinforcement" (e.g., tax credits, benefit reductions, benefit conditionality) (Bonoli and Natali 2012: 196). In short, they assert that "training and human capital accumulation no longer seem to be prerogatives in state regulation of the Swedish labor market" (Bengtsson and Berglund 2012, 102). Through assessing the degree of convergence in activation policies and governance, Graziano (2012) also argues that although there is limited evidence of full convergence, domestic activation policies are only partially converging towards an employment assistance type. However, he found that upskilling has not been obtained since expenditure on training has declined since 1995, despite the EU recommendations.

2.2.4 Analytic Framework

As reviewed above, many studies on ALMPs have focused either on the relationship between social democratic parties, the state, and unions (PRT) or quite different politico-economic configurations such as industrial structure and relations (institutionalist approaches). Recently, idea-oriented approaches have emphasized the role of ideas or the importance of cultural variables to analyze ALMPs and performance (Hall 1997). To explain policy choices of ALMPs, it must have analyzed the connection between policy and choice, in order words, between what could be done and the various factors that shape what decision-makers actually choose to do (Gourevitch 1986).

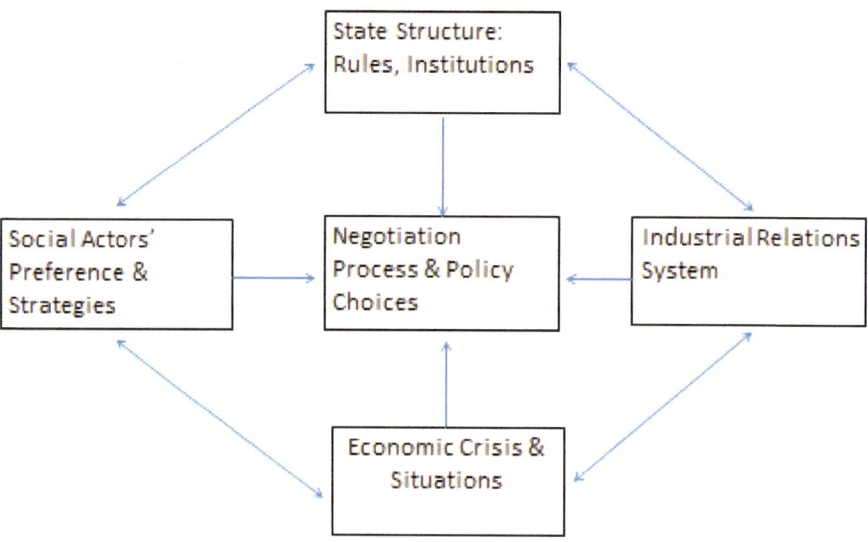

Figure 2.2 The Process of Policy Choices & Key Factors

Figure 2.2 shows the process of policy choices and the relationship between key factors. Social actors interpret economic crises and situations based on their own interests. Then, they try to link their preferences of policies to state institutions through political parties or interest groups such as labor unions or associations of employers.

On the other hand, social actors' strategies are restricted by institutional factors such as state institutions, bureaucracies, rules in defining and mediating their interests. The economic ideology also affects the role of perceptions, models, and values in shaping the understanding of the economic situation and political circumstance, which influence social actors' preferences and strategic behavior (Gourevith 1986). In short, new policy choices are made as a result of negotiation and political compromises between social actors based on their preferences and strategies.

In this regard, we can also broadly distinguish two sets of drivers of the change of policies: endogenous (domestic) and exogenous (international) factors. If studies on ALMPs in PRT and institutionalist approaches mainly focus on domestic and endogenous factors such as political interests and institutions, ALMP studies, based on the idea-oriented approach such as diffusion theory, emphasize exogenous factors such as neoliberal influences and emulation of new policies. To explain this difference and the change of expenditures of ALMPs, therefore, we need to consider both exogenous and endogenous factors.

In sum, the review of the literature suggests several determinant factors that could explain the adoption of ALMPs. First, political coalitions of social actors who act for their own interests in each economic situation may have significantly affected variation in ALMPs. Therefore, political factors, including partisan control, especially left-party or right-wing government, and union density rates, may have a very close relationship with ALMPs.

Second, the variations of ALMPs are closely linked to the ways in which countries differ in institutions and organizational structures. For instance, the corporatist structure and bargaining system under the coordinated market economics (CMEs) may have positively affected the level of expenditure of ALMPs. In countries where laborers and employers are coordinated by their organizations and have a cooperative relationship with the state, the expenditures of ALMPs are likely to be more than in other countries.

Third, the development of information technology and consequent changes in the industrial structure may have affected the expenditure or type of ALMPs. In this regard, upskilling in the knowledge-based economies needs more cost and time consuming than job training in the period of post-war industrial development. Therefore, some countries are likely to choose measures of ALMP, including short time-based employment incentives or job matching services, rather than upskilling through life-long education and higher education.

Lastly, the neoliberal influence and economic governance may be considered as an important determinant factor of ALMPs. In short, due to economic ideology such as neoliberalism, globalization (market openness), and influences of global economic governance such as OECD and EU, labor market policies in the OECD countries have changed from passive to active measures.

Chapter 3

RESEARCH DESIGN

This study aims to examine how and why countries chose particular ALMPs in response to the economic crisis. First, it will compare and analyze the changes and recent trends of ALMPs in OECD countries. At the same time, it will try to analyze determinant factors that caused the variations and differences in ALMPs within these countries. It also seeks to provide an in-depth understanding of how and why particular ALMPs have been shaped through the politics of job creation, given the economic situations and state structure and institutions.

Therefore, this study will use both quantitative and qualitative analysis (case studies) by focusing on policy choices and expenditure data analysis. This study consists of two parts. Based on the disaggregated OECD expenditures datasets, the first part of the study will analyze the trends in expenditures on ALMPs in the OECD countries. Then, it will also analyze causal factors that have resulted in the differences in spending on ALMPs in OECD countries. The second part of the study addresses the political processes that explain the variations in ALMPs. There is still an insufficient understanding of how domestic politics has influenced the adoption of various ALMPs. Therefore, these analyses of the changes in ALMPs will be supplemented by case studies of Sweden, Germany, and Korea. The case studies on the policy choices these countries have made in response to the economic crisis of 2008 will demonstrate how and why domestic partisan politics shaped the type of ALMPs adopted.

The first part of this study will analyze the expenditures and trends of ALMP in the OECD countries based on the updated pooling of OECD datasets (1985-2017). This study will use disaggregated OECD expenditure data and policy indicators to analyze the changes in the types of ALMPs. To visualize the changes and typical trends of ALMPs over time, it will use simple descriptive statistics. It will also use analysis techniques for the pooled cross-sectional OECD datasets, such as the fixed effects model and random-effects model, to assess the determinants of the differences in ALMP expenditures (See the following method session for more detail). For this, several determinants will be evaluated: government party, partisan control, union density rates, wage-setting coordination, collective bargaining system, industrial structure, and neoliberal influence.

Although the first part of the study will show trends of expenditures of ALMPs in the OECD countries and explain determinants that resulted in variations or differences in the expenditure of ALMPs, it is not easy to know in detail when, how, and why policy and institution have been changed and established. Variations on the expenditures of ALMPs in OECD countries will be more specific and conditional per the politics of job creation in each country. Therefore, the case studies in the second part will focus on the policy choices of Sweden, Germany, and Korea. The case study will analyze ALMPs that reshape how political actors understand and pursue their interests and, thus, how their political consequences unfold. A comparison of the policy choices that these countries have made in response to the economic crisis and unemployment will allow an analysis of differences and convergences of job creation policies in more detail.

3.1 Hypotheses and Method

3.1.1 Hypotheses

The literature review discussed several determinant factors that can explain changes and adoptions of ALMPs. Based on the previous discussion, this study suggests several hypotheses on ALMPs as follows.

First, the expenditure of ALMPs is likely to be different according to welfare regimes. Although there may be convergence in expenditures on ALMP within the same type of welfare regime, there will likely be differences in spending on ALMPs among the welfare regimes. In short, the expenditures of ALMPs in social democratic market countries(SMCs) are likely to be more than conservatism market countries(CMCs) or liberal market countries(LMCs). As discussed in chapter 2, there are several reasons why SMCs have traditionally emphasized ALMPs. As Katzenstein argues, small countries dependent on an unpredictable world market need to secure their workforce against the inevitable volatilities (Katzenstein 1985). Therefore, a small state in Nordic Europe, such as Sweden, has generally prompted the formation of democratic and corporatist arrangements to survive in the global market. As a result, SMCs under the control of the left party are the most likely to increase the expenditure of ALMPs in the economic crisis. For these reasons, a hypothesis is formulated:

Hypothesis 1: The expenditures of ALMPs in SMCs are likely to be more than CMCs or LMCs.

Second, this study hypothesizes that political actors based on their interests are likely to influence the spending of ALMPs. The political coalitions between laborers, employers, and states may have significantly affected variation in ALMPs. Partisan control, such as left-wing or right-wing governments, may also have a very close relationship with the level and scope of ALMPs' expenditure. Although, in principle, ALMP is a one-size-fits-all policy that is comparable with liberal, conservative, and left ideologies, it has been developed within the context of social-democratic strategies. It thus rests on the acceptance of state intervention in the economy (Armingeon 2007, 913). Hence, left parties and left-wing governments seem to be the most likely to support these policies (Boix 1998). From this, hypothesis 2 is presented:

Hypothesis 2: The left parties or left-wing government are more likely to approve the expenditure of ALMPs

Third, the variations of ALMPs are closely linked to the ways in which countries differ in institutions and organizational structures. For instance, the corporatist structure and bargaining system under the coordinated market economies (CMEs) may have positively affected the level of expenditure of ALMPs. In countries where laborers and employers are coordinated by their organizations and have a cooperative relationship with the state, the expenditures of ALMPs are likely to be more than in other countries. Therefore, hypothesis 3 is formulated as follows:

Hypothesis 3: The union density rate and coordination of wage-setting may have positively affected the level of expenditure of ALMPs

Fourth, this study also supposes that ideological factors such as neo-liberalism may significantly impact the level and scope of the expenditure of ALMPs according to the welfare regimes. As discussed in the literature review, neoliberal influence and economic governance may be considered important determinant factors. In this regard, Hemerijck argues, even though there are differences in the expenditure and policy choices among these countries, the greater influences of neo-liberalism and global economic governance, the more activation policies these countries have adopted (Hemerijck 2013). In short, neoliberalism, globalization (market openness), and economic governance through OECD and EU have changed the labor market policies from passive to active measures. The greater the impact of neoliberal economic ideology, the more likely short-term and pro-market oriented ALMPs such as PES and Employment Incentives will be preferred over traditional vocational training. Based on this discussion, hypothesis 4 can be derived:

Hypothesis 4: The greater the neoliberal ideology impact, the more likely it is that the expenditures of ALMPs will decrease.

Fifth, the development of information technology and consequent changes in the industrial structure may have affected the expenditure or type of ALMPs. According to Bonoli, traditional job training has a relationship with manufacturing economies (Bonoli 2010). As Bengtsson (2014, 67) argues, however, "upskilling might not have the same effect today as it did in the mid-20th century." The upskilling policies in the knowledge-based economies need more cost and time. In the transition from manufacturing to digital service economies, OECD countries have faced two job creation pathways: the High-road and the Low-road (Milberg and Houston 2005). In the Low-road, the countries are more likely to rely on short-term and temporary

ALMPs, such as job-matching services and job-creation policy through public work. On the other hand, the countries headed to the 'High-road' are more likely to adopt ALMPs directed towards skill-upgrading and human capital development through lifetime training (or retraining) and higher education. In short, countries on the low road are likely to choose measures of ALMP, including job matching services or employment incentives, rather than upskilling through life-long education and higher education. Based on the above discussion, hypothesis 5 is presented.

Hypothesis 5: Under the countries in the Low-road, training expenditures for upskilling are more likely to decrease.

To analyze the hypothesis, I will compare the changes in expenditures of ALMPs among welfare regimes and/or between countries within welfare regimes from 1985 to 2017. This study will use simple descriptive statistics to visualize the changes and typical trends of ALMPs. This study is also interested in the variation of ALMPs over time. Therefore, it utilizes the analytic method of the pooled OECD panel data to assess the difference of expenditures of ALMPs between welfare regimes (Van Vliet 2011). [1]

Though, this study does not stop at simply analyzing changes in the expenditure of ALMPs expenditure according to the welfare regimes. It will also focus on whether the trend of ALMPs' expenditure according to the welfare system has changed since the 2008 global economic crisis. As noted above, the expenditure and change of types of ALMP may have a relationship with the economic downturns and crises.

---

[1] The difference-in-difference (DID) method is called the 'controlled before and after study' in some social sciences such as the field of econometrics. DID is a quasi-experimental design that makes use of longitudinal data from treatment and control groups to obtain an appropriate counterfactual to estimate a causal effect (source: www.columbia.edu).

Since the 2008 Great Recession, the expenditures and types of ALMPs that the OECD countries funded to address unemployment are more likely to be different according to their economic context and labor market institutions.

To analyze the changes of types of ALMP after the economic crisis, I will classify four types of ALMP, based on Bonoli's work (2010): Public employment services (PES) consist of placement & related services and benefits administration; Upskilling includes institutional training, workplace training, alternate training, and special support for apprenticeship; Employment incentives consist of recruitment incentives, employment maintenance incentives, job rotation, and sharing, supported employment, rehabilitation, and start-up incentives; Direct job creation covers job creation schemes in the public sector such as public works programs. Then, this study will use simple descriptive statics to compare the changes in the expenditure by the OECD countries and across time after and before the 2008 global economic crisis. Besides, to compare active and passive benefits, this study will add the type of unemployment benefits that includes unemployment benefits, early retirement benefits, and bankruptcy compensation. In particular, to assess the pathways of job creation (high or low road), this study will divide four types of ALMP into two groups: Upskilling and the others. In this study, human capital investment is considered as the pathway of the high road. Other types of expenditures are assumed as the pathway of the low road (Milberg and Houston 2005).

At the same time, to assess determinant factors that resulted in different expenditures of ALMPs, this study estimates the following equation:

$$EXP\ of\ ALMP_{it} = \alpha + \beta_1\ EXP\ of\ ALMP_{it} + \beta_2\ PV1\ (Government\ Party)$$

$_{it}$ + β_3 *PV2 (Union Density Rates)* $_{it}$ + β_4 *PV3 (Coordination of Wage-Setting)*$_{it}$ + β_5 *Neo-liberalism (Openness)*$_{it}$ + β_6 *Dummy (Time)* + β_7 *Dummy (Welfare Regime)* + ε_{it}

Where *EXP of ALMP* is the change in the dependent variable (expenditure of ALMP) in the country *i* and year *t* from one year to the next, α is the constant, and β is the coefficient. *EXP of ALMP* $_{it}$ is the lagged level of each dependent variable multiplied by its estimated coefficient β_1 and ε_{it} is the error term.

3.1.2 Method

This study will perform analytical procedures that tap into two different aspects of the dependent variables: Total ALMP spending and the expenditure of ALMP by the types. The expenditures on ALMPs are measured as spending on ALMPs as a percentage of GDP. The other dependent variable is the expenditures on ALMPs by Bonoli's (2010) types as a percentage of GDP. In this regard, two aspects are considered as the reasons for dividing the dependent variable into total ALMP expenditure (variable name: soex_amlp) and type-specific ALMP expenditure by the public and mandatory private spending (variable name: almp-pmp, almp-pub). The first is to examine the differences in the types of welfare countries by analyzing the trends in ALMP expenditure in OECD countries. Second, through the analysis of the ALMP expenditure type, it will examine what job strategies OECD countries are pursuing, what is called either the high road or low road.

Then, to explore the main determinants that resulted in differences in the expenditure of ALMPs, it will analyze the causal effect of the independent variables affecting overall ALMP spending. As discussed in the previous section of the hypothesis, there are also key explanatory variables that serve as independent variables, including partisan government control (government party), collective bargaining coverage, union density rates, coordination of wage-setting, industrial structure(service economy), and economic openness.

  The partisan government control (government party) is based on the cabinet composition (Schmidt index 1992).[2] The higher the cabinet composition (Schmidt index), the higher the hegemony of social-democratic and other left parties. The union density rate is measured by net union membership as a proportion of wage and salary earners in employment. The collective bargaining coverage, as Visser (2011) defines, is calculated for "employees covered by wage bargaining agreements as a proportion of all wage and salary earners in employment with the right to bargaining, expressed as a percentage, adjusted for the possibility that some sectors or occupations are excluded from the right to bargain (removing such groups from the employment count before dividing the number of covered employees over the total number of dependent workers in employment)"(Armingeon *et al.* 2012, 15). The coordination of wage-setting is an indicator of the "degree of coordination, based on a set of expectations about which institutional features of wage-setting arrangements are likely to generate more or less coordination" (Kenworthy 2001:78, 80).[3]

---

[2] Cabinet composition (Schmidt-Index): (1) hegemony of right-wing (and centre) parties (gov_left=0), (2) dominance of right-wing (and centre) parties (gov_left<33.3), (3) balance of power between left and right/centre (33.3<gov_left<66.6), (4) dominance of social-democratic and other left parties (gov_left>66.6), (5) hegemony of social-democratic and other left parties (gov_left=100). (Amingeon et al. 2019, 4)

[3] Codings: 1 = fragmented wage bargaining, confined largely to individual firms or plants, no coordination;

The industrial structure is measured by civilian employment in agriculture, industry, and services from 1960 to 2017 (Armingeon *et al.*, 2014). This study uses data from the service industry. Independent variables related to political factors such as government party, collective bargaining coverage, employment protections, and union density rates are based on the Comparative Political Data Set 1960-2017 (Armingeon *et al.* 2019).

On the other hand, it is not easy to measure the influences of neo-liberalism and global economic governance. Therefore, this study uses the degree of market openness as a substitute variable to measure these factors because the degree of a country's trade and financial openness can indirectly consider the effects of neo-liberalism and global economic governance. In this study, the degree of economic openness is measured by the index for the degree of openness in capital account transactions from 1970 to 2017. The higher the value, the more open a country is to cross-border capital transactions (Chinn and Ito 2008, Armingeon *et al.* 2014).

The welfare state regime types (Esping-Andersen1990) are measured as dummy variables for social democratic market countries (SMCs), conservatism market countries (CMCs), and liberal market countries (LMCs). The reason for measuring the welfare regimes as dummy variables is to see the causal effect of the independent variables on the dependent variable according to the types of welfare regimes.

---

2 = fixed or alternating industry- and firm level bargaining, with weak enforceability of industry agreements; 3 = industry-level bargaining with no or irregular pattern setting, limited involvement of central organizations, and limited freedoms for firm-level bargaining; 4 = mixed industry and economy-wide bargaining: a) central organizations negotiate non-enforceable central agreements (guidelines) and/or b) key unions and employers associations set pattern for the entire economy; 5 = economy-wide bargaining, based on a) enforceable agreements between the central organizations of unions and employers affecting the entire economy or entire private sector, or on b) government imposition of a wage schedule, freeze, or ceiling. Years: 1960-2017 (Kenworthy 2001).

There are also several control variables: GDP growth, employment rates, unemployment rates, income inequality, and atypical labor rates. The GDP growth is measured as the annual percentage change of real GDP. The unemployment rate is calculated as standardized unemployment according to OECD definitions. A set of variables relating to efficiency is the employment rate (persons employed in the percentage of the total population, aged 15 to 64) and the share of long-term unemployment (over six months of unemployment) in total unemployment. Income inequality is measured by the Gini index and atypical labor rates in the employed workers, based on the OECD dataset (OECD 2013).

The datasets in this study are composed of panel data. This is a mixture of characteristics of pooled time series and cross-sectional data. Therefore, the datasets in this study have the characteristics of panel data that is especially cross-sectional by countries and repetitively measured by year. Therefore, in this study, it will use the panel data analysis method. Using the pooled crossectional data of OECD countries, regression analysis will be performed to verify the hypothesis discussed above (commend: xtreg). Considering that the error term has a high possibility of autocorrelation within the panel data, this study will run the regression analysis through the Hausman test.

The Hausman test is a kind of test to determine which model is to choose between the random effects model and the fixed effects model by examining the assumptions of the random effects model (Hausman 1978). The random-effects model provides more efficient estimates than the fixed-effects model but provides a biased estimate when the fixed-effects of individual economic entities are correlated with independent variables. Therefore, in the Hausmann test, the difference between the estimated parameters is examined to know if the estimated values of the fixed-effects model and the random-effects model are significantly different. The null hypothesis sets that if the assumptions of the random-effects model are satisfied, it will provide the same parameter estimates as the fixed-effects model. If rejecting the null hypothesis fails, the estimate of the random-effects model is selected. However, if the null hypothesis is rejected, the estimate of the fixed-effect model is selected.

At the same time, this study will analyze panel datasets with a time dummy variable to examine whether there is a structural change in the expenditure of ALMPs for every 10 years from 1998 to 2017 before and after the 2008 economic crisis. The dummy variable will be used to analyze structural changes in the expenditures of ALMPs before and after the 2008 global economic crisis.

3.1.3 Datasets

The data in this study are culled from the OECD datasets (1960-2018), Comparative Political Data Set I (Armingeon *et al.* 2019: 1960-2017), Institutional Characteristics of Trade Unions, Wage Setting, State Intervention and Social Pacts (ICTWSS) Data Set (Visser 2014: 1960-2018), and Comparative Welfare States Data Set (Brady et al. 2020: 1960-2017). Although these datasets are partially over-lapped, they provide good data sources and information for specific areas or variables. The statistical analyses are implemented in version 16.0 of the STATA statistics program.

The sample of data sets includes a total of 1,475 cases that were extracted from the OECD database, including 24 OECD countries (OECD 2020). Especially in this study, the 24 OECD counties are classified into three states' groups, based on Esping-Andersen's (1990) classification of welfare states.

Table 3.1 Datasets

Name	Period	Key variables	Source
OECD Data Set	1960-2018	ALMPs, Growth rate, the Unemployment rate	OECD.org
Comparative Political Data Set I	1960-2017	Governments, Party system Institutions, Openness of the economy, Labour force, Trade unions, Social expenditure, Labour market policy, Income inequality	Armingeon et al. 2019
Institutional Characteristics of Trade Unions, Wage Setting, State Intervention and Social Pacts (ICTWSS) Data Set	1960-2018	Right of Association and Strike, Coordination of wage setting, Minimum wage, Social pact, Works council, Sectoral organization of employment relations, Union density	Visser 2019
Comparative Welfare States Data Set	1960-2017	Wage and Income, Social spending, ALMPs, Revenue, Welfare State Institutions, Labor force, and labor institutions	Brady et al. 2020

According to Esping-Andersen (1990), welfare capitalism is classified into the three worlds according to the concepts of de-commodification and social stratification indices, such as social democracy, conservatism, and liberalism (Esping-Andersen 1990: 9-12).[4]

---

[4] According to Esping-Andersen, de-commodification is defined as the extent to which individuals and families can afford an acceptable standard of living independently of market participation (Esping-Andersen 1990: 47). Instead, social stratifications are captured through a wide range of indicators of how welfare state key institutions operate in structuring class and social order (Esping-Andersen 1990: 55). Esping-Andersen captured social stratification with seven indicators directly related to three political movements that dominated the Western World in the 20th century. First of all, socialist principles measured through: (1) the degree of universalism, (2) the equality of benefits among citizens. Second, conservative principle measured through: (3) the level of corporatism, (4) the level of statism. Third, liberal principle measured through the spending for: (5) means-tested poor relief, (6) private pension and (7) private health care.

Table 3.2 Classification of Welfare Regimes

Welfare Regimes	Characteristics	Country
Social Democracy (SMCs)	Universal Welfare Benefit equality	SWE, NOR, DNK, FIN, ISL
Conservatism (CMCs)	Christian Democracy Corporatism	BEL, NLD, AUT, FRA, DEU, ITA, ESP, GRC, PRT, LUX, CHE
Liberalism (LMCs)	Means-tested poor relief Private Pe	IRL, NZL, AUS, GBR, CAN, USA, KOR, JANnsions & health spending

Source: Esping-Andersen (1990)
Note: SMCs = Social Democratic Market Counties, CMCs = Conservatism Market Countries, LMCs = Liberal Market Countries

According to Esping-Anderson's classification, social democratic countries have developed under the considerable influence of socialist principles such as low social stratification and high de-commodification. Under the social-democratic regime, the trade unions have exercised their power to support the interest of the working class. Where the elites established their power over the working-class movement, liberalism and Christian democratic regimes have been established based on the characteristics such as high social stratification, low de-commodification, and minimal interference of the state. Instead, with medium social stratification and de-commodification, continental European countries have developed Christian democratic welfare regimes and perpetuated conservative Paternalism. Most of the Scandinavian countries are predominantly social-democratic. However, liberalism is strong in the USA, UK, and Australia. Instead, European conservative regimes have incorporated both liberal and social democratic characteristics. Esping-Andersen's classification of OECD countries into three groups is provided in Table 3.2.

3.2 Case Study

The case study research method, as one of five qualitative approaches (with narrative research, phenomenology, grounded theory, and ethnography), can be useful to analyze how or why an issue or a policy is discovered through one or more cases within abound (Creswell 2007). Based on the case study method, this study will analyze how or why ALMPs have been shaped and changed in three different countries, Sweden, Germany, and Korea, representing three different types of countries identified in the varieties of capitalism literature (Hall and Soskice 2001).[5] As Kingdon (2002) argues, the crisis would open political windows of opportunities for change and the further development of ALMPs. Specifically, economic theory suggests that market pressures would compel governments to converge in terms of the type of policies that they adopt (Vis 2009; von Vliet 2010; Taylor-Gooby 2013; Shahidi, 2015). When and where these pressures are particularly severe, governments will confront a policy agenda and fiscal crisis of the welfare state (Hay and Wincott 2013; Streeck 2011; O'Connor 1973). In this study, therefore, the case studies will describe how these three countries have responded to the 2008 financial crisis and

---

[5] Although Sweden has been known as a draft country of ALMP at first, the trend of expenditures of ALMPs in Sweden has largely changed from traditional job training to PED and employment incentives. Since the late 1990s, ALMP in Sweden has placed significant emphasis on employment incentives and public employment assistance. This is in sharp contrast with the past when the expenditure of job training had been strongly emphasized. In Germany, the trend of ALMPs has been also changing. In the process of Hartz Reforms, the German government has not only benchmarked the case of the UK, as known as a pivotal country of neoliberal economics, but also recently focused on the wage subsidies and new start-up subsidies after the 2008 economic crisis (Zimmerman 2013, OECD 2012). Meanwhile, after the 1997 IMF economic crisis, the South Korean government has emphasized new job creation policies but the expenditure of ALMPs is still low, when compared with the previous two countries.

whether there appears to be pressure for convergence or divergence. The case study will specifically focus on ALMPs that they chose in the 2008 economic downturn: Why did they choose these policy measures? How were ALMPs different among the three countries; What are institutional factors that resulted in differences of ALMPs? In this regard, it shows several institutional factors that will be significantly considered in the case study (See Table 3.3).

Table 3.3 Comparing Institutions and Organizational Structures of Three Countries

	Sweden	Germany	Korea
Welfare Regime	Social Democracy (SMC)	Conservativism (CMC)	Liberalism (LMC)
Ruling Party (2008-2016)	Right-wing	Right-wing	Right-wing
State	Weak	Medium	Strong
Unionization Rate	High	Medium	Low
Employer Organization	Strong	Medium	Low
Tripartite Commission	So	Corporatismcial Partnership	Government-led
Collective Bargaining by Industry	Yes	Yes	No
Vocational Training	Strong	Strong	Weak
Financial Crisis (negative) after 2008	None	None	None
Unemployment Benefit (Generosity)	High	Medium	Low
Employment Strictness	High	Medium	Low
Labor and Management Cooperation	High	Medium	Low
Labor Market Issues	Refugees & Youth unemployment	High & Long-term unemployment	Irregular Workers & Youth-unemployment

The case study will use multiple sources, such as e-mail interviews; websites of governments, organizations, and institutes; observations, documents (legislative debates or policies passed), and debates or articles in journals, newspapers, and pieces of literature. It will analyze and compare data sources through the description of the case and themes of the case as well as cross-case themes (Creswell 2007; Yin 2008).

The case studies will be a descriptive approach to understand government approaches to developing labor market policies. Thus, the case studies can be used to identify what the forces and arguments were for the continuation and/or change in ALMPs in these countries. These accounts can be used to see if similar or different approaches were being advocated in these different countries. The case studies can thus help identify potential forces driving the type of ALMPs and could provide directions for future research. The case studies will be descriptive accounts that can help bolster the quantitative analysis by showing that these mechanisms identified in the quantitative analysis are at work in these three cases. Through these case studies, it can also help identify what sorts of questions we should be asking going forward when examining ALMPs and related policies.

Chapter 4

TRENDS AND CHANGES
OF EXPENDITURE OF ALMPs

This chapter analyses trends and changes in the expenditures of ALMPs in the OECD countries based on the updated pooling of OECD datasets (1985-2017). This chapter uses disaggregated OECD expenditure data and policy indicators to analyze the trend of changes in types of ALMP.

4.1 Trends and Changes in Expenditure of ALMPs

4.1.1 Welfare Regimes and Expenditures of ALMPs

The expenditures of ALMP have a relationship with the economic downturns and crisis. As shown in Table 4.1, the expenditures of ALMPs in OECD countries increased sharply during the economic crisis. While the economic crisis subsides, spending on ALMPs tends to decline naturally. However, the expenditures of ALMPs that the OECD countries funded to address unemployment in hard times were different according to their economic context and labor market institutions.

As shown in Figure 4.1, the expenditure on ALMPs in Sweden has been higher than all other OECD countries until 2000. However, the expenditure has been greatly reduced in recent years. Nevertheless, ALMP expenditures in SMCs such as Denmark, Sweden, and Finland are still higher than other types of welfare states. ALMP expenditures in CMCs such as Germany and France remain moderate. On the other hand, the expenditures of ALMP in the LMCs such US, UK, and Canada are low all the time.

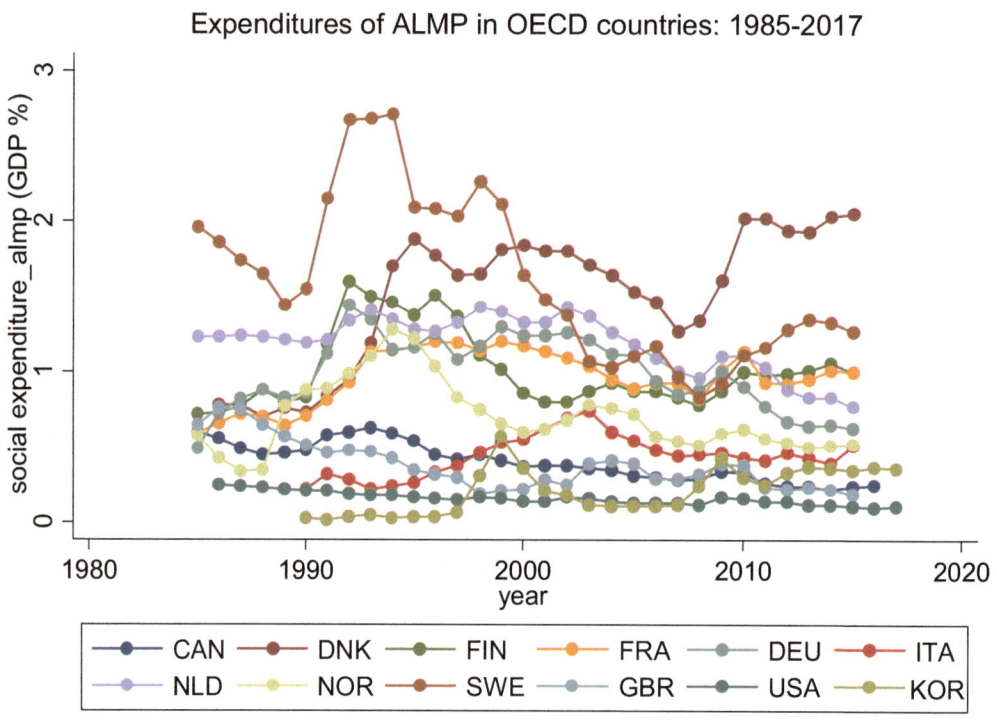

Figure 4.1. Expenditures of ALMP in OECD countries: 1985-2017

As noted above, although ALMP expenditures are partly converging within the same type of welfare regime, ALMP expenditures are still different among the welfare regimes. As shown in Figure 4.2, the ALMP expenditures of SMCs as a percentage of GDP are generally higher than those of CMCs or LMCs.

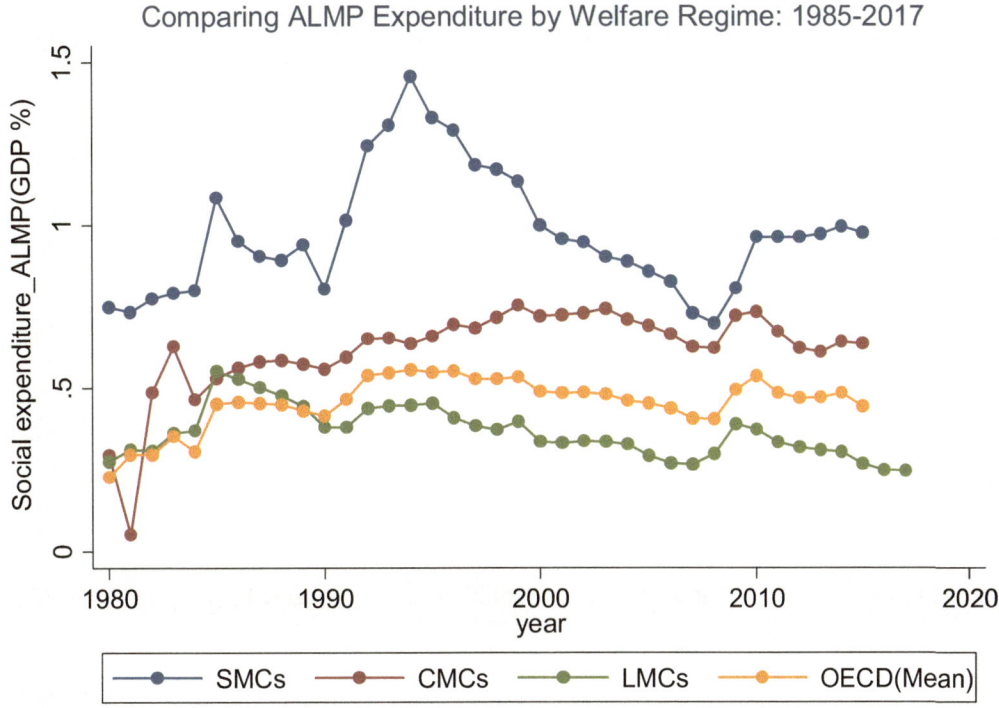

Figure 4.2. Comparing ALMP Expenditures by Welfare Regime: 1985-2017

The expenditures of ALMP have a relationship with the economic downturns and crisis. However, the expenditures of ALMPs that the OECD countries funded to address unemployment in hard times were different according to their economic context and labor market institutions. Even before and after the 2008 global economic crisis, there was no cross-variation in the level of ALMPs expenditure by welfare regime type (See Figure 4.2). Figure 4.3 compares the three countries of each welfare type. The proportion of ALMP expenditure in Sweden's GDP has gradually decreased, except after the 2008 global economic crisis.

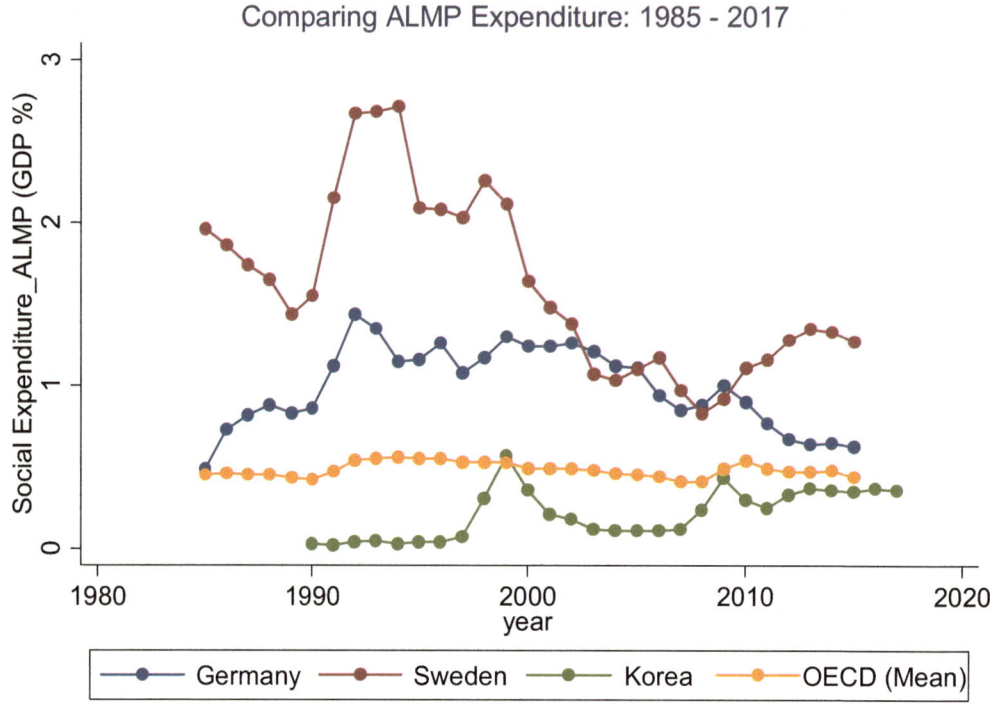

Figure 4.3. Comparing ALMP Expenditure in OECD countries: 1985-2017

On the other hand, Germany's ALMP spending moderately increased after the 2008 financial crisis and has reduced again. In Korea, which is considered an LMC, the proportion of ALMP spending in GDP remains low. In particular, the case of Korea shows a temporary increase in the timing of the IMF (International Monetary Fund) economic crisis in 1997 and the global economic crisis in 2008. However, the spending of ALMPs has been declining sharply after the economic crisis.

4.1.2 Expenditure of Training

The expenditure on training has gradually decreased except for the period of the recent economic crisis among OECD countries. The expenditure of training has a high share in SMC countries, especially in the 1990s. It has rapidly reduced in the 2000s, but after the global economic crisis in 2008, it temporarily increased again. On the other hand, although the expenditures of training in CMCs do not reach the level of SMCs, they have remained constant. However, the proportion of training spending in LMCs has been very low when compared to the other two economic regimes.

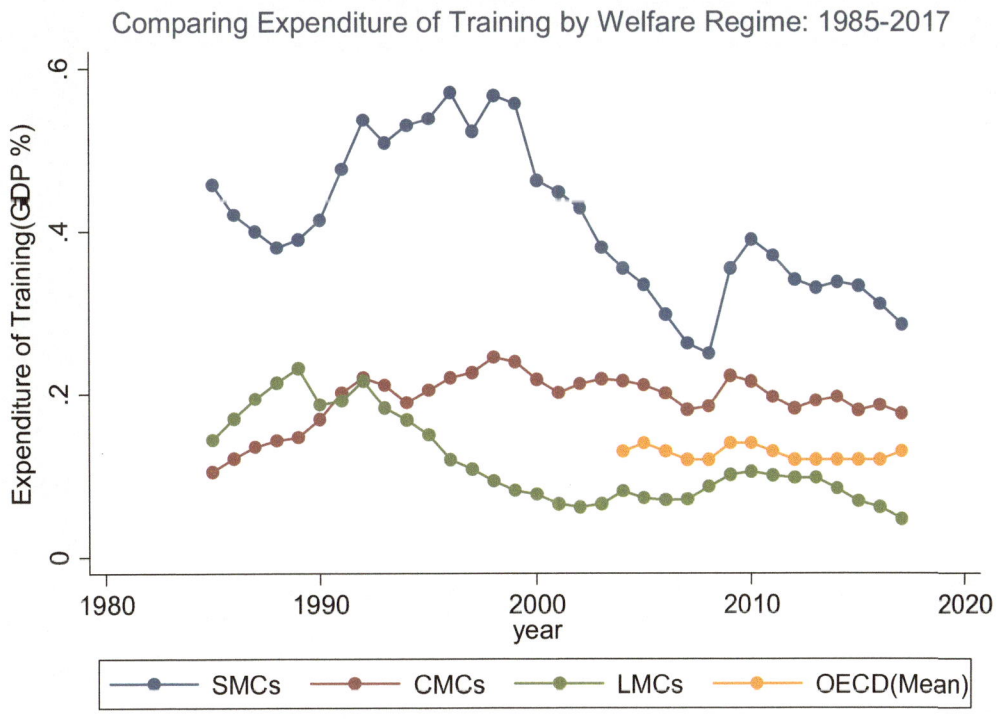

Figure 4.4. Comparing the Expenditure of Training in OECD countries: 1985-2017

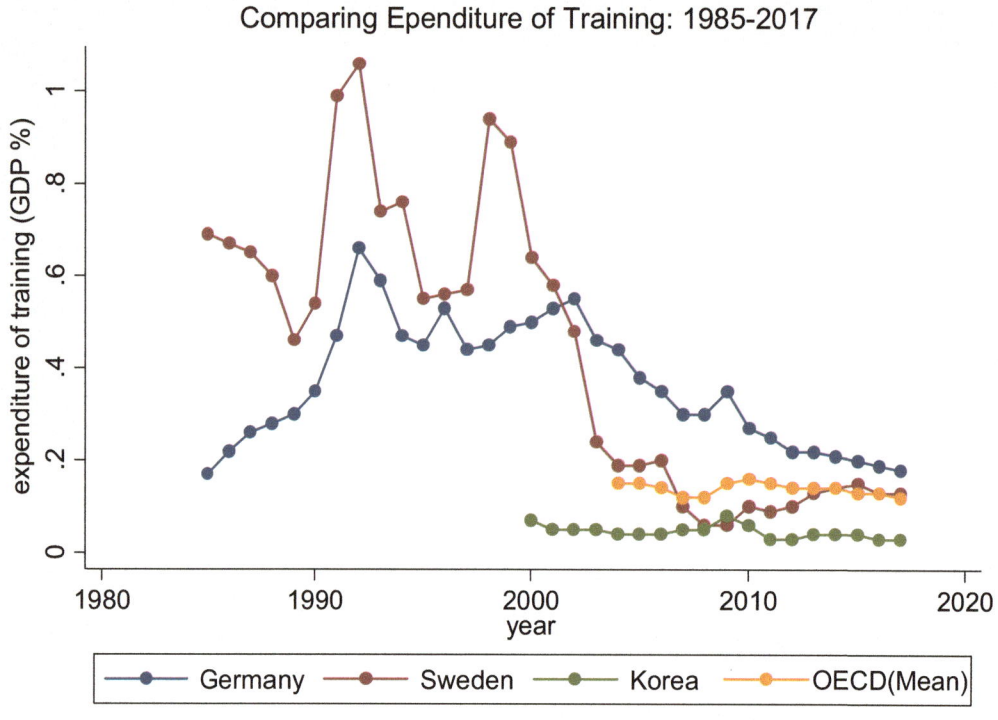

Figure 4.5. Comparing Training Expenditure in Case Countries: 1985-2017

As shown in Figure 4.5, the expenditure on ALMPs has largely decreased (especially job training) in Sweden, where it has been traditionally well-known as a leader in implementing ALMPs. In recent years, the main reason why the proportion of vocational training spending in ALMPs has decreased significantly seems to be a change in the industrial structure, and the effect of neo-liberalism deepened in the 2000s. As discussed in the previous chapter, the transition from manufacturing to service economies has largely affected the expenditure of training in OECD countries. Jobs in service economies are typically organized around very simple and/or narrow tasks, often highly routinized. In this case, the countries are more likely to rely on short-term and temporary ALMPs, such as job-matching services and public work, rather than vocational training that takes money and time. As Bengtsson argues, "up-skilling might not have the same effect today as it did in the mid-20th century" (Bengtsson 2014, 67).

Upskilling in the knowledge-based economies needs more cost and time consuming than job training in the period of post-war industrial development. In short, traditional vocational training is fundamentally required by many budgets and training hours. However, many countries that want a quick policy effect in a neoliberal economy that emphasizes competitiveness and flexibility within the labor market are reluctant to increase the budget for vocational training and education. Above all, extreme changes in the labor market structure are favoring short-term job placement and job-matching rather than longer-term-based job training that requires more policy attention and spending.

4.1.3 Public Employment Services and Employment Incentives

While the expenditures on training have decreased, the expenditures on PES and subsidies such as the employment incentives and subsidized employment have been relatively growing. As shown in Figure 4.6, this trend has been more prominent among SMCs since the 2008 global economic crisis. However, the trend of expenditure on PES has sharply decreased in LMCs.

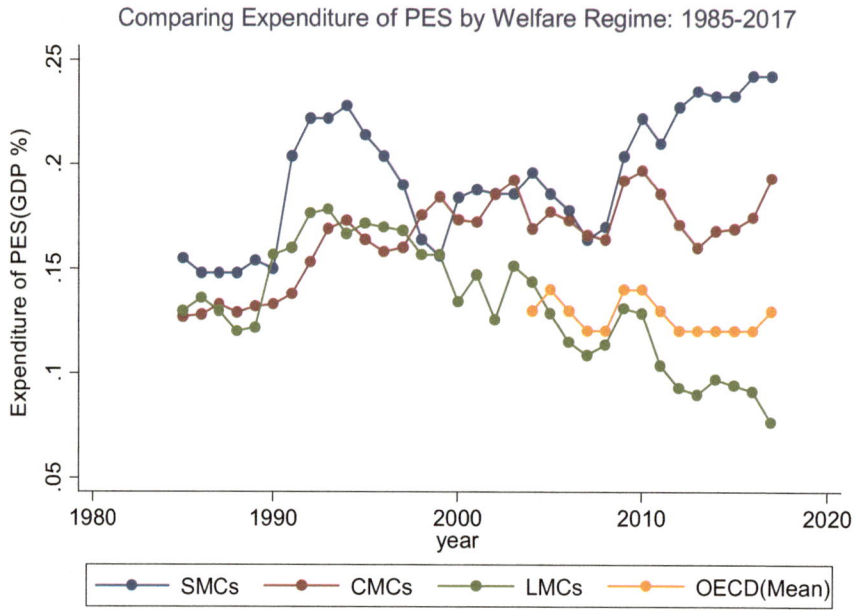

Figure 4.6. Comparing the Expenditure of PES in Case countries: 1985-2017

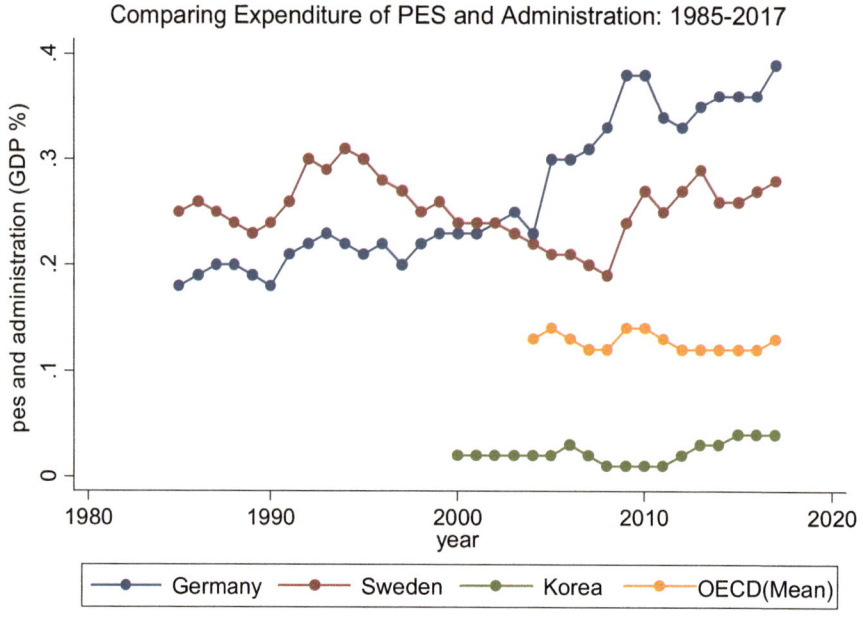

Figure 4.7. Comparing the Expenditure of PES by Welfare Regime: 1985-2017

In the Nordic European countries such as Denmark and Sweden, PES spending has increased significantly since the 2008 economic crisis. In Figure 4.7, PES spending in Germany has increased significantly since 2005, when the Hartz reform began. The German government has made efforts to further systematize the public employment system through the Hartz reform (See Chapter 6 in more detail).

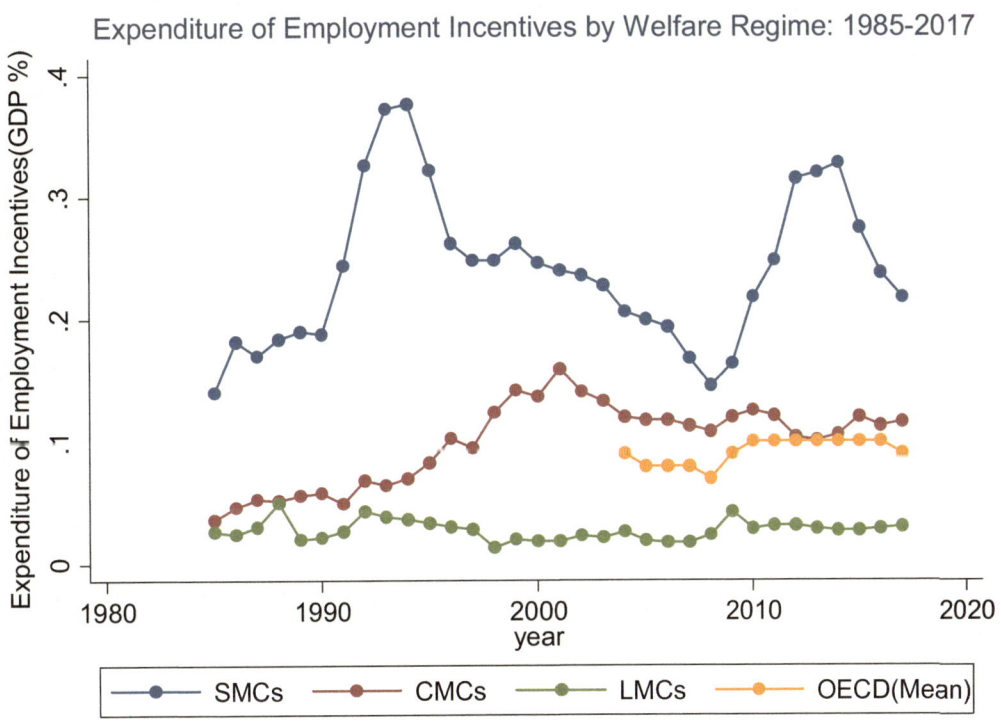

Figure 4.8. Comparing the Expenditure of Employment Incentives: 1985-2017

The expenditures of employment incentives in SMCs are also much higher than those of CMCs or LMCs. This trend of expenditure shows that SMCs have relied on the spending of economic incentives to maintain employment during the

2008 economic crisis. In terms of employment incentives spending, Sweden is still relatively high compared to other countries. As shown in Figure 4.9, Sweden's employment incentive spending has remained above 0.4% of GDP since the 1980s.

In Germany, on the other hand, employment incentives are relatively low. In the case of Korea, employment incentives are still relatively small but have recently shown a gradually increasing trend.

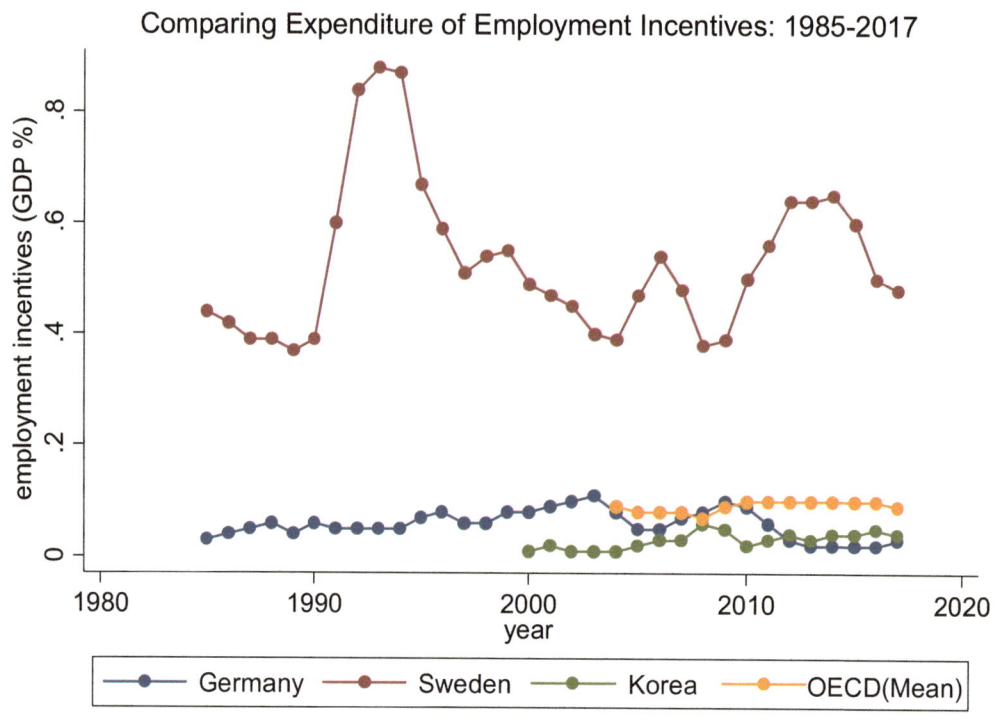

Figure 4.9. Comparing Employment Incentives in Case countries: 1985-2017

4.1.4 Direct job creation and Start-up incentives

The opposite trend in ALMPs' spending trends is spending trends for direct job creation and start-up. The Expenditures of Direct job creation was one of the leading ALMPs in the 1990s with vocational training. However, it has been declining significantly in recent years (See Figure 4.10).

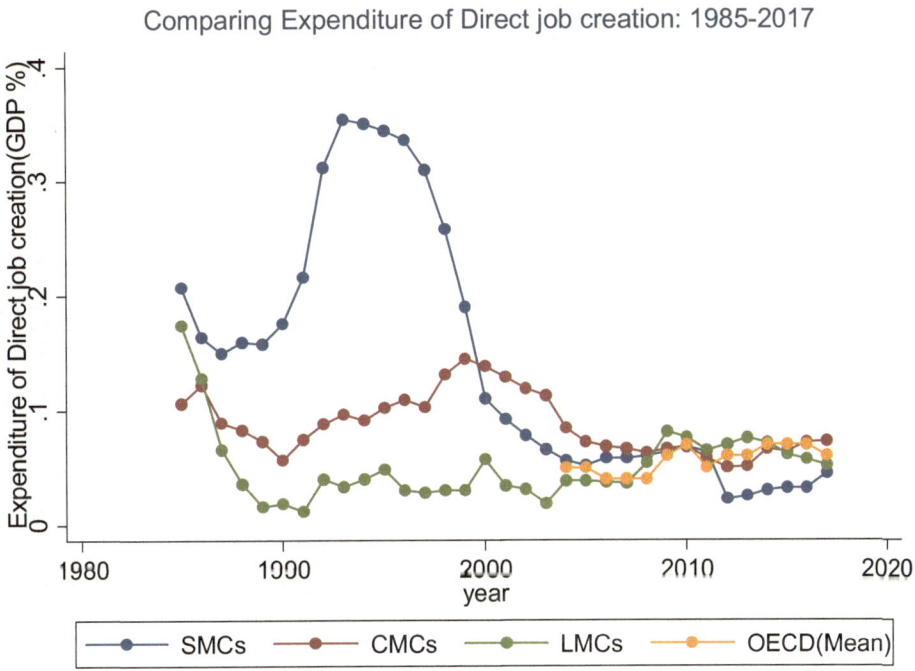

Figure 4.10. Comparing Direct Job Creation by Welfare Regimes: 1985-2017

Expenditures of direct job creation that have been mainly selected among CMCs in the early 1990s have also sharply decreased. Even France, which relied heavily on direct job creation policies during the economic crisis by the first half of the 2000s, has recently reduced its budget.

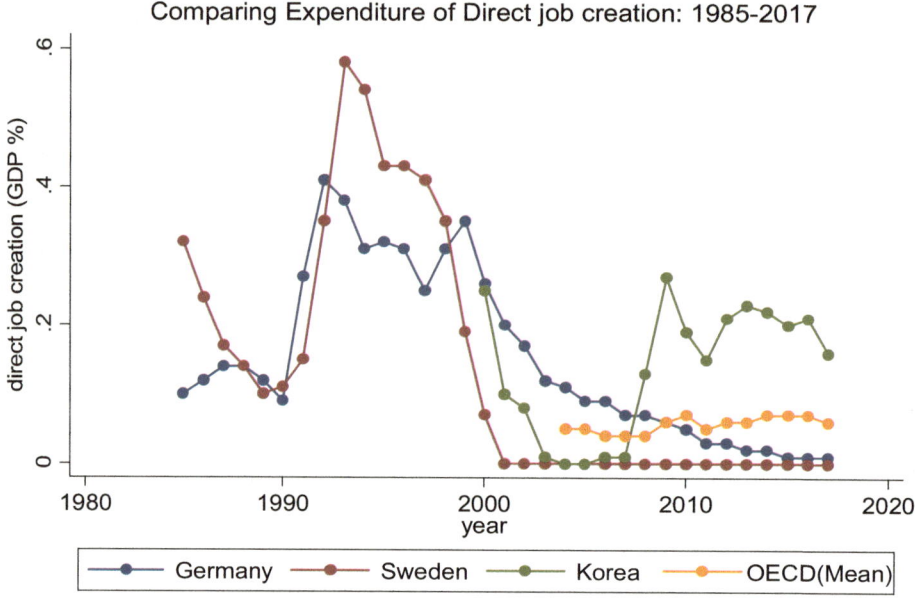

Figure 4.11. Comparing Direct Job Creation in Case countries: 1985-2017

This change in the spending of ALMPs has also been shown in research findings that direct job creation policies have not achieved the desired policy results for stable jobs. For instance, as Kluve and Schmit (2002) argue, while job training is most likely to improve employment probability, direct job creation in the public sector is likely to fail to turn temporary jobs into stable jobs.

In the period of an economic crisis, the Korean government has also largely relied on direct job creation. A typical example is public work employment such as internships at public institutions and urban environment improvement work. As seen in the case of Korea, most of the public works in the economic crisis were mostly short-term jobs of less than six months or one year, making the jobs very unstable and failing to guarantee the sustainability of employment. However, when the economic crisis settled, public work budgets have been dramatically reduced.

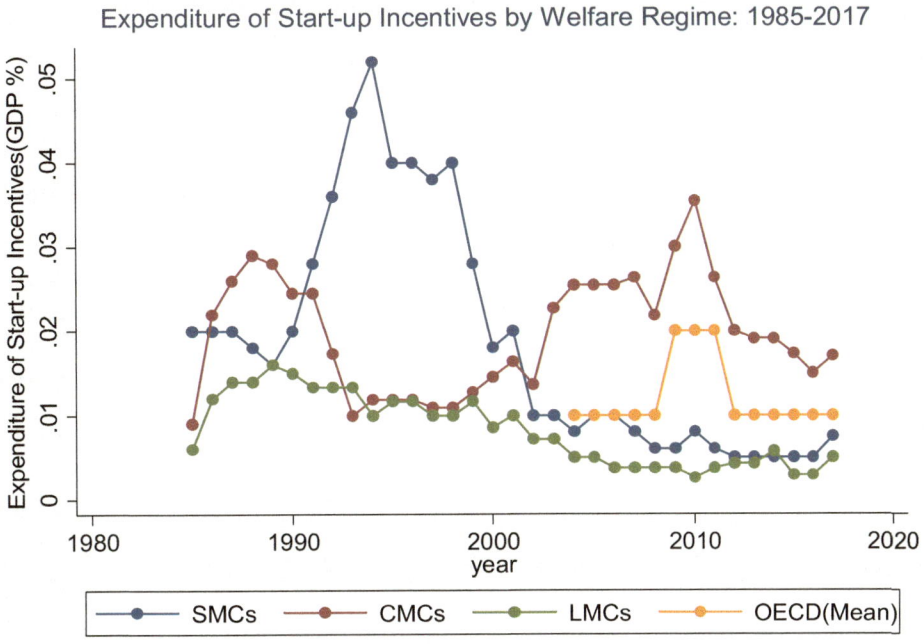

Figure 4.12. Comparing Start-up Incentives by Welfare Regimes: 1985-2017

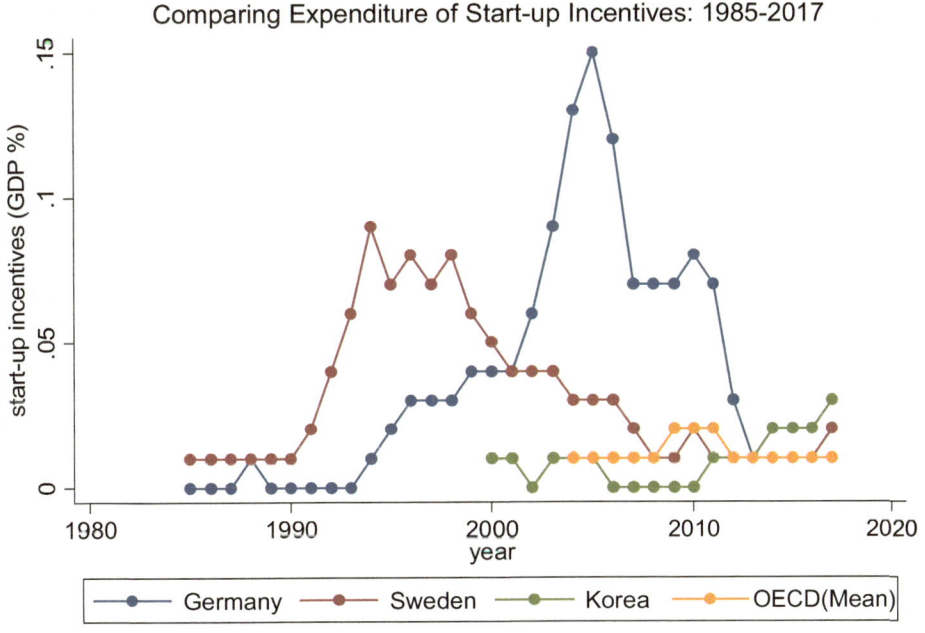

Figure 4.13. Comparing Start-up Incentives in Case countries: 1985-2017

On the other hand, the expenditure of start-up incentives shows to be relatively low but increase. As shown in Figure 4.12, the average expenditure on startup incentives in CMCs countries is much higher than that of SMCs and LMCs since the early 2000s. The expenditure of startup incentives is related to the industry 4.0 policy, which has been promoted by the German government after the Hartz reform. Germany, which relied heavily on direct job creation policies from the 1990s to 2000, has significantly reduced its spending. However, the German government has recently increased the start-up incentive spending after the Hartz reform. The Korean government has also recently increased Start-up spending (See Figures 4.13).

In short, inconsistent with the EES recommendations, the data on ALMPs shows that in OECD countries, spending on short-term and pro-market-based policies such as PES and employment incentives has increased, rather than increasing spending on traditional vocational training. There are two possibilities why this has happened. First, in the face of the economic crisis, each government is more likely to prefer job matching or incentives to retain employment with short-term policy effects. Second, another possibility is that the need for traditional manufacturing-oriented vocational training has been relatively reduced due to the recent digital transformation and the transition to the knowledge service industry. This will be discussed in more detail in the next section.

4.1.5 Trends of ALMPs within Welfare Regimes

As discussed in the previous section, the expenditures of ALMPs differ depending on the policy type as well as the welfare system. In this section, it will be examined in more detail how the policy measures of ALMPs appear differently according to the welfare regime. Regarding analyzing trends of ALMPs within welfare regimes, it will explore it based on Bonoli's typology (Bonoli 2010) and the concept of two pathways of capitalism (Milberg and Houston 2005; Wright and Rogers 2010): "high road" or "low road." According to Bonoli (2010), there are four types of ALMPs: incentive reinforcement (tax credits or benefit reductions and conditionality), employment assistance (PES), occupation (job creation schemes in the public sector or direct job creation), and human capital investment or up-skilling (through vocational training) (See Chapter 2 in more detail). This typology can be very useful to understand the trends and characteristics of ALMPs within welfare regimes.

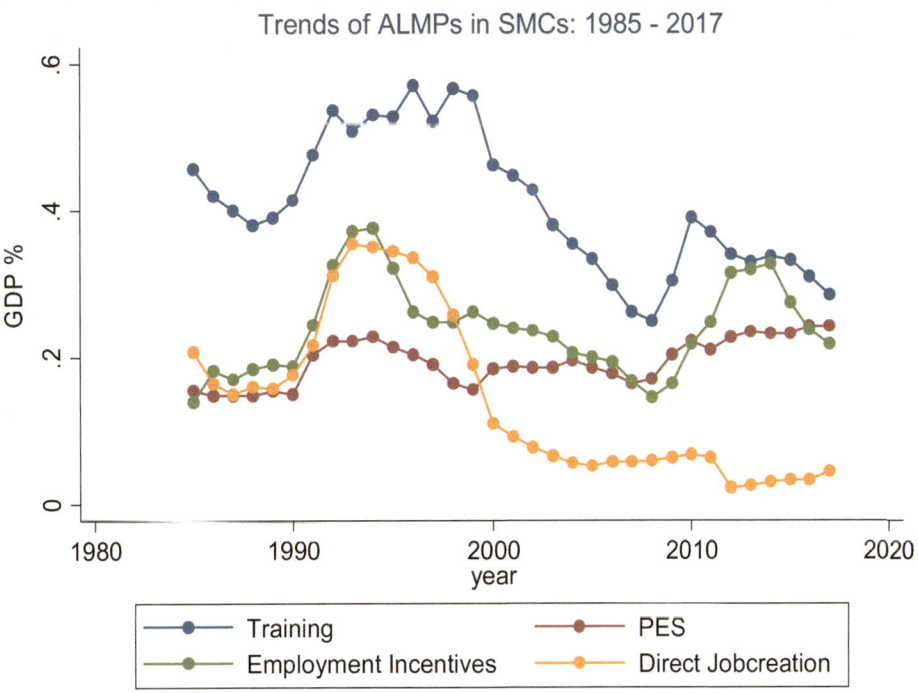

Figure 4.14.   Trends of ALMPs by types in SMCs: 1985-2017

As shown in Figure 4.14, looking for the trend of expenditure according to the type of ALMPs under SMCs, training spending occupies the highest proportion of ALMPs over the entire period. Next, the expenditure of employment incentives accounted for a second large proportion after the global economic crisis in 2008. However, recently, the expenditure of PES has outpaced spending on employment incentives since 2016. On the other hand, the expenditure on direct job-creation has increased significantly between the early and mid-1990s, but after then has continued to decrease and now occupy the bottom of the four types.

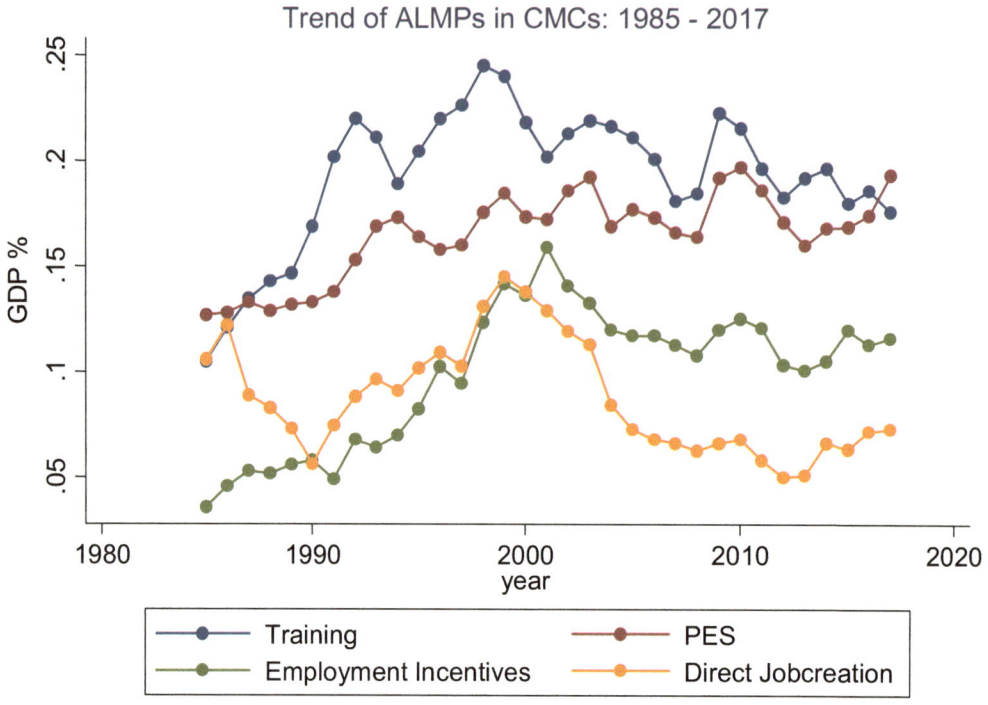

Figure 4.15. Trends of ALMPs by types in CMCs: 1985-2017

Figure 4.15 shows the trends and changes in the expenditure by ALMPs' type under CMCs. Traditionally, in CMCs, training spending has occupied the highest proportion among the types of ALMPs. However, recently, the expenditure of PES has outpaced the spending on vocational training. Next, the expenditures of employment incentives and direct job creation are followed by a large difference.

On the other hand, looking at the trend of spending by type of ALMPs in LMCs, the expenditure of PES has outpaced vocational training spending since the mid-1990s. Unlike SMCs and CMCs, under LMCs, it has been highly dependent on direct job creation after the 2008 global economic crisis. On the other hand, the expenditure on employment incentives has occupied a relatively small proportion in LMCs (See Figure 4.16).

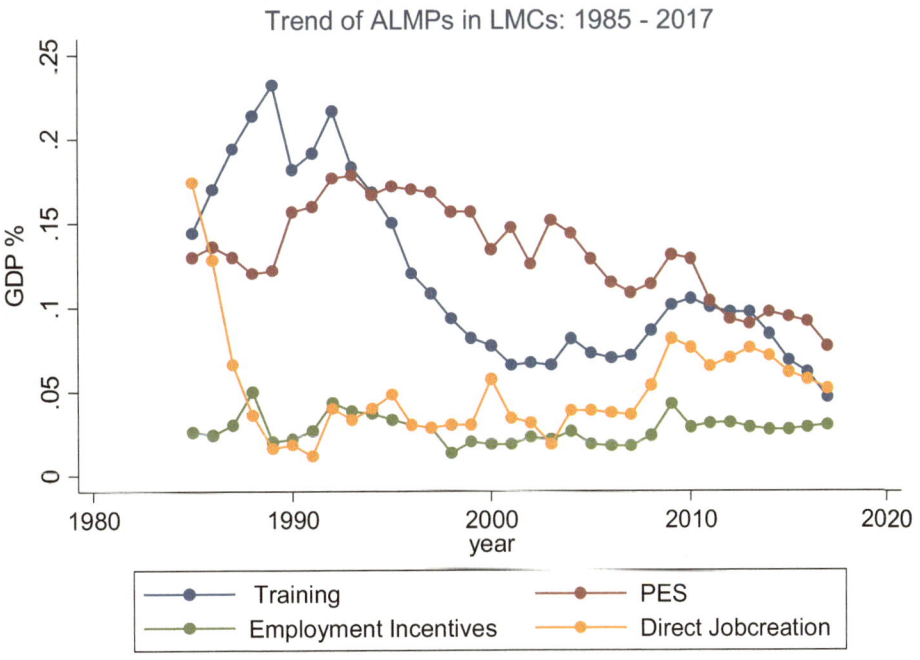

Figure 4.16. Trends of ALMPs by types in LMCs: 1985-2017

Based on Bonoli's typology of ALMPs, these analytic results show that spending on upskilling and human resource development in SMCs is more than CMCs and LMCs. On the other hand, the role and importance of PES have gradually increased under CMCs and LMCs since the 2008 global economic crisis. The results confirm that the trend of expenditure of ALMPs in three welfare regimes has been changed with short-term job policy through PES spending, which is directed by more pro-market measures than investment for traditional human resource development.

4.2 Determinants of ALMPs

In the previous section, we have analyzed the trends in ALMPs spending by welfare regimes. As a result, several points are confirmed.

First, the ALMP expenditures of SMCs as a percentage of GDP are generally higher than those of CMCs or LMCs, while the expenditures of ALMP have a relationship with the economic downturns and crisis. It supports *Hypothesis 1 (H1: The expenditures of ALMPs in SMCs are likely to be more than CMCs or LMCs)*. Second, the expenditure on training has gradually decreased except for the recent economic crisis among OECD countries. Although the expenditures of training in CMCs do not reach the level of SMCs, however, they have remained constant. Third, while the overall expenditures on training have decreased, the expenditures on PES and subsidies such as the employment incentives and subsidized employment have been growing. Fourth, in the period of an economic crisis, particularly LMCs, in particular, the Korean government has considerably relied on direct job creation, unlike counties in SMCs and CMCs. Fifth, the average expenditure on startup incentives in CMCs countries is much higher than that of SMCs and LMCs since the early 2000s.

Why is there the variation of spending on ALMPs among OECD countries, and why did the change of trend in ALMPs happen? As discussed in the previous chapter, this study assumes that the expenditures of ALMPs to address unemployment in hard times are likely to be different according to their economic context and labor market institutions. To explain the differences and changes in expenditures of ALMPs, one needs to analyze several determinant factors that could explain the adoption of ALMPs.

In this regard, political coalitions of social actors who act for their interests in each economic situation may have significantly affected variation in ALMPs. Therefore, political factors, including partisan control, especially left-party or right-wing government, and union density rates are more likely to have a relationship with ALMPs (*H2: The left parties and/or left-wing government are more likely to approve the expenditure of ALMPs*). At the same time, the variations of ALMPs are closely linked to how countries differ in institutions and organizational structures. The corporatist structure and wage-setting coordination system under the coordinated market economies (CMEs) may have positively affected the level of expenditure of ALMPs. In countries where laborers and employers are coordinated by their organizations and have a cooperative relationship with the state, the expenditures of ALMPs are likely to be more than in other countries (*H3: The union density rates and coordination of wage-setting may have positively affected the level of expenditure of ALMPs*).

The development of information technology and consequent changes in the industrial structure may also have affected the expenditure or type of ALMPs. Upskilling in the knowledge-based economies needs more cost and time than job training in the period of post-war industrial development. Therefore, some countries are likely to choose measures of ALMP, including short time-based employment incentives or job matching services, rather than upskilling through life-long education and higher education. In this regard, the neoliberal influence may be considered as an important determinant factor of ALMPs (*H4: The greater the impact of neoliberal economic ideology, the smaller the expenditures of ALMPs*).

In this regard, several determinant factors can be pointed out. In particular, this section analyzes the causal effect of independent variables affecting overall ALMP spending as a dependent variable (soex_almp). These independent variables include partisan government control (gov_party, leftcum), collective bargaining coverage (adjcov1), union density rates (ud_1), and coordination of wage-setting (coord), economic openness (kaopen), industrial structure (emp_ag, emp_ind, emp_serv).[1] At the same time, this study used a dummy variable to examine whether there was a structural change in the expenditure of ALMPs before and after the 2008 economic crisis.

As discussed in Chapter 3, this study used the panel data analysis method. Using the pooled crosssectional data of OECD countries, regression analysis was performed to verify the hypothesis discussed above (commend: xtreg). First, the Hausman test was performed to find out which model is right between the random

---

[1] See the previous chapter for details on how these variables were measured.

effects model and the fixed effects model (Hausman 1978). Through the Hausmann test, the difference between the estimated parameters was examined to know if the estimated values of the fixed-effects model and the random-effects model were significantly different. As a result of the Hausman test, the fixed effect model was confirmed to be suitable, except for the case of SMCs. Table 4.1 shows the results of the regression of panel data about determinants of ALMPs.

Overall, it can be seen that the cabinet composition (Schmidt-Index) (gov_party) is also showing a positive direction to the expenditures of ALMPs at the level of significance of 0.01. It supports *Hypothesis 2* that the left parties and/or left-wing governments are more likely to approve the expenditure of ALMPs. Also, the union organization rate has a positive effect on ALMPs expenditure at a significance level of 0.01 (*Hypothesis 3*). Although the degree of market openness and wage-setting coordination have a positive effect on the expenditures of ALMPs, however, it is not statistically significant. In the case of the dummy variable, it is also significant at the 0.01 level. It means that the overall expenditures of ALMPs have positively changed since the 2008 economic crisis compared to the pre-2008 period. However, there is a possibility that the overall analysis results and the analysis results according to welfare regimes may show some differences. Therefore, in order to examine more objective analytical implications, it is necessary to examine the analysis results according to welfare regime types.

Table 4.1 Results of Regression of Panel Data: Determinants of ALMPs

Welfare Regime (soex_almp)	ALL	SMCs	CMCs	LMCs
	Model 1	Model 2	Model 3	Model 4
Government Party (gov_party)	0.026***	0.011	0.031***	0.033**
	(2.81)	(0.44)	(3.24)	(2.26)
Left Party (leftcum)	-0.002	0.021***	-0.009	0.024***
	(-0.33)	(2.81)	(-1.00)	(3.08)
Union Density (ud_1)	0.036***	0.075***	0.023**	0.032*
	(6.81)	(11.39)	(2.25)	(1.96)
Bargaining Coverage (adjcov1)	-0.004	-0.094***	0.002	0.002
	(-1.00)	(-7.54)	(0.56)	(0.20)
Coordination of Wage-setting (coord)	0.048	0.235**	0.041	-0.040
	(1.41)	(2.36)	(0.83)	(-0.90)
Market Openness (kaopen_1)	0.071	-1.778**	0.	0.0000
	(0.93)	(-2.24)	(0.84)	omitted(.)
Employment Rates (employmentrates)	-0.022***	-0.058***	-0.008	-0.009
	(-3.57)	(-2.77)	(-1.20)	(-0.58)
Dummy	0.082***	0.237***	0.036	0.023
	(2.98)	(3.06)	(1.02)	(0.79)
_cons	0.951	10.485***	0.385	-0.235
	(1.54)	(3.39)	(0.50)	(-0.15)
r2	0.4965	0.7593	0.3946	0.4446
No of Obs.	150	29	78	43

Note: * $p<.1$; ** $p<.05$; *** $p<.01$, t-value ( )

As shown in Table 4.1, the cabinet composition (Schmidt-Index) under SMCs has a positive relationship with the expenditure of ALMPs, but it is not statistically significant. Though, the leftcum variable, which means cumulative leftcab(share of seats in parliament held by leftist parties in the most recent government as a percentage of all seats held by the government) score, has a positive effect on ALMPs at the 0.01 significance level. Also, institutional variables such as the labor union organization rate (ud) and wage-setting coordination (coord) have a positive effect on the expenditure of ALMPs at a significance level of 0.01 and 0.05 each. On the other hand, contrary to the expectations, it was found that the collective bargaining coverage rates (adjcov) gave negative results(-0.094***) on the expenditure of ALMPs. In this regard, further analysis is required later. In regard to market openness (kaopen), it has a negative effect on the expenditure of ALMPs at the significance level of 0.05. In SMCs, the market openness appears to be putting pressure on reducing ALMPs' spending. In particular, the dummy variable representing the change in ALMPs expenditure before and after 2008 is significant at the 0.01 level, indicating that the expenditure of ALMPs increased after than before the 2008 global economic crisis. This is also confirmed in Figure 4-2 in the previous session.

Under CMCs, the institutional variables such as cabinet composition (Schmidt-Index) and union organization rate have a positive effect on expenditures of ALMPs at levels of 0.01 and 0.05, respectively. The degree of wage-setting coordination (coord) and market openness (kaopen) are also shown to have a positive effect on ALMPs spending. However, it is not statistically significant. The dummy variable is not statistically significant. It means that the expenditure of ALMPs in CMCs has not changed significantly before and after the 2008 economic crisis. Under LMC, the cabinet composition (Schmidt-Index) and union organization rate have a positive effect on ALMPs spending at levels of 0.05 and 0.1, respectively. However, other influence variables are not statistically significant. In particular, the dummy variable is not significant statistically. It is analyzed that the expenditures of ALMPs in LMCs have not changed significantly before and after the 2008 economic crisis.

In short, based on the panel datasets, the regression analysis between the expenditure of ALMPs (socex_almp) and the several independent variables reveals several analytical implications. First, the cabinet composition (Schmidt-Index) (gov_party) also shows a positive direction to the expenditures of ALMPs. It means that the left party and/or left-wing government has positively affected the expenditure of ALMPs. In this regard, while the left-wing party under SMCs is expected to have a great influence on ALMPs spending, the analysis result is not significant statistically. However, the leftcum variable has a positive effect on ALMPs at the 0.01 significance level. Second, it is confirmed that institutional factors such as union density rate and wage-setting coordination system have a positive relationship with the expenditure of ALMPs expenditure. Third, the effects of neoliberal ideology on the spending of ALMPs are also mixed. Though it shows a positive relationship under CMCs, it shows a negative relationship in SMCs. It means that the effect of neoliberal ideology on ALMPs expenditure depends on domestic institutional conditions. Lastly, the analysis results for dummy variables show that the ALMPs spending has significantly changed only under SMCs. Therefore, it is confirmed that the ALMPs expenditure still shows a difference according to the type of welfare regimes.

4.3 Summary

In hard times of the global economic crisis, the OECD countries have focused on ALMPS rather than passive labor market measures such as unemployment benefits and assistance. However, ALMPs expenditure differs from the type of welfare state. In general, SMCs have manifestly spent more on ALMPs than CMCs or LMCs. Also, the gap of ALMP expenditures among types of the welfare state is getting a little bigger after the 2008 economic crisis. Above all, the expenditure of ALMPs in Sweden which has been traditionally well-known as a frontier of ALMP, has largely decreased (especially job training) since 2000 but has again increased after the 2008 economic crisis.

In general, the decreases in ALMP expenditures after the 2000s are attributed to the global neo-liberal influence. Even in the same welfare regimes such as SMCs, ALMPs expenditures still show differences depending on political institutions and economic conditions. In general, the ALMP expenditure during the left-wing rule was greater than that of the right-wing government. The expenditure on training has gradually decreased except for the period of the recent economic crisis among OECD countries. While the expenditure on training has decreased, the expenditures of PES and subsidies such as the employment incentives and subsidized employment have been growing. With this, it needs to note that in the case of Sweden, the expenditure on vocational training, which has traditionally been strong, has already declined sharply, except during the temporary economic crisis. It is unclear whether these vocational training expenditures are due to changes in the policies of the right-wing government in 2006 or the changes in the industrial structure during the 4th Industrial Revolution, which means that the existing vocational training is no longer valid. The sharp decline in spending on vocational training has to do with the emergence of a right-wing coalition government. However, even after the SPD government took power in 2014, the budget for vocational training has not increased significantly. Therefore, it needs to analyze why the trend of expenditures of ALMPs in Sweden has largely changed from traditional job training to PES and employment incentives. It will be examined in more detail in Chapter 5.

The expenditure of ALMPs in Germany, a key country in the CMCs, shows different characteristics from Sweden. In general, the expenditures of ALMPs such as PES, Training, and employment incentives are bigger in SMCs than in CMSs. Though, the expenditures of PES and Training in Germany are bigger rather than in Sweden. Especially, the expenditures of PES since the mid-2000s have been higher than spending on vocational training in Germany, which has a strong vocational training system traditionally. Here, it cannot help but wonder how and why the changes in expenditures and types of ALMPs happened in Germany. In Chapter 6, it will examine why these changes occurred and what it means in more detail.

On the other hand, the expenditures of direct job creation that have been mainly selected among CMCs in the early 1990s has also sharply decreased, except for Korea. For example, public finance expenditures on direct job creation policies, which were shown in CMCs in the early 1990s, such as Germany and France, are shrinking significantly. Direct job creation during the economic crisis is dominated by temporary effects that lower the unemployment rate, but it does not lead to long-term stable and persistent jobs. For this reason, countries that have traditionally made many financial allocations to direct job creation are also reducing spending on these policy measures. However, it is paradoxical that Korea has relied on direct job creation in every economic crisis. This indicates that Korea's active labor market policy is pursuing only a short-term, temporary policy effect rather than a long-term plan (See Chapter 7).

Unlike recommendations of EES, the measure of ALMPs has shown short-term and pro-market characteristics, such as PES and employment incentives. Overall, most countries are seeing a gradual increase in spending on government subsidies, such as short-term, pro-market PES, and employment incentives and subsidies, instead of financial spending on vocational training. This clearly shows that neoliberal economic ideology has a major impact on ALMPs in OECD countries. Under the neoliberal economic system, governments and corporations tend to emphasize flexibility and efficiency within the labor market. Therefore, they prefer short-term education and job matching rather than vocational training, which requires a certain amount of time and social cost.

On the other hand, recent changes in the industrial structure, such as the advent of the fourth industrial revolution era, are likely to be related to changes in the financial spending patterns of ALMPs. Because service sector jobs are typically organized around very simple and/or narrow sets of tasks, often highly routinized, it does not require long-term vocational training. As the industrial structure changes from traditional manufacturing to the service industry, the type of ALMP is also shifting to financial spending on short-term employment services and employment incentives rather than on financial expenditure on vocational training. However, as a result, short-term and pro-market-oriented policy measures such as job matching and employment incentives have produced negative consequences such as low-wage job creation, job instability, and social inequality.

As a result of the panel datasets, the left party and/or left-wing government has positively affected the expenditure of ALMPs. Also, institutional factors such as union density rate and wage-setting coordination system have a positive relationship with the expenditure of ALMPs expenditure. However, the effects of neoliberal ideology on the spending of ALMPs are also mixed. It shows a positive relationship under CMCs but is not significant. However, it shows a negative relationship in SMCs at the 0.05 significance level. It shows that the effect of neoliberal ideology on ALMPs expenditure depends on domestic institutional conditions. The analysis results for dummy variables show that the ALMPs spending has significantly changed only under SMCs. In short, the ALMPs expenditure still shows a difference according to the type of welfare regimes.

In sum, the influence of neoliberal economic ideology makes it difficult for the OECD countries to solve the fundamental job problem of high youth unemployment rate and new job creation, which ALMPs alone face in these countries. Now, these OECD countries must go beyond active labor market policy and actively establish integrated job policies through linkage with macroeconomic and industrial policies. In the transition from manufacturing to service economies, OECD countries have been faced with a choice between two types of job creation pathways, that is, the high road and low road (Milberg and Houston 2005). Instead of taking the 'high road' to employment, wage moderation and policies with less training and human capital development and stronger work incentives point towards the 'low road' to employment and work as an impetus towards an expanded low-wage service sector (Bengtsson 2012, 18-19). The low road through workfare means low-skilled labor, low productivity, unstable jobs, low wages, low consumption, dual labor market, and a vicious cycle leading to low growth due to insufficient human capital and vocational training investment. Unlike this, the high road through learn-fare is the route to a virtuous cycle that leads to high skills, good jobs, high wages, high income, and high growth through higher education and long-term vocational training. However, the analytic results show that the expenditures on training have decreased among the OECD countries. On the other hand, the expenditures on PES and subsidies such as the employment incentives and subsidized employment have been growing.

Chapter 5

SWEDEN: ECONOMIC CRISIS AND ALMPs

5.1 Introduction

Sweden has been regarded as one of the most successful social models in terms of economic development and social welfare among OECD countries. With an export-oriented economic structure, Sweden has sensitively responded to external competition and economic conditions in the global economy. As Katzenstein argues, Sweden has a small state with a strong economy. Sweden has formed a social democratic economic system that manifests both political stability and economic flexibility in the face of periodic economic crises in the global market. Sweden's economic openness and vulnerability have prompted the formation of democratic and corporatist arrangements to survive in the world market (Katzenstein. 1985).

The Swedish model later contributed to the rapid growth of the economy and the development of mature social security systems from the 1950s to the 1970s. Since the 1980s, however, the emergence of neoliberalism in the global economic system and intensifying competition among countries by global corporations have gradually affected it. Since the 1980s, the deregulation of capital and financial markets and the devaluation of currencies have resulted in inflation and wage growth in Sweden. Since 1983, the wage decision at the national level has been shifted to the wage decision method at the industry level or the enterprise level. The solidarity wage policy based on the principle of same value labor and same wage at the national level gradually began to crack.[1]

In the early 1990s, Bildt Cabinet (1991-1994) tried to reform the labor market based on neo-liberal ideas, including measures to reduce welfare expenditure, privatize social services, and reform the pension system. However, Sweden faced a serious economic crisis in 1993 due to deregulation since the 1980s and rising real estate prices and bubbles following the Swedish currency devaluation. Even after the Social Democrats took power again, changes and reforms of the labor market had continued. In 2006, Reinfeldt's cabinet, a center-right coalition government, began more drastic labor market policies, welfare, and tax reforms.

The shock of the 2008 global economic crisis was no exception for Sweden. In the aftermath of the global economic crisis, Sweden's economy has deteriorated rapidly since the second half of 2008, and real GDP fell by 5 percent in 2009. The unemployment rate rose from 6.2 percent in 2008 to 8.3 percent in 2009 (Anxo 2015). Nevertheless, Sweden has recovered faster than other OECD countries. In 2010, the Swedish real GDP increased by 6.6 percent, compared to the previous year. The number of employed also increased by 25,000 in 2010, followed by 100,000 in 2011. However, despite the gradual increase in employment rates since

---

[1] In 1987 the liberalization of the capital market by the Social Democrats and the deregulation of the credit market led to a significant increase in Swedish capital's foreign investment, and the Swedish giants gradually became multinational corporations. As a result, global capitalists no longer valued negotiations with domestic labor. Consequently, the third path taken by the Social Democratic Party in 1980 failed to combine its goals of solidarity and equality, economic stability, and growth, further weakening existing corporatism with only rising inflation and wages.

2010, the unemployment rate in Sweden was relatively high at 8 percent. The youth, including the low-educated, unskilled, and refugees, were exposed to long-term unemployment and temporary employment.

This chapter analyzes how Sweden has overcome and responded to the 2008 global economic crisis. This chapter also focuses on why it has shown a rapid economic recovery compared to other OECD countries. First, what was the Swedish government's response and ALMPs to the global economic crisis in 2008, and what were the strategies of major actors in social dialogue? What were the main contents of the ALMPs presented in response to the 2008 global economic crisis? Why has the trend of expenditures of ALMPs in Sweden largely changed from traditional job training to PES and employment incentives? This chapter tries to answer these questions.

5.2 Economic Crisis in Sweden

5.2.1 Pre-2008 Economic Crisis: Formation and Change of The Sweden model

The Saltsjöbaden Agreement (1938) and the Rhen-Midner model were the product of this global market competition and responses to the economic crises. The model was a self-regulating mechanism to resolve conflicts of interest between the export-oriented industrial sector and the domestic manufacturing sector in the competition of the global market. It was a comprehensive policy system to simultaneously achieve various goals, such as full employment, price stability, and industrial restructuring through the solidarity wage policy, social security institutions, and active labor market policy (see Figure 5.1).

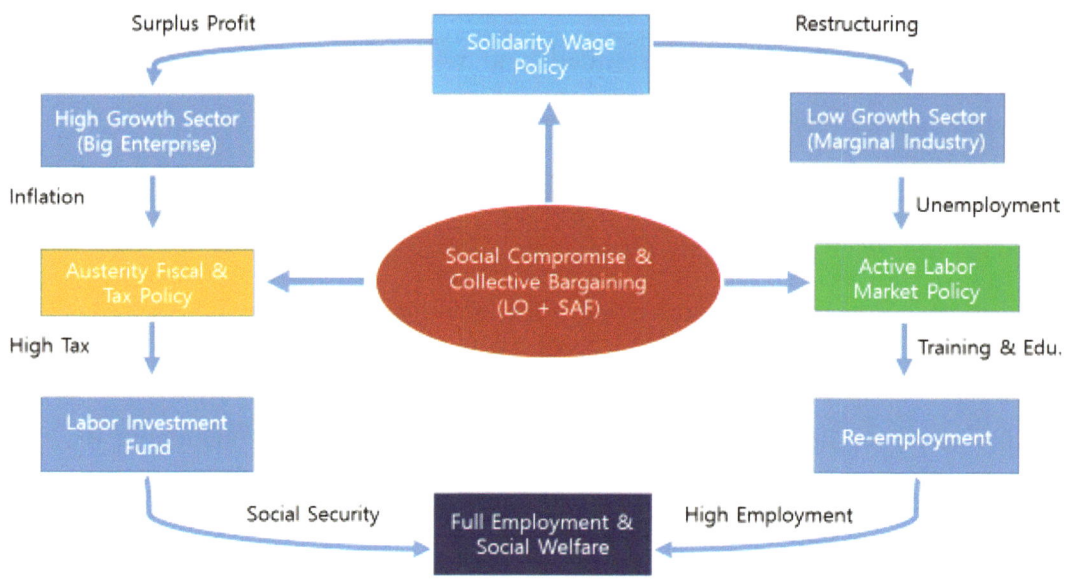

Figure 5.1. The Swedish Model

As shown in Figure 5.1, it consists of three policy pillars: solidarity wage policy, social security system, and active labor market policy. Since 1956, LO and SAF have pursued a solidarity wage policy that provides equal pay for the same kind of job through central bargaining regardless of the profit of the enterprise. It had a prioritized wage increase in the low-wage sector. At the same time, it reduced the wage gap among industries and companies in the same industry. Efficient companies under the solidarity wage policy had been expanded and developed by increasing profits and investments. Inefficient companies were forced out of the market or attempted to increase efficiency and productivity for survival.

Active labor market policies (ALMPs) were introduced to solve unemployment problems that could arise from solidarity wages. ALMPs have eased the constraints on labor mobility and have led to the rapid movement of unemployed people from inefficient sectors into highly productive ones. Therefore, solidarity wage and active labor market policies made possible industrial restructuring while realizing full employment, macroeconomic stability, and equality in complementary relation.

Meanwhile, the Swedish government of the Social Democratic Party (SAP, Sveriges socialdemokratiska arbetareparti) supported the labor union's wage restraint, absorbed the corporate profits into the tax system and various social fund systems, and invested in the productive sector through the state control on the central bank and the financial market. And it was possible to supplement the direct wage restraint with indirect social wages such as pension system, family allowance, medical insurance, housing subsidy, disease allowance, etc.

The Swedish Trade Union Confederation(LO) and the Swedish Employers Association(SAF) had agreed to suppress wage increases through the solidarity wage. Instead of minimizing the direct distribution conflict between labor and management by breaking a connection between company profits and wages, it was transformed into a social redistribution issue. LO, on the other hand, accepted the wage restraint at national negotiations for macroeconomic stability. Instead, the companies have increased employment by investing their profits in domestic production, and the government has tried to create a virtuous cycle of future income increase through the expansion of the national tax and social welfare system.

In other words, the reason for the class compromise in Sweden is that the Social Democratic government, supported by the union, absorbed the increased profits from the union's wage restraint into the tax system and social fund system. The government has encouraged corporate profits to invest in the production sector through control over central banks and financial markets. Compensation for direct wage restraints was provided through indirect social wages in the form of public service provision and income transfer, such as pension schemes, family allowances, medical insurance, *housing subsidies*, and sick pay.

In short, to curb inflation and sustain appropriate profits, the Swedish model implemented long-term fiscal policies and promoted the solidarity of the working class by narrowing the wage gap among companies and industries under the principle of equal pay for equal work. To improve the competitiveness and productivity of the industry, it suppressed excessive wage increases in competitive industrial sectors. On the other hand, it weeded out non-competitive industries and marginal firms. The excess profits of competitive high value-added industries were absorbed into investment funds and ATP funds (general supplementary pensions) and used as funds for enhancing technological development and corporate competitiveness, and welfare costs. The unemployed in the wake of the restructuring of the marginalized firms were absorbed through active labor market policies and relocated to new industries. This mechanism of the Swedish model became a stepping stone to the economic success of Sweden. Until the 1960s, the Swedish labor market achieved wage stabilization and full employment based on the central bargaining of LO-SAF and maintained high economic performance. Then, the Swedish central bargaining had continued for almost 27 years since 1956.

Oil Shock and the Crisis of the Swedish Model: 1970s – 1980s

The crisis of the Swedish economic model in the 1970s began with the global recession caused by the first and second oil shocks. The OECD countries, the trading partners of Sweden, have experienced extreme recessions since 1973, including high prices, low productivity, and low growth rates. The global economic environment made it difficult for Sweden to implement its full employment policy. In the aftermath of the oil shocks, the cost of living in Sweden had also risen relatively, which again had been the pressure for wage increases. And these wage pressures had lowered Swedish export price competitiveness, which in turn led to higher unemployment rates. At the same time, the collapse of the Bretton Woods system in the early 1970s was another factor in the crisis of the Swedish economic model. The fixed exchange rate regime for the dollar collapsed, resulting in a significant increase in capital flows between countries. As a result, it became important for Sweden to have a lot of foreign exchange to stabilize its currency, and it was forced to implement a high-interest rate policy.

The Swedish Social Democratic Party proposed 'the third way' in 1982 as an economic election pledge. At that time, the 'Third Way' policy core was maintaining full employment and the deregulation of the financial market. In other words, the central economic wage negotiations were to retain the past Swedish economic model to curb wage increases while taking some of the neo-liberal policies like devaluation of the currency value to drive economic growth and recreate past economic performance. However, the deregulation of capital and financial markets and the devaluation of currency values had led to inflation and real-wage decrease.

The Swedish Social Democratic Party's liberalization and deregulation of the capital market in 1987 became another cause for Sweden to implement low-price and high-interest rate policies. Sweden had been forced to pursue them to maintain its export price competitiveness and foreign exchange reserves. This had made it impossible for Sweden to adhere to its previous full employment policy. The large Swedish corporations started to transform themselves into multinational corporations gradually by increasing foreign investment beyond the control of the state. Above all, Sweden's high progressive income tax rate had led to the incentive to reduce labor supply due to the transfer of overseas factories of large Swedish companies. With the increasing reliance on foreign markets, large Swedish corporations gradually began to avoid central negotiations with labor organizations (LO).[2]

In 1983, the employer organization of big companies (VF), which had the most extraordinary dependence on the foreign market, proposed to the metal union (Industrifacket Metall, IF Metall) to break away from the central bargaining system. It tried to set up independent industrial bargaining, arguing about securing skilled workers and raising wages higher than the central wage agreement. As IF Metall accepted this VF's proposal for resolving metalworkers' dissatisfaction with wage equalization policy, the central bargaining system of LO-SAF collapsed. Since then, the influence of SAF, a partner of LO, has been sharply weakened, and in 1990, SAF abandoned collective bargaining with a central labor organization, LO.

As shown in Figure 5.2, changes in the Swedish industrial structure have also weakened negotiations at the central level. In the previous large-scale manufacturing industry, which was made of relatively homogeneous labor, the collective bargaining power at the central level was very strong because of the high degree of solidarity

---

[2] In the case of the solidarity wage policy, the equal wage for equal work started as a policy to practice the wage rule of a fully competitive market. Sweden's wage gap narrowed in all respects, from industry to enterprise size, gender, education, years of service, and the wage gap between careers (Forslund, 1997). However, the solidarity wage policy served as a mechanism to restrain the wage increase of skilled workers despite the relative wage increase effect on unskilled workers. This deepened both the lack of skilled workers in Sweden and their complaints about wages.

of labor. However, as the proportion of the service industry increases, the labor union has been relatively weakened.

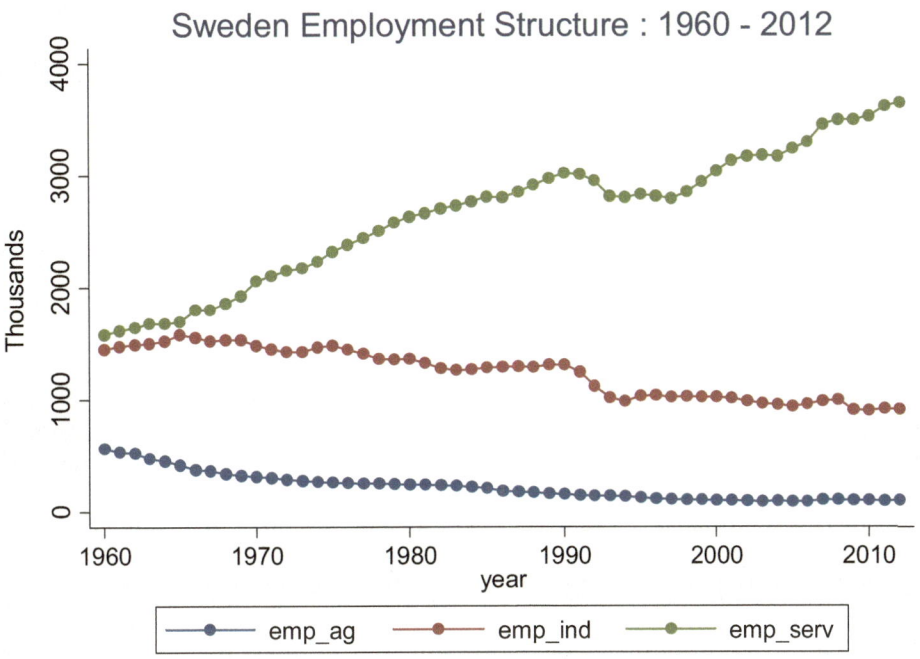

Figure 5.2. Change of Swedish Industrial Structure

In short, based on solidarity and full employment policies, the Swedish model was in crisis in the 1970s due to the global economic downturn, the liberalization of capital markets, and the weakening of unionism. Despite these crises, Sweden has maintained full employment policies, increasing spending on the public sector. As the public sector expanded, the participation rate of women increased rapidly. Unemployment rates in Sweden remained at around 2 percent until the end of the 1980s. The third-way policy of the Social Democratic Party became the opportunity to dismantle the Swedish model and implement neo-liberal policies in earnest. The third-way policy failed to combine the goals of solidarity with equality, economic stability, and growth and only weakened the existing unionism while raising inflation and rising wages. The capitalist forces, which had the opportunity to challenge the existing Swedish model due to the political weakening of Union and SPD, and deregulation, supported a right-wing coalition with competitive and market-friendly policy lines. It opened a political opportunity for the right-wing coalition to take power in the early-1990s.

Centre-Right Alliance and Market-oriented Reform: 1990s

The Bildt cabinet, based on the central-right coalitions, declared its 'transition to the economic system' and started revising the Swedish model in February 1991 (Shin 2007). The conservative right-wing coalitions, which took power from 1991 to 1994, tried various policy changes based on the neo-liberal economic ideology. They put austerity, monetarism, and market-oriented reforms as the core of policy. They have implemented measures to reform the welfare system, such as reducing welfare spending, privatizing social services, and reforming the pension system. In 1993, the government enacted the 'Competition Act,' which allowed state-owned enterprises, which had been in the monopoly status, to enter the competition.

However, the market-oriented reform measures and deregulation measures of the center-right coalitions had resulted in an economic crisis in Sweden. The reforms of the center-right alliances had significantly increased the domestic real estate prices along with the adverse effects of economic stimulus policies in the late 1980s, such as capital market opening, **credit expansion**, and low-interest housing purchase.

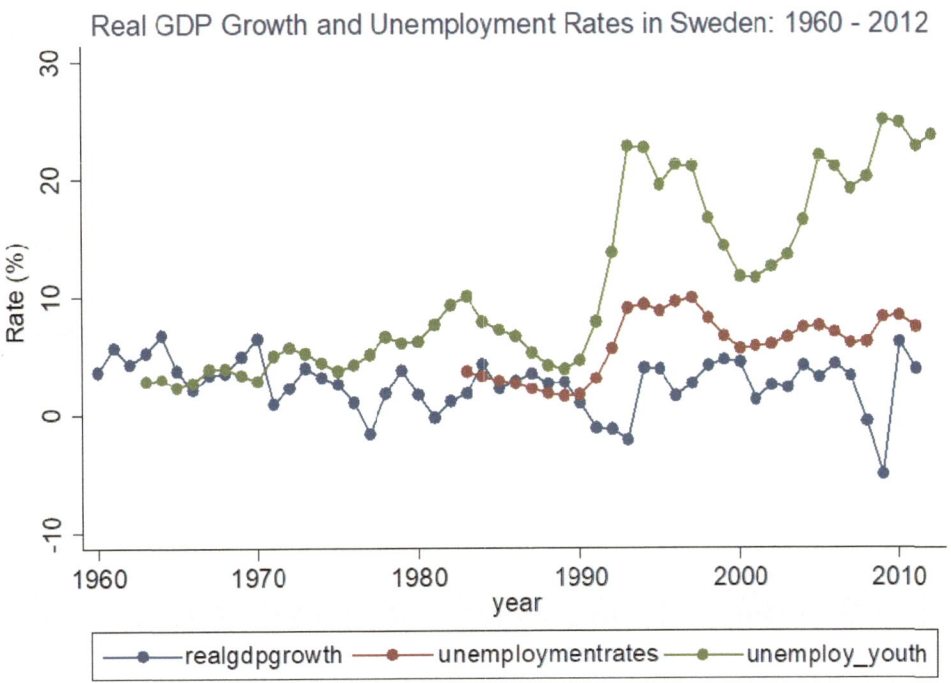

Figure 5.3. Changes in Real GDP Growth and Unemployment Rates

With the fall of the world economy in the early 1990s, the bubble burst, and Sweden faced a severe economic crisis with real estate and financial assets plunging and banks suffering from bad debt accumulation. Sweden's total gross domestic product recorded negative growth from 1990 to 1993. Unemployment rates rose sharply from 2 percent in the late 1980s to 10 percent in the mid-1990s. Unemployment rates under the age of 25 soared from 3 percent to over 20 percent (See Figure 5.3).

As a response to the economic crisis, the Swedish government was actively investing in the nationalization of insolvent banks, the reorganization of insolvent assets, and investments in the future, including reform of welfare systems, fiscal austerity, and university education. Expenditure on labor market policies largely increased. Above all, the proportion of financial expenditure on active measures such as income preservation measures through subsidies and the use of various employment programs was relatively high. Vocational training programs were linked to unemployment insurance and local employment offices, and most workers were required to undergo a vocational education program if they were unemployed for more than six months.

Swing between Social Democratic Party and Centre-right Alliance: After the 2000s

The Social Democratic government, which came back thanks to the policy failure of the Bildt cabinet, pursued reform policies of the tax, welfare, and labor to overcome the economic crisis. However, the Social Democratic government tried to progressively reform the Swedish way rather than accept neo-liberalism (Woo et al., 2014). Rather than reducing the size of public social services and privatization of social services, the Swedish government tried to induce citizens to provide more efficient and better social services through core values of marketization. For example, it allowed the participation of private companies in education and health services to expand options and improve service quality through competition. The flexibility of the labor market had increased, and incentives for labor market entry (or reentry) or sanctions had been strengthened by policy measures, such as strengthening unemployment insurance qualification requirements and reducing benefits.

However, in 2006, Sweden had its first majority government in decades as the Centre-right Alliance defeated the incumbent Social Democratic government, based on the rapid growth of the anti-immigration atmosphere and the failure of new job creation under the Social Democratic government(Ahn 2007). SDP failed to meet the expectation of new job creation, which had caught a great deal of public interest. It promised only the maintenance of the welfare system through subsidies but failed to provide concrete alternatives.

Prime Minister Fredrik Reinfeldt, who took power in 2006, strongly pushed the reforms of labor market policies. The Swedish government focused on reducing the number of unemployed people receiving unemployment benefits and increasing the real employment population. Starting with the abolition of wealth tax in 2008, the Swedish government announced policies, such as reduction of unemployment assistance, real estate tax and income tax, and downsizing of labor representative members in small-scale businesses. The Centre-right alliance government sought ways to increase employment by lowering the company's mandatory tax rate, strengthening market competitiveness, and lowering wage costs for enterprises. It also pursued a smaller, more efficient government, which laid out a typical supply-oriented economic policy. The sharp decline in Swedish ALMP expenditures had closely related to these reform policies of the Centre-right alliance government.

5.2.2 2008 Economic Crisis

The 2008 global financial and economic crisis from Wall Street in the United States has caused a significant shock to the Swedish economy. Since the second half of 2008, the Swedish economy has deteriorated rapidly. Sweden's growth rate was negative 0.6 percent in 2008, followed by a negative 5.2 percent in 2009. In particular, the unemployment rate increased significantly from 6.2 percent in

2008 to 8.6 percent in 2010. The youth unemployment rate also increased significantly from 20.2 percent in 2008 to 24.9 percent in 2009. Since then, the economic growth rate in 2010 has rebounded to 6.0 percent very quickly, in line with the Swedish government's fiscal and active labor market policies.

The unemployment rate has also been on a modest decline, peaking at 8.6 percent in 2010. However, since the 2008 economic crisis, the unemployment rate has not reached the level of 6.1 percent in 2007, just before the economic crisis. In particular, the youth unemployment rate was 16.7 percent in 2018, roughly three times the total unemployment rate of 6.3 percent, but down considerably from 24.9 percent in 2009 (See Figure 5.4)

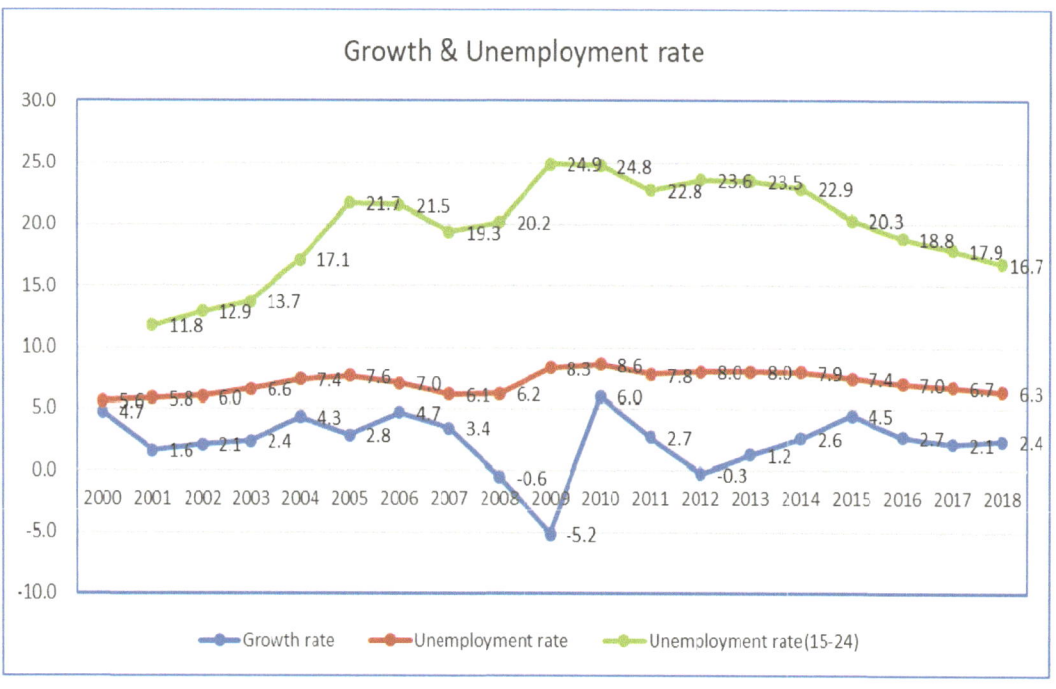

Figure 5.4. Changes in GDP Growth and Unemployment Rates

The 2008 economic crisis hit the manufacturing sector, particularly the male-centered industry and workplace. The fall in output and employment was particularly marked in the male-dominated manufacturing industries, with 25 and 20 percent decreases, respectively (Anzo 2017). Sweden had a significant impact on the manufacturing industry, especially the automotive industry. In Sweden, where large companies like Volvo and Saab were the employers of many workers, the crisis in the automotive sector, which accounted for a large size of jobs and had a high backward linkage effect, soon led to a decline in employment.[3] The employment rate in Sweden fell by about 10 percent from the second half of 2008 to the first half of 2009, resulting in 100,000 job losses (Anzo 2017).

The 2008 global economic crisis affected the recession in manufacturing and related industries, such as the distribution and service sectors. Besides, the 2008 global financial crisis has also deteriorated the quality of employment in Sweden. The number of workers and short-term contract workers in local government agencies, which were relatively budget-constrained by the 2008 global economic crisis, significantly decreased. In the early phase of the recession, adjustment essentially took the form of a reduction of overtime and a dramatic reduction in the number of dispatched workers and short-term contracts, particularly among male employees.

The Swedish government rapidly responded to the global economic crisis

---

[3] In the case of Volvo, Volvo Passenger Cars laid off about 3,000 people in 2008, and Volvo Trucks about 1200 in 2007, and Volvo Construction Equipment about 1350. Volvo's cooperation companies and subcontractors also cut approximately 1,000 employees in 2007. In the case of Shab owned by GM of the United States, instead of reducing jobs, the company shortened operations to change from two-time production to one-time production per day and reduced wages of 1200 employees. Saab's subcontractor Adecco, on the other hand, cut 50 of its 145 employees as Saab's production decreased (Anzo 2017).

in 2008, and its economy has stabilized since 2010. However, as shown in Figure 5.4, Sweden's unemployment rate has peaked at 8.6 percent in 2010 and has remained 6 to 7 percent thereafter. The youth unemployment rate has remained at 20 percent until 2015.[4] In particular, the youth unemployment rate was nearly three times the total unemployment rate. Along with youth unemployment, the increase in the number of long-term unemployed (27 weeks or longer) became a key issue in the Swedish government's job policy (Anxo 2017). Furthermore, one of the most problematic issues in the Swedish labor market in recent years is refugee unemployment.

5.3 Responses to the Economic Crisis

5.3.1 Political Responses

The Swedish government's response to the 2008 global economic crisis has emerged as an expansionary fiscal policy to alleviate economic shocks and activate labor market policies to overcome the unemployment crisis. In the face of the 2008 global economic crisis, when the economic situation deteriorated sharply, the Swedish government implemented financial and fiscal stimulus measures at the end of 2008. In particular, the Swedish government has decided to make extensive financial investments in the maintenance activities of roads and rail networks to boost the economy.

---

[4] In Sweden, there are some reasons for the high youth unemployment rate, compared to the overall unemployment rate. First, it results from the application of the seniority principle (Last in, First out, LIFO) of the Swedish Employment Protection Act. Another reason is that employers tend to be hesitant to hire young people with low skills because of high initial wages. For this reason, the youth with a short employment period has been the first to be fired when economic downturns occur. In addition, a mismatch between jobs and vocational education is also cited as the cause of high youth unemployment (Anxo 2017).

To prevent the downturn in the construction sector, the Swedish government provided tax deductions to repair, maintenance, and improvement of residential and tenant homes to promote construction activities and maintain labor demand.

The Swedish government announced further fiscal expansion measures to respond to the 2009-10 economic crisis. The new fiscal expansion resulted in more resource investment, primarily in the growth of government subsidies to the local governments and counties and in active labor market policies. In 2010, the Swedish government decided to increase the government subsidy for municipalities and county councils by an additional 10 billion Swedish krona (SEK). To maintain and stabilize employment in the public sector, it decided to expand its investment in infrastructure to 1 billion kronor and then expanded social transfers, such as child and housing allowances for low-income workers, to continue household consumption (Anxo 2017).

With fiscal expansion policy, the Swedish government has also sought to mitigate the impact of the global economic crisis on the export industries through a variable exchange rate regime. At the same time, the Swedish government promoted tax cuts for corporate and individual earners and social security reforms, including improvement of unemployment benefits, health insurance, etc. While reforms to the social security system helped to save fiscal budget, the government tried to strengthen labor supply and incentives through the tax deduction for employees and reduction of marginal income tax for high-income earners.[5]

---

[5] The Swedish government abolished the inheritance tax and the wealth tax in 2005 and 2008 respectively, and the tax burden of the citizens also dropped from 56 percent to 46.4 percent in ten years. In the last decade, the amount of tax cuts reached about 17.5 trillion (SEK). At the time of the economic crisis, Sweden implemented policies to lower interest rates and boost corporate investment through bailouts for the auto industry, special loans, employer tax relief and tax credits. In Sweden's view of accepting a welfare model of high level of welfare and high burdens, lowering corporate tax

In particular, the labor market policy of the government of the center-right alliance emphasized the supply side of the labor market. The Swedish government sought to reduce the income tax, property tax, and corporate tax to ease government regulations on enterprises and encourage them to increase their investment and employment. It also encouraged companies to carry out voluntary wage restraints and employment training programs. In 2007, the New Start Job (the Nystartsjobb) Program allowed employers to be exempt from social welfare contributions if they employed long-term unemployed or socially subsidized persons. It also cut the social welfare contributions of employers in half when they hired young unemployed people (ages 19 to 25), which was aimed at employment promotion effects.

The government of the center-right alliance abolished or cut off the 'Plus Job,' the Sabbatical year program, some employment subsidies, and unemployment benefits implemented by the Social Democratic Party.[6] For example, in the case of unemployment benefits, the benefit period was limited to a maximum of 300 days since 2007. The replacement rate of unemployment benefits was also lowered to 80 percent of their income by the 200th day and 70 percent after the 201st day. Another 300-day extension of benefits was abolished on July 2, 2007. Instead, after 300 days, the government helped the unemployed find new jobs or motivated them to participate in the job and development guarantee program, including coaching,

---

burdens was an unprecedented attempt to overcome the economic crisis of the time.

[6] The 'plus job' policy was to allow unemployed people who have been registered for more than two years in a public employment agency to work for the state, local governments, and related companies. This was mostly assigned to immigrants who had difficulty finding employment. Also, this was done to expand employment opportunities and enhance work experience for long-term unemployed workers. However, the new government abolished the job creation policy because it aimed to reduce the unemployment rate.

education, and job search activities. If job seekers previously had a right to income-linked unemployment insurance benefits, they would receive 65 percent of their previous income. Otherwise, individuals may receive a minimum compensation of SEK 223 per day in support of their activity (Anxo 2015).

In 2006, Prime Minister Reinfeldt focused on reducing the number of unemployed people receiving unemployment benefits and increasing the real workforce, and initiating measures for tax reforms and cut in unemployment benefits. In 2008, starting with the abolition of wealth taxes, the Swedish government released neo-liberal policies, including reducing unemployment benefits, real estate and income tax cuts, and the reduction of the number of labor commissioners in workplaces of a small size. Employers generally welcomed these social security reforms, tax cuts, and supply-oriented measures of the right-wing government. However, the unions on the other side pointed out the problems of rising youth unemployment and social polarization under neoliberal policies. They emphasized that the employment increase by 80,000 to 85,000 in 2009 thanks to the 'new start' program was attributed to the increase in the number of non-regular workers. Moreover, there was a problem that regular workers had continued to decrease.

5.3.2 Economic Responses

The response of economic actors to the 2008 economic crisis can be summarized in two ways. First, wage reduction was one of the responses to the 2008 global economic crisis. Second, the effort to shorten the working hours and job sharing was among those. As we have seen above, the Swedish economic model was based on a solidarity wage policy. Sweden's economic actors have adapted to the external economic environment through the solidarity wage policy instead of strikes over economic interests after the Saltsjöbaden Agreement. The solidarity wage policy made it possible to secure competitiveness through industrial restructuring. The problems of frictional or structural unemployment, which are inevitable to be seen in the industrial restructuring process, have been solved through a social security system and active labor market policies. The solidarity wage system was broken by the collapse of central wage bargaining and inter-industry agreements at the national level in 1983, which had been in place for the past 20 years. Since then, collective bargaining has been carried out at two levels: the industrial sector and the corporate unit.

In particular, the wage hikes and increase of unemployment during the severe economic recession of the early 1990s had a decisive impact on new compromises on wage decisions. New compromises in the private and public sectors represented a clear trend to reorganize businesses and sectoral wage decisions (Anxo 2015). In short, unlike the mid-1970s, public sector wages did not affect private-sector wages since the mid-1990s. The new spirit of the agreement was to re-establish the role of the pace set by the sectors exposed to international competition. As a result, Sweden experienced different wage increases in the following decade.

The new procedures and rules of wage-setting have played a role in ensuring industrial peace and coordinating wage negotiations in the industrial sector since the second half of the 1990s. At the regional level, there was a clear trend for individualization and decentralization of wage bargaining in both the private and public sectors. Wage negotiations at the local level played a central and significant role in setting wages, as well as terms and conditions of employment. Most wages in the public sector were set locally and personally by monitoring performance. This trend was in stark contrast to the seniority-based wage system, which prevailed until the mid-1990s.

Social partners in the private and public sectors recognized that wage increases would result in limited monetary policy (an interest rate hike) with potentially adverse effects on employment and unemployment. This reorientation of macroeconomic policy played a decisive role as an institutional mechanism against excessive wage growth. As far as wage settings and wage increases were concerned, experience from the severe economic crisis of the early 1990s has shown that wage moderation characterized wage increases during the late 1990s and early 2000s. Thus, in the wake of the 2008 global economic crisis, the wage restraint agreement served as a mechanism for maintaining employment stability and preventing further unemployment. Indeed, the results of the 2009-2011 bargaining round had been dominated by wage restraint in Sweden. As a result, these wage restraints helped the economic recovery by reducing the negative impact of the economic downturn on production and employment and slowing down the rise of labor costs.

Sweden's employment rate was higher than other European OECD countries even during the economic crisis. It resulted from allowing part-time work. Today, part-time is one of the most common forms of employment in Sweden. According to the Survey of the workforce by the Swedish Bureau of Labor Statistics in 2012, a total of 4,657,000 people participated in the labor market, of which 24 percent (1.2 million) were part-time workers. Female workers had a high rate of part-time employment: 12.9 percent of male workers were part-time workers, while 36.4 percent of female workers were those (Sweden Statistics 2012).

Part-time work in Sweden shows a distinctive characteristic from that of other OECD countries. In general, employers preferred it to reduce incidental social costs and labor costs due to economic fluctuations. However, Sweden's part-time work aimed to increase the employment rate through women's social advancement. In addition, it was promoted as part of a policy for work-life balance along with public childcare and parental leave. In particular, the Swedish government has made various policy efforts to ensure that part-time work of good quality is established in the labor market.[7] As part-time jobs expanded, the employment rate for Swedish women increased significantly.[8]

The characteristic of Swedish part-time jobs is that the proportion of 'convertible part-time' is very high, which comes from reducing working hours by full-time workers. These part-time workers are predominantly female workers who voluntarily shorten their working hours by 20 percent to 50 percent by exercising their claim for shortened working hours during the period of childcare.[9] One of the reasons

---

[7] The tax reform in 1971 transformed the combined taxation of couples into individual taxation, reducing the tax burden on double- income families. In 1976, the marginal rate of part-time workers (32 percent) was significantly lowered compared to the marginal rate of full-time workers (up to 64 percent). In 1997, the Employment Protection Act was amended to greatly strengthen the rights of part-time workers. After childcare leave, if the child is eight years old or older, the worker could reduce her working hours to 10 hours per week while maintaining her full-time status. It also laid out the legal basis for solving part-time unemployment problems for part-time workers by specifying their right to claim additional work. In 2002, the Anti-Discrimination Act was enacted to prohibit indirect disadvantages as well as direct discrimination on economic compensation and treatment of part-time workers (Kim, UK, 2011).

[8] As of 2012, the female employment rate in Sweden was 71.8 percent, far ahead of 53.5 percent in Korea, as well as Spain (51.3 percent), France (60.0 percent) and Germany (68.0 percent) (OECD data 2014).

[9] According to the Swedish union LO's part-time survey, 27 percent of all part-time workers were convertible part-time workers who could return to full-time work at any time. The high rate of regular part-time workers means that there are many voluntary part-time workers, and in the same survey report, 54 percent and 65 percent of the TCO and SACO part-time workers voluntarily chose

that 'transitional part-time' was high was that it was difficult to use part-time workers in Sweden to reduce costs. Employers must pay social insurance contributions regardless of working hours, except if working days are too small to qualify for social benefits. Since the social benefits of part-time workers were not significantly different from those of full-time workers, there was little incentive to use part-time workers because of price demand. Also, in Sweden, the need for flexible workforce placement was very high. Part-time workers were mostly converted from full-time regular workers to part-time workers. Part-time workers could choose from two different types of work: two hours of work each day or a weekly day off. On the other hand, most temporary part-time workers were students who worked part-time and took ultra-short time work in service centers or call centers to earn money (Yang et al. 2014, 33).

In general, however, during the 2008 global economic crisis, the government and social partners did not consider shortening working hours as a useful policy tool to overcome unemployment (Anxo 2017). In Sweden, the widespread consensus between stakeholders and decision-makers was that unemployment depended on factors other than working hours and that there was no clear correlation between the country's unemployment rate and the length of working hours. Therefore, the labor market imbalance in Sweden was attempted to be fundamentally solved through dependency on external quantity and active labor market policies.

In the 2008 global economic crisis, non-regular workers did not increase significantly in Sweden. Above all, Sweden did not experience the development

---

part-time (Kim Young Mi. 2011; 300-301).

of mini-jobs or zero-time contracts. Unlike other EU member states, such as France and Germany, Sweden has hardly embraced public measures in favor of the retention of employment and the saving of working hours during periods of economic downturns and structural changes, such as reduction of working hours, part-time work, or job sharing. Traditionally, employment adjustments in Sweden took the form of the dependency on external quantity and active labor market policies, and relatively generous income support. However, with the 2008 global economic crisis, there were signs of change in this policy flow. In the next section, I will discuss it in more detail.

5.3.3 Labor Responses

Labor's response to the 2008 global economic crisis in Sweden was very different from that of the early 1990s. As shown in Figure 5.5, the number of labor-management conflicts had increased significantly since 1983, when national bargaining ceased. This surge in labor-management disputes continued until 1990. They declined considerably with the economic crisis in early 1990 but continued until the mid-1990.

In contrast, the 2008 global economic crisis did not have a direct impact on labor-management relations. The 2008-13 period was characterized by industrial peace, unlike the late 1980s and previous recessions (1992-95). The number of labor-management conflicts in the same period was about five, which can be said very rarely (See Figure 5.5). Why was the labor response after the 2008 global economic crisis contrasted with the situation during the early 1990s economic crisis? Answering this question requires an understanding of the Swedish industrial relations system, and an analysis of how labor responded is required. One of the basic features of the Swedish labor relations system is a strong social concertation tradition based on the presence of strong social partners with considerable autonomy from the government.

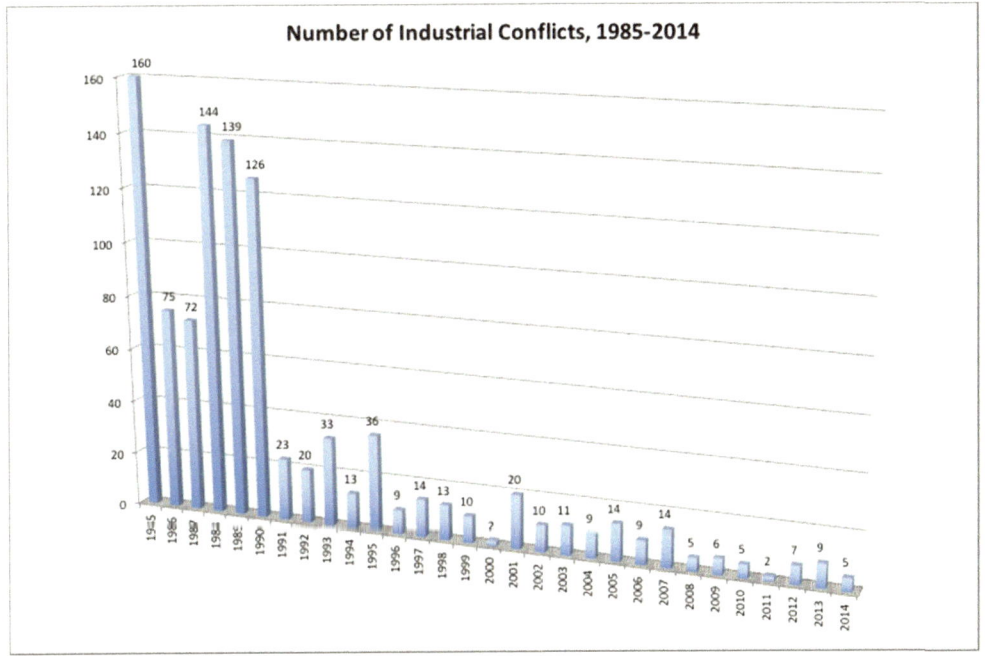

Note: Number of conflicts (upper panel, Statistics Sweden 2015), number of lost days (lower panel, Mediation Offices 2014).
Source: Anxo (2017)

Figure 5.5. Industrial conflicts, Sweden, 1985–2014

The Swedish labor relations model, or bipartite, has played an important role in the labor market since the mid-1950s, especially in the mechanism for regulating wage formation and working conditions. Since 2007, however, there has been a great change in the unionization rate. As shown in Figure 5.6, Sweden's unionization rate has declined slowly since 1990 but has declined significantly since 2007. The union organization rate, which was in the mid-80 percent before the economic crisis in the early 1990s, fell to 71 percent in 2008. In particular, the downward trends in union organization rates of the blue-collar workers in the manufacturing sector were more significant than that of the white-collar workers (See Table 5.1).

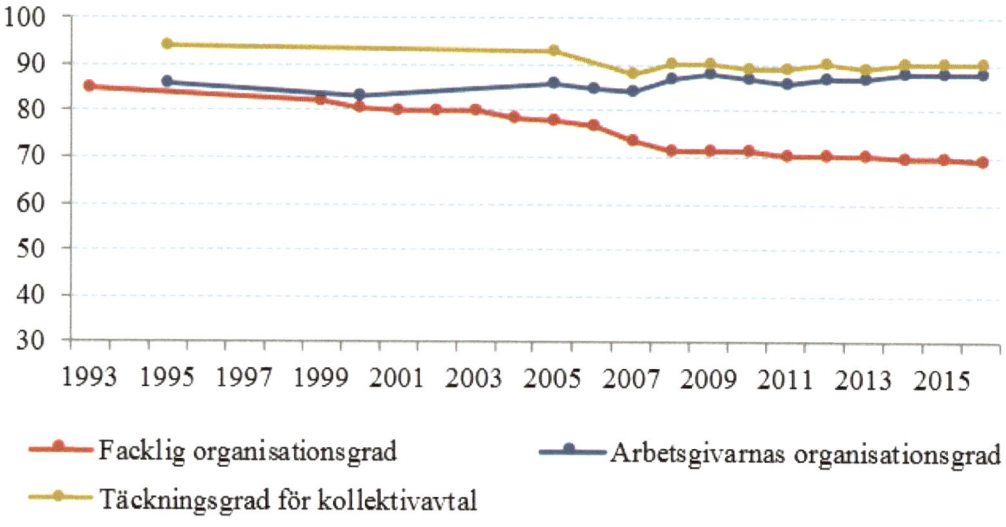

Source: Kjellberg (2017) & National Mediation Office (2018)

Note: Facklig organisationsgrad (union organization rate), Arbetsgivarnas orgainsationsgrad (Employer Organization Rate), Täckningsgrad för kollektivavtal (Coverage rate for collective agreements)

Figure 5.6. Organization rates and Coverage ratio

The global financial crisis in 2008 affected especially the sectors exposed to international competition and of blue-collar workers. However, it also affected white-collar workers in unskilled and low-wage sectors such as hotels, restaurants, and retail, having high turnover rates.

Table 5.1. Trends in union density by industries, Sweden: 1990 - 2014

	1990	1996	2006	2008	2010	2014	Variation 2008–2006	Variation 2010–2008	Variation 2014–2010	Variation 1990–2014
Blue-collar workers										
Manufacturing industry	89	92	84	81	79	76	−3	−2	−3	−13
Construction	90	90	81	73	71	67	−8	−2	−4	−23
Retail	68	74	64	57	57	53	−7	0	−4	−15
Private services	70	77	67	58	57	53	−8	−1	−4	−17
Public services	92	96	87	83	83	77	−4	0	−6	−15
All	84	87	77	71	69	64	−6	−2	−5	−20
Non-manual/white-collar workers										
Manufacturing industry	82	83	80	75	77	80	−5	2	2	−2
Retail	60	63	62	56	61	62	−6	5	2	−2
Private services	66	73	65	60	63	65	−5	3	2	+1
Public services	94	93	89	85	86	89	−4	1	−2	−5
All	81	83	77	72	73	77	−5	1	1	−4
All sectors/ occupations	82	84	77	71	71	70	−6	0	0	−12

Source: Mediation Office (2014) and Kjelberg (2015), Anxo (2017) p. 21.

The decrease in the unionization rate in Sweden was due to structural factors such as the decrease in the number of manufacturing workers in the wake of the change in the industrial structure, the decrease in employment in the public sector due to the fiscal consolidation and cutbacks in the 1990s, and the change in social and cultural norms emphasizing individual values (Anxo 2015, Kjellberg 2017). However, the accelerating decline in union organization rates since 2006 was closely related to changes in policy, particularly the Unemployment Insurance System (UI) reforms initiated by the right-wing government in 2007 and 2008.

The newly revised Swedish UI system in 2007 lowered the replacement rate from 80 percent to 70 percent after 200 days of unemployment and reduced the period of unemployment benefits to 300 days (450 days if there are dependents under 18). Also, the UI financing method was revised to differentiate and rapidly increase the contribution of various unemployment funds managed by trade unions (Ghent) according to the level of unemployment in the sector/industry. In other words, a system of experience rating was introduced, and the contribution of personal unemployment insurance increased or decreased depending on whether the unemployment rate increased or decreased in an industry. This reform led to a significant increase in individual monthly contributions. As a result, union membership decreased significantly, and the number of employees covered by the UI system dramatically reduced. After the UI reform, about half a million employees left the unemployment insurance system between 2007 and 2008. The unionization rate dropped by six percentage points from 77 percent in 2006 to 71 percent in 2008 (Kjellberg 2015). The right-wing government's main objectives with these UI reforms were to strengthen incentives for job seekers and indirectly influence the outcome of wage bargaining by weakening trade unions' bargaining power, thereby inducing wage restraint that refrained from raising wages (Anxo 2017).[10]

---

[10] Sweden's average unionization rate was 70 percent in 2014, which was still the highest among OECD countries. In particular, the coverage rate of collective agreements was also very high about 84 percent in the private sector and 100 percent in the public sector. This high coverage rate of collective agreements in Sweden, unlike European countries such as Germany and France, is not due to the existence of mandatory statutory provisions for collective bargaining, but high organizing rates of employers' organizations and trade unions (Anxo 2015).

As noted above, the 2008 economic crisis did not hurt Swedish industrial relations, although the unionization rate was significantly reduced due to unemployment insurance reform. Despite falling unionization rates, both labor and management remained two agents of social dialogue. Both actors had played a crucial role in labor market regulation and wage-setting during economic downturns. Though there were trends in the decentralization of wage decisions over the past two decades, Sweden's bargaining system has been centralized and coordinated as a two-stage bargaining model, basically at the industry/sector and company/organization level. In particular, strong trade unions have also promoted more equal relationships between workers and employers, making them more autonomous and independent of employers. Social partnerships also played a central role in carrying out major reforms in Sweden. As Anxo (2013) argues, Sweden can be a model of a negotiated flexibility regime in which social partners are widely involved in the formation of vocational training and the regulation of working conditions and wage settings at the industry and individual firms and the local level.

In the global economic crisis of 2008, the IF Metall (Industrifacket Metall) and Manufacturing Employers Association (Teknikforetagen) signed the framework agreement on March 2, 2009, in which employers agreed to stop further layoffs and workers decided to reduce their wages. The social pact in response to the crisis was achieved in a way that labor and capital traded off labor flexibility and employment security. In other words, labor made concessions on working hours and wage flexibility, while capital guaranteed employment.

At the time, the Swedish government rejected the tripartite social pact in response to the economic crisis, despite the requests from the IF Metall and

Manufacturing Employers Association. The conservative government maintained its policy stance that it would not support inefficient companies that had lost their competitiveness. The right-wing government saw the 2008 economic crisis as a natural process in the capitalist economy and a process of restructuring, in which industries or companies with weak competitiveness withdrew, and new businesses and companies grew at the same time. In short, the conservative government adhered to the labor market flexibilization policies focused on external and numerical flexibility instead of internal and functional flexibility through reducing working hours (Cho 2019).

Social agreements signed by the trade unions of the IF Metall and the manufacturing employers' association have made wages payable according to actual working hours. In particular, the working hours can be shortened to less than 80 percent of regular working hours, but the minimum wage was set at 80 percent of ordinary wages, including various allowances. The social agreement was a framework agreement at the industry-level that allowed the establishment of a subsequent agreement at the enterprise level. Originally, the social agreement in 2009 was signed for 12 months, but since then, it has been extended until the end of 2010 by extending the validity period in collective agreements. In 2014, with the proposal of IF Metall and the Manufacturing Employers' Association, the framework agreement was enacted into legislation (effective January 1, 2014) that enabled labor and management to respond to the crisis by minimizing the layoffs of workers through reduction of working hours in the future economic crisis. Also, on February 4, 2014, a tripartite agreement was signed, including the conservative government. If the social agreement in 2009 was a way for labor and management to share the wage burden according to the reduction of working hours, the tripartite agreement in 2014 allowed employers to receive financial support from the government with the reduction of working hours when it determined that it was an economic crisis.[11]

In general, wage restraint has been a key feature of collective bargaining between Swedish labor and management since the 2008 global economic crisis to stabilize employment and limit further growth in unemployment. Indeed, with the weakening labor market, the results of the wage negotiations in the final round resulted in a modest rise of wages in both the private and public sectors for four years (2009-2013). Wage stabilization and decrease in labor cost, along with the devaluation of the Swedish currency under the expansionary monetary policy by the Swedish Central Bank in 2008-10, helped alleviate the negative impact of the recession on production and employment. It was also helpful that exports had increased during the period of recovery in 2010.

In short, unlike countries with weak industrial relations systems and unbalanced bargaining power between the two sides, Sweden's labor-management relations system has involved a more balanced sharing of crisis costs. Therefore, Sweden still has the highest quality level of jobs. The 2008 global economic crisis did not negatively affect working conditions like other European countries despite wage cuts, longer working hours, heavy workloads, and increased work intensity in Sweden (Anxo 2011, 2013).

---

[11] In the case of tripartite crisis agreements provided by the government, workers' wages can be reduced by up to 12 percent, 16 percent, and 20 percent, respectively, when the labor union shortens working hours by 20 percent, 40 percent and 60 percent. In this case, the share for cost by businesses is 1 percent, 11 percent, and 20 percent of the costs, respectively, in accordance with the reduction of working hours, and the government will bear 7 percent, 13 percent, and 20 percent of the costs, respectively (IF Metall 2014)

5.4 Labor Market Policies for Job Creation

5.4.1 ALMPs in the 2008 global economic crisis

In the 2008 global economic crisis, the active labor market policy has played a vital role in reducing the unemployed and securing economic stabilization. In particular, the preference for the principle of employment promotion (work-first principle) has predominated over passive measures for the unemployed.

As shown in Table 5.2, most of the ALMP measures implemented during the period 2008–13 targeted people with a weak attachment to the labor market, such as long-term unemployed, young dropouts, foreign-born immigrants, and disabled people. Regarding unemployed youths, particularly those who have not completed upper secondary school, the government priorities have been to increase the number of participants in previously established youth programs, such as Youth Guarantee.

The government has also emphasized the role of the Swedish PES in easing the matching process in the labor market, in particular intensive monitoring of job-search and activation measures, as well as additional resources to the PES (increase in the ratio of staffing). The increase in the level of appropriation and the allocation of resources in the various ALMPs attests to the reinforcement of ALMPs towards labor-supply-oriented matching measures, greater monitoring of job-searching, and activation measures administrated by the PES.

Table 5.2. ALMP Programs in Sweden: 2008 – 2013

Program	Purpose	Measures
Special Measures for the Disabled	Supporting people with disabilities to be able to work	Wage subsidies for employers who hire persons with a disability Sheltered employment for persons that cannot get jobs About 70,000 participants per year during the period 2008–13
Employment Support	Stimulating employment of persons with difficulties by finding a job in the regular labor market	Employment support for persons with a background of long-term sickness absence Various types of employment support for long-term unemployed by reducing the employers' wage costs
New-start Jobs	Supporting the employers' costs of social fees for a limited period	Abolishing the employer's costs of social contributions Introduced in 2007
Preparatory Actions and Activation	Guiding, rehabilitating, or informing and preparing persons for a new program or job	Various types of extended assessment and guidance Labor market training for newly arrived immigrants Complementary training for persons without any grade from primary or secondary schools
Labor Market Training	Facilitating people to get or keep a job and preventing emerging labor shortage	Various occupational training that is procured by the PES or other authorities Directed towards occupations with a short supply of workers in the local labor market.
Work Experience	Obtaining work experience to stay in the labor market or be able to enter the labor market	Directed towards unemployed persons with previous educational attainment in Sweden as well as newly arrived immigrants
Youth Programs	Helping unemployed persons aged 16 to 25 to obtain early work experience or training	Job-guarantee for youths which is implemented after 90 days of unemployment Tax cut for Swedish employer-paid payroll concerning the youth workers (16–25 years) in 2007 and 2009
Business Start-up	Paying for the livelihood of persons that are judged to have good prospects to start a business and obtain a sustainable employment	Support for the start-up of businesses Normally restricted to 6 months
Job and Development Guarantee	Persons who have been employed for a long period have been able to obtain individually adapted measures to obtain a job (since 2007).	Introduced after 300 days of unemployment benefits Coaching and job-searching activities for 150 days Directed to employment which is mediated by the PES for a maximum period of two years

Source: Swedish Public Employment Service (2014) and IFAU (2014); Anxo (2015)

In the aftermath of the global economic crisis, the Swedish government also increased the number of businesses for work experience, trainee schemes, and labor market training (Anxo 2015).

Table 5.3. Participants in ALMP programs: 2008 – 2013 (percent)

Year	2008	2009	2010	2011	2012	2013
Special Measures for Disabled	41	31	24	24	24	23
Employment Support	8	3	2	2	2	4
New-Start Jobs	9	9	12	15	14	13
Preparatory Actions and Activations	6	6	7	8	9	11
Labor Market Training	3	2	2	2	2	2
Work Experience	1	4	6	2	2	2
Youth Programme	6	16	16	13	13	12
Start-up Business	1	1	2	2	1	1
Job and Development Guarantee	24	27	27	31	31	31
Total Number of Participants	171,300	213,500	286,410	294,300	303,000	318,200

Source: Swedish Public Employment Service (2014b).

Overall, to counteract the increase in unemployment, especially long-term unemployment, the number of participants in the various ALMPs had gradually increased. As shown in Table 5.3, ALMPs' participants were mainly the disabled who were disadvantaged in the labor market and long-term unemployed who needed new jobs and the development of vocational skills. However, the share of ALMPs participants has changed since the 2008 global economic crisis. While the share of participants in special measures for the disabled has decreased from 41 percent in 2008 to 31 percent in 2009, the share of youth programs has increased from 6 percent in 2008 to 16 percent in 2009. The share of participants in the measures of 'Job and Development Guarantee' and 'New-Start Jobs' also increased during the period 2008-2013, compared to other policy measures.

While the proportion of participants in the 'Special Measures for Disabled' has been decreasing, that of participants in the 'Job and Development Guarantee' program is increasing every year. With the Job and Development Guarantee, since 2007, those who have been unemployed for a long period have been able to obtain individually adapted measures to get a job. The measures were normally introduced after 300 days of unemployment benefits. The measures progress in three phases, where phase one includes coaching and job-searching activities for 150 days, phase two includes work experience up to 450 days, and in phase three, the unemployed are directed to employment which is mediated by the PES for a maximum period of two years. (Anxo 2015, ILO)

Employment support aimed to stimulate the employment of persons with difficulties in finding a job in the regular labor market. The measures included employment support for persons with a background of long-term sickness absence and various types of employment support for long-term unemployed by reducing the employers' wage costs. In contrast to other forms of employment support, the New-Start Jobs program was a special form of employment support, which was introduced in 2007. It was implemented by abolishing the employers' cost of social contributions for a limited period.

Preparatory Actions and Activations were individually adapted measures to guide, rehabilitate, or inform and prepare persons for a new program or job. The measures included various types of extended assessment and guidance, labor market training for newly arrived immigrants, and complimentary training of persons without any attainment from the primary or secondary schools. Labor market training was to facilitate people to get or keep a job and to prevent emerging labor shortages. The measures included various occupational training procured by the PES or other authorities and directed towards occupations with a short supply of workers in the local labor market.

Youth Programs helped unemployed persons 16 to 25 years old to obtain job training and early work experience. Since 2007 the measures have been organized within the job guarantee for youths which was implemented after 90 days of unemployment. In this regard, to better meet the labor market and skills needs and improve the quality of the educational and training system, the Swedish government has undertaken several educational reforms since the mid-2000s, placing more emphasis on vocational training and apprenticeship programs. A major upper secondary reform began in the fall 2011 with a reinforced emphasis on vocationally-oriented subjects in high school. To better prepare students for working life, a permanent apprenticeship program was introduced in 2011 as a standard course of vocational studies in upper secondary school, manifesting the government's intention to move from a mainly school-based occupational training system towards a vocational training system with a stronger component of workplace-based training.

The Swedish government also took several measures to enhance the quality of vocational training through closer cooperation, at the local level, between high-school authorities and social partners (employers, unions, and so on). More recently, to favor the development of a dual system in Sweden, it decided, in 2013, to strengthen the apprenticeship training programs by permanently extending the allowances for apprentice providers and raising the part of the allowance paid to employers.

Work Experience aimed to obtain work experience to stay in the labor market or be able to enter the labor market. The measures were directed towards unemployed persons with educational attainment in Sweden as well as newly arrived immigrants. In the latter case, it was often combined with labor market training for immigrants. Also, in 2007 and 2009, the tax cut for Swedish employer-paid payroll was enforced on a large scale for young workers (16–25 years), substantially reducing the labor cost for this group (Anxo 2015). The program of Start-up of Business aided the livelihood of persons that were judged to have good prospects to start a business and obtain sustainable employment. However, the support was normally restricted to 6 months (Anxo 2015). The next section will take a closer look at how the various institutional arrangements of the ALMPs were operated to solve the problem of unemployment in the economic crisis.

5.4.2 Main Measures of ALMPs

Youth Guarantee

The Youth Guarantee Policy in Sweden aimed to provide employment, academic, and vocational training opportunities to meet the needs of the individuals so that young people could be out of unemployment.[12] The policy played a key role

---

[12] The 'Youth Guarantee' that was first introduced by the Swedish government in 1984, spread to Norway in 1993, Denmark and Finland in 1996.

in the active labor market policy that Sweden and the Nordic countries had long emphasized. It enabled Swedish and Nordic countries to effectively deal with youth unemployment even in the 1990s economic crisis.

The Youth Guarantee has received new attention due to the 2008 global financial crisis. In 2010, two years after the economic crisis, the average youth unemployment rate in Europe exceeded the unprecedentedly high 20 percent, as the youth guarantee policy of Nordic Europe did not exist at the European level.[13] The Swedish youth guarantee had two important characteristics. First, the state must guarantee unemployed youth the provision of jobs or training opportunities. Second, the state had an obligation to provide quality jobs and opportunities to study further or pursue an apprenticeship or professional training within up to four months from the time when youth left employment or education.

The Swedish government has implemented youth guarantee policies through the provision of jobs, continuing education, and guaranteeing training opportunities. Specific programs included youth employment subsidies, internship programs, public job programs, and employment incentive support. On the supply side, there were specialist training programs, apprenticeship programs, and plans to reduce disruption to the youth. On the operational side, the central government was engaged in education and training and vocational training, and the local governments were in charge of lifelong education.

In the spring of 2015, the 'Job Guarantee for Youth' was revised to '90-day

---

[13] In 2012, the EU Commission announced that it would institutionalize the Youth Guarantee through a 'Youth Employment Package' and spend € 60 billion (75.17 trillion won) in the Youth Guarantee Program from 2013 to 2020. The number of countries among the 28 member nations that had developed it increased from 9 countries in 2013 to 17 countries in 2014.

Guarantee for Youth Unemployed.' To prevent the prolongation of youth unemployment, the Swedish government decided to support job seeking or vocational training within 90 days. Within these amendments, Trainee Jobs and Education Contracts were suggested as programs to cope with youth unemployment. These two systems were intended to complement the mismatch between education and jobs, which had been identified as the main cause of youth unemployment in the meantime. These policies were designed to help the unemployed youth who were not adequately educated and to provide an opportunity for education.

The apprenticeship program aimed to hire unemployed youth in occupational fields that lacked human resources, including the welfare sector, to kill two birds with one stone, i.e., youth employment and solution of manpower shortage. The scheme operated in a way that granted government subsidies to employers. Wage subsidies can be supported for up to one year. In the welfare sector, the government provided 85 percent of apprenticeship wages, with the subsidy for an apprenticeship supervisor amounting to up to 2,200 Krona per month. In areas other than the welfare sector, up to about 50 percent of the apprenticeship wage could be supported. The youth was able to work receiving vocational training while combining 50 percent of working and 50 percent of training under the apprenticeship.

The education contract system was for young unemployed people aged between 20 and 24 who had not been educated in high school or higher. The goal of this system was to help them to establish a career by allowing them to be educated in adult education institutions and Folk high schools at the local level. According to this system, young people were able to receive full-time education depending on the individual situation or were able to both work and be educated as a part-timer.

This system was devised because young people who had not completed high school or lower education were at high risk of falling into long-term unemployment and were likely to be excluded from the labor market(Song, 2015).

The Swedish government has recognized the diversity of young people and implemented various youth guarantee programs. A variety of policies in the areas of education and training, such as supplementary education, reduction of school interruptions, employment matching services, and employment subsidies, has been implemented. The one-to-one matching program that took into consideration the level of education, age, language, qualifications, and work experience for the unemployed youth was used for individual human resources management to consider individual differences and special circumstances, including the disabled and women. It also took into consideration the various problems of young people.

Vocational Training and Unemployment Benefits

The unemployment insurance system in Sweden has operated as the Ghent system, in which unions have organized unemployment insurance funds and operated them under legal regulations, but with government funding. In the Scandinavian countries that have developed the Gent system, unemployment insurance was not a duty but a voluntary option for workers. Therefore, non-union members were also allowed to join (Cho 2015).

The Swedish people, if they did not resign, were able to receive at least 70 percent of the monthly salary (averaging 12 months before unemployment) from the previous job as unemployment benefits by immediately reporting to the State Employment Office. The Swedish Employment Agency (Arbetsformedlingen) helps unemployed people who have sought their jobs or who have been suddenly dismissed to find new jobs. In addition to the unemployment report, unemployment benefits were provided by submitting a specific job search plan and a report on the specific job situation once a month while receiving benefits. Unemployed workers were able to be paid up to 300 days (450 days if they have children under 8) when they meet the conditions encouraging active job-seeking activities. The maximum amount they were able to get in Sweden was up to 27,000 kronor a month.

Also, the Job Security Council(JSC) paid unemployment benefits for income compensation, which has coordinated the opinions of employers and trade unions and carried out employment support services. The JSCs, established in 1974 in Sweden, are nonprofit organizations that provide comprehensive services such as financial support, counseling, vocational training, and career support to workers laid off in the wake of restructuring.[14] The allowance was paid out from the fund accumulated with contributions by enterprises at the premium rate of 3 percent of the monthly salary of workers.

Sweden's policy of emphasizing vocational education was not just economic support for the unemployed. Unemployment benefits were paid to ensure the economic security for the employed and, at the same time, to increase the likelihood of re-employment through aggressive vocational education. Therefore, as soon as they registered as unemployed, they received appropriate re-education and training after consultation with a dedicated counselor for employment. Sweden's vocational training focused

---

[14] There are about 15 JSCs in Sweden, including TRR (white collar) and TSN (civil servants), operating in each industrial sector. In the case of TRR, unemployed people over 40 years of age are paid up to 2 years.

on the characteristics of the individual unemployed and operated in an effective way to provide practically helpful services. In short, Sweden shows that social consensus and social intervention are important for solving unemployment problems through unemployment benefits and education, in which a strong sense of responsibility for unemployment was shared by the state and enterprises, and the government tried to fulfill its responsibilities.

Part-time Work

Part-time work has become one of the most common forms of employment in Sweden today. According to the Labor Force Survey in 2012, a total of 4.46 million people participated in the labor market in Sweden, of which 24 percent (1.12 million) were part-time workers. Particularly, for female workers, the part-time employment ratio was high. While 12.9 percent of male workers were part-time workers, 36.4 percent of female workers were part-time workers (Statistics Sweden, 2012). In Sweden, a great deal of policy effort has been made to ensure that 'good quality part-time jobs' were established.[15]

As part-time work expanded, the employment rate of women increased. In the 1970s and 1980s, the participation rate of women in the labor market in Sweden

---

[15] In the 1971 tax reform, the combined taxation of married couples was converted into individual taxation, which reduced the tax burden on dual-income families. In 1976, the marginal tax rate for part-time workers (32 percent) was significantly lower than that of full-time workers (up to 64 percent). Two reforms in the tax reforms in the 1970s have positively impacted on improving the employment security of part-time workers while raising awareness of part-time workers. In 1997, the Employment Protection Act was also amended to significantly strengthen the rights of part-time workers. Even after childcare leave, if a child was younger than 8 years old, he or she was able to maintain his full-time status and shorten working hours to 10 hours per week. Since 2002, the Anti-Discrimination Act has made direct discrimination as well as indirect penalties for the subject of the economic compensation and pursued better treatment of part-time workers.

increased sharply, coupled with the rate of women's part-time work increasing sharply. As of 2012, the female employment rate in Sweden was 71.8 percent, far ahead of Korea (53.5 percent) and Germany (68.0 percent). Sweden's part-time jobs were characterized by a high proportion of 'transition-type part-time' jobs, which were made up of short-time working full-time employees. These full-time, part-time workers were workers who voluntarily shortened their working hours by 20 percent to 50 percent according to the claim for short-term work during childcare, and they were mostly female workers. According to the Swedish union LO (the Swedish Trade Union Confederation) part-time work report, 27 percent of all part-time workers were convertible part-time workers who could return to full time at any time. In the same survey report, the percentage of workers who voluntarily selected part-time workers among TCO (The Swedish Confederation of Professional Employees) and SACO (the Swedish Confederation of Professional Associations) part-time workers was 54 percent and 65 percent, respectively (Kim Young-mi, 2011: 300-301). One of the reasons for the high proportion of 'convertible part-time' was that it was difficult to use part-time workers in Sweden in terms of cost reduction. The employer has to pay social insurance contributions regardless of working hours, except when working hours were too short to meet the eligibility requirements. Since the social benefits enjoyed by part-time workers were not significantly different from those of full-time workers, the incentive to use part-time workers due to a cost-related demand was not great, and the demand for flexible workforce placement was very high.

Providing New Temporary Jobs to the Public Sector

The biggest problem in Sweden was the high unemployment rate of low-educated people. Therefore, the Swedish government has tried to provide jobs that can work with low qualifications and education levels with public institutions. Their main tasks included simple jobs such as file organizing, copying, administrative processing, digitalization of records, environmental beautification, etc. They were able to extend contracts for up to two years, and the experiences of temporary jobs have also provided opportunities to get regular jobs.

Training of Short-term Workers in the Field of Health and Senior Care

There was traditionally a shortage of labor in health care, geriatric care, and teachers in Sweden. Teachers have received a relatively low salary compared to other occupations, making them unpopular jobs. To improve this, the Swedish government has a plan to raise the wage of teachers, and at the same time to expand the process of educating teachers and childcare teachers. It aims to train the employees who have worked in the short-term work and help them stay in the labor market for a long time.

5.4.3 Labor Market Policies on Youth Unemployment

In Sweden, youth unemployment has been a big problem. As of June 2009, the overall unemployment rate was 9.8 percent, while the youth unemployment rate was 29.7 percent. A high youth unemployment rate had been a significant contributor to a relatively high unemployment rate. Above all, the youth unemployment rate in Sweden was severe, considering that Denmark's was about 10 percent and

Norway's about 9 percent in the same period.[16]

In general, several are pointed out as significant causes for Sweden's high youth unemployment rate. First, there is the 'Last-in & First-out Principle' by the employer, based on the Employment Security Act in Sweden. For many years, the Act and high levels of early wages have played an excellent role in protecting the labor market insiders, but they have been a major obstacle for young people and immigrants who have not yet entered the labor market. This is because the youth and staff having a short employment period have been the first to be laid off at the time of the economic downturn. Besides, employers were hesitant to hire young people with short experience due to high starting wages. Some labor market experts also point out mismatches between jobs and education as a major cause.

Among the measures to solve the serious youth unemployment, various labor market programs assist young people in job searching in state-run job centers as the following. As discussed in the previous section, the new start job program was introduced in 2007 as a system in which the government subsidizes employers when they hire young workers who have been unemployed for more than six months. However, as the number of employers utilizing the program has increased in tandem with the increase in youth unemployment, the government decided to reduce the subsidies given out to those who had been unemployed for less than two years.

---

[16] Unemployment generally affects livelihoods regardless of age, but youth unemployment can be more severe than other age groups. The reason is that if you experience long-term unemployment in adolescent years, it can lead to a decrease in lifetime income due to lack of human capital formation, in addition to other usual costs. Also, in terms of national finance, long-term unemployment of youth can increase social assistance expenditures for young people and on the contrary, it can reduce earned income taxes.

Instead, it decided to pay more subsidies if they hire long-term unemployed people or hire immigrants for more than three years.

The Youth Guarantee was a representative policy of ALMPs for unemployed young people under the age of 25 who were unemployed for 90 days during the four months and registered as unemployed in the state employment agency. Under the youth guarantee system, employers can allow the youth to have practical training for at least four hours a week to three months in their companies. Then they can decide whether to hire them after three months. The interns can receive the internship grant or the self-improvement subsidy from the state job placement center. In this case, there occurred no employer costs. In the state-run job centers, the youth who lacked labor market experience were required to sign contracts for job training.

The matching program aimed at job seekers who were at least 20 years old and ready to work in a workplace with no or limited experience in the Swedish labor market. During the workplace or company introduction, job placement consultants assisted job seekers and workplaces at the same time. Usually, when a job seeker found a job that suited his or her career and knowledge, the employer must agree on how to provide a workplace or company program for the job seeker. In this process, the state-run job centers assisted jobseeker in carrying out specific tasks in the workplace or company. Such support was provided for up to six months, and as the end of the support period neared, the level of support for state-run job centers was gradually reduced. With the workplace or company introduction during the program period, participants were expected to be hired by the workplace.

Another policy for solving the unemployment problem of young people was an apprenticeship. An apprentice program can be done by private or public corporations and non-profit corporations. There were four types of interventions practiced in state-run job centers, such as work practice, on-the-job training, vocational skills examination, and practical skills development. Meanwhile, support for self-employment was provided to young people on the condition of self-employment, which included financial support during the period of self-employment preparation. Support for self-employment was usually provided to young people over 25 years of age, excluding those under 25.[17]

There were also other labor market education programs. Young people who were unemployed during a crisis of unemployment or those who were registered in the state-run job centers and were seeking jobs were encouraged to participate in labor market education programs at state-run job centers. In recent years, state-based job placement centers have entrusted such programs to public institutions and private institutions through open bidding rather than directly operating them. Besides, the labor market education program has been greatly reduced in size due to the increase in the education level of young people and the introduction of other private vocational education programs, and the vocational education college system that started in 2009. In this regard, labor market education programs were mainly conducted in the industries of manufacturing, health and welfare, and transportation.

---

[17] Exceptions include those whose work ability was reduced due to functional disabilities; Those with short experience in the labor market and over 20 years old were registered in state-run job centers as the unemployed for 3 months; although they were under 25 years of age, but tried to get a job for long period, they were eligible to participate in the labor and development guarantee program for young people.

5.4.4 Job Policies for Immigrants

In the 2010s, the refugee problem emerged as an important social issue that significantly impacted the Swedish labor market.[18] The problem of immigrant unemployment in Sweden is considered very serious.

As shown in Figure 5.7, the number of unemployed foreigners since 2015 has been higher than that of registered unemployed people born in Sweden. Therefore, the Swedish social policies to solve these identified challenges among new immigrants were to improve the integration of immigrants into the labor market and take appropriate measures to increase the labor supply of the foreigners (in particular female immigrants), through both labor market and educational policy and anti-discrimination measures, particularly regarding recruitment of non-natives.

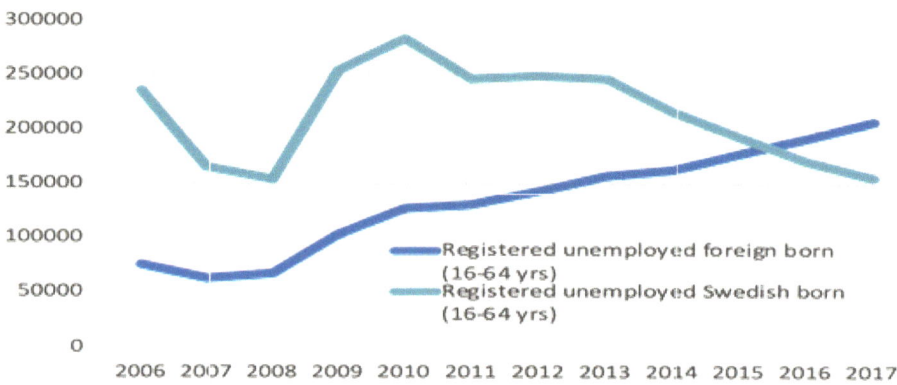

Source: Statistics & Public Employment Service (2018)

Figure 5.7. Unemployment Rate, 16-64 Years of Age

---

[18] Sweden, unlike other Nordic countries, has been an active country in accepting immigration and refugees. In 2016, 110,000 refugees were accepted, and a total of 310,000 refugees were granted residence permits for five years from 2012 to 2016. Given that Sweden has a total population of about 10 million, the refugee issue and its related policies have become the core of its social policy. Recently, anti-immigrant sentiment has become stronger in Sweden due to a large proportion of foreigners compared to the entire population.

To cope with the unemployment problem of immigrants, the Swedish government has introduced various job policies. The three main immigrant and refugee job policies implemented by the Swedish government included measures such as the immigrant certification and integration scheme, the new apprenticeship job model, the abolition and integration of refugee settlement programs.

First, the Fast Track was a policy implemented in 2015 to integrate immigrants. The immigrant certification system itself has been around for some time, but it was implemented to achieve certification and integration at the same time. The policy aimed to overcome the labor shortage by allowing immigrants to adapt to Swedish society and find employment in their most suitable jobs. The Swedish government provided various programs such as job training, career counseling, support for language and skills certification at work, to help immigrants adapt to the Swedish community and vocational community. As Margherita Bussi and Jon Pareliussen (2017) argue, this system reduced the discrepancy between the quality of work requirements and the quality of immigrant or refugee workers and expanded employment possibilities.

The second was the 'new apprenticeship job model.' In March 2017, the Swedish Confederation of Trade Unions(LO) proposed a new training job model for recruiting low-cost refugees, such as those who graduated from a junior high school or under high school. The model was for new immigrants, such as refugees aged 25-45, or other unemployed persons who were registered as job seekers in the employment service center and who have received basic education (nine years) but did not have the level of education at Swedish high school. The maximum period of contracts between immigrants with the Swedish Federation of Businesses was five years, and employers were able to hire apprentices at low wages for two to three years, depending on the sector. However, to prevent companies from abusing immigrants' apprentices at low wages, employers must hire apprentices during a full two- to three-year period, and the government ensured that apprentices received the education they need for work within the formal adult education system. These policies show that the Swedish Confederation of Trade Unions, representing Sweden's progressive force, expressed its willingness not to unconditionally adopt an inclusive immigration policy, considering the strengthened anti-immigrant sentiment in Sweden.

The third was policies about the abolition and integration of refugee settlement programs. In December 2010, the Swedish government implemented the Swedish Establishment Reform for newly arrived immigrants and asylum-seekers and their families. In addition to traditional wage subsidies targeting the foreign-born, the PES has been given a clearer role and a coordinating responsibility for speeding up the establishment of newly arrived people into the labor market. The main objective of the reform was to improve and speed up the labor market integration of immigrants by shifting responsibility for activation measures from the municipalities to the PES. The PES has the overall responsibility to coordinate various measures and draw up an individual introduction plan, including Swedish for Immigrants (SFI), civic orientation, and employment preparation activities. From 2011 onwards, the Establishment Reform has been broadened to cover more newly arrived refugees, and the PES has therefore received additional resources. To encourage employers to hire newly arrived immigrants, the Swedish government amended the already implemented wage subsidy for the foreign-born (Instegjobb), with the period of subsidy extending from six to twelve months. The change in regulation took effect in 2013. It became possible to renew a subsidized period of employment without the requirement of having successfully passed the Swedish for Immigrants (SFI) examination.

The Swedish government has also implemented policies to help immigrants in their early settlement, including immigrants in labor market programs such as 'New Start Job' (Nystartjobb) and 'Extra Job' (Extrajobb). The Swedish government has failed to fulfill the role of the Employment Service Center due to the rapid increase in refugees and immigrants. Therefore, the government has tried to streamline the job placement system in the employment service center so that job seekers were able to quickly find jobs or choose to study. However, the Swedish Ministry of Employment announced in March 2017 that it would abolish the Employment Settlement Program in the Office of Refugees and their Families. Starting from January 2018, their employment was looked for through the same Employment Program. Also, a warning and reduction of settlement support were planned for refugees who did not actively participate in job searching activities, including not applying for jobs recommended by the Employment Agency. Although the anti-immigration sentiment in Sweden has spread recently and the policy has shifted into a passive mood. However, Sweden still provides more welfare and education for immigrants and refugees than other European countries, based on the inclusive policy. In short, the positive effects of these Swedish immigrants and refugee policies have contributed to the social integration between immigrants and non-immigrants.

5.4.5 Trends and Changes of ALMPs

Since the 1970s, the economic crisis and the increase in the unemployment rate have changed the characteristics of active labor market policy in Sweden. In the early period, an active labor market policy responded to the frictional unemployment that temporarily appeared in the industrial restructuring process. Therefore, an active labor market policy was primarily aimed at providing the unemployed with new jobs in growing industries through vocational training. However, the oil shock in the 1970s and the opening of the capital markets through the 'third way' in the 1980s greatly impacted the structure of the Swedish labor market. The high unemployment rate due to the economic crisis in the early 1990s immediately turned job creation into a significant issue in society.

The Swedish government's policy on unemployment is illustrated in Figure 5.8. Unlike other OECD countries, Sweden's unemployment policy has emphasized active labor market policies than passive labor market policies like unemployment benefits. As a result, expenditures for the active labor market policies exceeded the spending on the passive labor market policies, except for 2003, 2004, and 2005. As Sweden faced a severe economic crisis and a very high unemployment rate in the early 1990s, the Bildt cabinet significantly increased spending on ALMPs, even while the welfare spending was shrinking. For solving the unemployment and economic crises, the Bildt cabinet utilized active labor market policies.

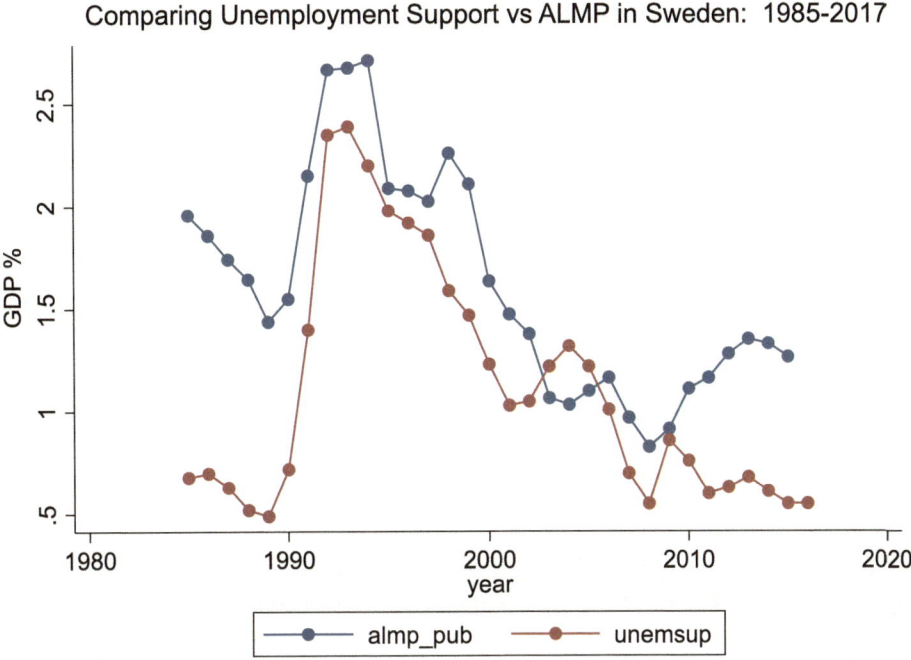

Figure 5.8. Comparing Expenditure of Unemployment support and ALMPs in Sweden: 1985-2017

The main goal of the active labor market policies in the Bildt cabinet was the creation of short-term jobs through subsidy payments and employment incentives and the absorption of unemployment through training programs. Spending on active labor market programs increased until the early 1990s and peaked in 1994, and overall spending on labor market programs declined since the late 1990s as the economic crisis subsided.

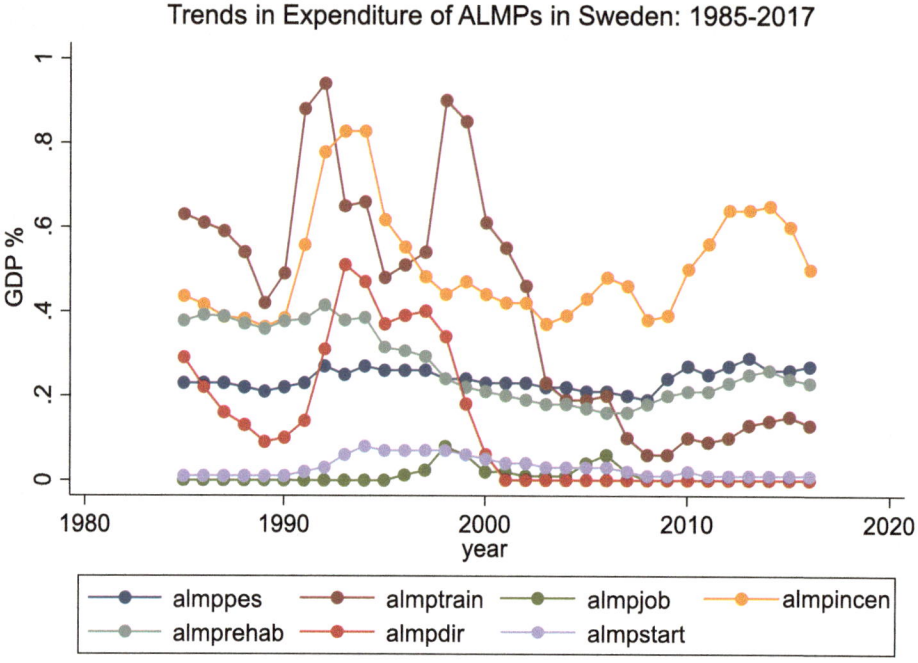

Figure 5.9. Trends in Expenditure of ALMPs in Sweden: 1985-2017

As shown in Figure 5.9, the trends of ALMPs spending had changed over time. First of all, vocational training, which was a representative policy of Swedish ALMPs, had been used as an important policy mechanism in the economic crisis period. However, the expenditure on training had been shrinking since the 2000s. Especially in 2004, the spending on vocational training conceded the first and second place to the expenditure on employment incentives and PES. These changes in the ALMP expenditure structure can be a very big change in Sweden. After the ruling Centre-right regime was installed in mid-2006, spending on ALMPs had been reduced to the proximity of other comparable countries. The expenditure of ALMPs, which was 2.35 percent of the national GDP in 2004, gradually decreased to 1.37 percent in 2008, reaching the lowest level. Although the Social Democratic Party regime was re-elected in 2014, it remained at 1.25 percent of GDP in 2017.

The reasons why the proportion of aggressive labor policies had sharply fallen include the following points. First, Sweden's fiscal crisis in 2008 was the biggest factor. At the time, the Centre-right wing government significantly reduced financial support for vocational training. It had blocked many young people from going to vocational schools, in the name of reform, by preventing them from going to college when they choose to go to vocational schools (Interview with LO officials in Sweden, July 8, 2018). In fact, in 2008, the youth unemployment rate in Sweden skyrocketed from 19 percent to over 24 percent. The increase in employment from 80,000 to 85,000 since 2009, thanks to the 'new start' program as the government's job creation program, was due to the increase in non-regular workers, and regular jobs had been reduced.

As it was pointed out that the vocational training programs operated by private institutions entrusted by the central vocational training institute were less effective, the Swedish government under the Central-right Alliance focused on reducing budgetary support for these private tutoring programs and instead of seeking jobs directly without job training. Today, jobs in Sweden are being bi-polarized with low-educated jobs and highly educated professional jobs. Especially, there have been a lot of refugees with a poor educational background from the Middle East to escape the Syrian war for several years. On the other hand, the workforce with higher education and expertise is in short supply. Therefore, it has become a big policy issue for the Swedish government to educate these young refugees and provide them with jobs.

As shown in Figure 5.4, another characteristic of the Swedish ALMPs spending trend is that expenditure on vocational training has significantly decreased, while expenditure on employment incentives has notably increased. It is analyzed that this change in the trend of expenditures of ALMPs has a relationship with the government's support for wage cuts due to the reduction of working hours according to the framework agreement (on March 2, 2009) between IF Metall and Manufacturing Employers Association.

5.5 Summary

The Swedish model has been symbolized by the concept of a 'people's house' that emphasizes equality and mutual understanding among social partners. The Sätchevaden convention, which was the background of the Swedish model, made it a core principle of cooperation, mutual recognition, and respect. This spirit has sometimes been shakily faced with economic crises, but it still serves as the basis for the Swedish socio-economic policy. In Sweden, the rights of workers are respected, governments and businesses have a strong sense of responsibility for workers' problems, and in the economic crisis, tripartite social actors have worked together to solve problems. The cooperation and active participation of labor and management in Sweden's labor market policies were possible because of the sense of responsibility through social consensus and the will to solve problems actively.

The Swedish active labor market policies have also been characterized by the fact that the government's public spending on active labor market policies was larger and more responsive than other countries. The main function of active labor market policies was to alleviate the impact of unemployment, not to create rapid re-employment or overall employment growth. The focusing on active labor market policies was possible because the vocational training program was linked to the unemployment insurance and regional employment offices, and most workers were required to go through vocational education programs if they were unemployed for more than six months.

The Youth Guarantee Policy in Sweden showed a sense of duty and various policies and efforts for youth security. The burden of unemployment benefits for the preservation of income was a good example of the social consensus that companies should take responsibility for unemployment problems. This aspect can also be found in efforts to ensure the good quality of part-time workers in Sweden. In Sweden, the 'Anti-Discrimination Act' was enacted in 2002 to guarantee the rights of part-time workers, and active measures have been taken to protect vulnerable workers, including women. This allowed Swedish part-time workers to receive treatment that is not significantly different from full-time workers.

Sweden's active labor market policies were not without problems. In the 1990s, despite the continued implementation of vocational training programs, criticism continued that the unemployment rate did not decrease and that the cost of vocational training programs was a financial burden. It also pointed out that vocational training did not have a significant effect on job creation, while the subsidy-type employment policy had the effect of temporary unemployment mitigation (Calmfors *et al.*, 2002). Besides, as the number of unemployed people who wanted to reapply for unemployment benefit status through job training programs instead of working has increased, and the problem of chronic moral hazard has been raised, such as the question of the reemployment effect and cost hikes.

In sum, the main factors that Sweden was able to overcome the economic crisis in the earliest stages include social dialogue based on the social trust between labor and management and active labor market policies that have been operating since the Sätchevaden convention. Despite the neoliberal reform attempts by center-right governments in the early 1990s and mid-2000s, the Swedish tradition of social consultation remains largely unspoiled. Faced with the economic and unemployment crises, the Swedish government has still focused on ALMPs such as employment incentives and PES. In particular, the government's public expenditure on active labor market policies was larger than that of other European or OECD countries, and they were carried out in a responsive way to the crisis of unemployment. In this regard, the main function of active labor market policies was to alleviate the shock of unemployment and provide new jobs to the unemployed. A key feature of the change in response to the crisis and job policies that emerged before and after the 2008 global economic crisis was the shift from traditional external and quantitative flexibility to internal and functional flexibility. As a result, supports for job retention and sharing through shorter working hours and wage cuts have increased more than expenditures on vocational education and training for unemployed people. Though, the high youth unemployment rate and the integration of refugees into the labor market, which have emerged around the 2008 economic crisis, have remained challenges in Sweden.

Chapter 6

GERMANY: ECONOMIC CRISIS AND HARTZ REFORMS

6.1 Introduction

While many countries faced recession and unemployment problems due to the global financial crisis in 2008, Germany has attracted much attention for its "job miracle," including rapid economic recovery and reduced unemployment. It is also doing well on the issue of youth unemployment, which is a key policy issue for European countries.

What is the reason for Germany's doing better in overcoming the 2008 global economic crisis compared to other OECD countries? Many scholars have cited the Schröder government's labor market reforms that had been implemented before the 2008 global economic crisis (Schmid 2008, Hudter 2015). These measures for labor market flexibility were called the Hartz reforms. Through the Hartz reforms, the German government promoted the mitigation of layoff requirements, reduced unemployment benefits, and expanded part-time jobs. Thanks to the preemptive labor market reforms, Germany was relatively less injured by the impact of the 2008 global economic crisis, and it was possible to overcome it quickly.

The Hartz reform has also effected changes in expenditures of ALMPs in

Germany. Before the Hartz reform, the spending of ALMPs in Germany traditionally emphasized vocational training. However, after the Hartz reform, it has been changed trends and types of ALMPs spending in Germany. While the expenditure on vocational training has decreased, PES spending has significantly increased since the 2008 economic crisis. Job placement and matching services measures for the unemployed were greatly strengthened.

In this chapter, I will examine why these changes occurred and what it means. This chapter looks at how Germany's economic situation developed during the 2008 global financial crisis and what political, economic, and labor measures were taken to respond to the crisis. It will look at which ALMPs were proposed to overcome it.

6.2 Economic Crisis in Germany

6.2.1 Pre-2008 Economic Crisis

After World War II, the German economy developed rapidly due to the Marshall Plan, the European Recovery Program (April 1948 – December 1951). With the spread of the Cold War, the German economy became a show window of East-West regime competition. At that time, the US government considered economic aid to Germany an essential policy to prevent the spread of the communist revolution in European countries and create a stable political system and democratic institutions. As a result, Germany recorded a GNP growth of 11.9 percent per year and the unemployment rate below 1 percent in the 1950s. In the 1960s, it expanded its welfare policy based on the growth trends fueled by full employment.

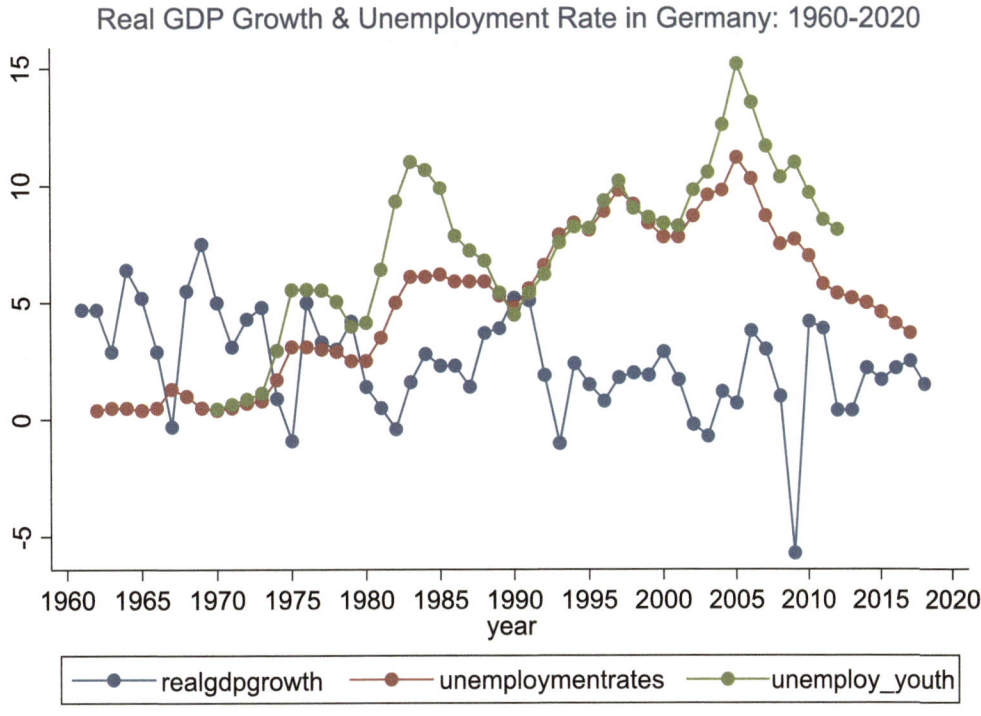

Figure 6.1. Growth and Unemployment rate in Germany: 2000 - 2018

However, in the 1970s, due to two oil shocks, the German economy had to go through stagflation and the unemployment rate gradually increased. In the late 1980s, Germany's employment conditions improved, including increases in economic growth rate and drops in the unemployment rate. However, German unification in 1990 resulted in the economic downturn caused by the collapse of the foundation of the East German economy and the cost of the unification. Above all, exchanging West and East Germany's currencies in the one-to-one ratio increased the labor cost in the East German region. It weakened the competitiveness of local companies in these areas. Rising wages for East German workers far beyond productivity disrupted the industrial base in eastern Germany, resulting in mass unemployment.

Since the reunification of Germany, the number of unemployed people has continued to increase, surpassing 3,907 thousand in 1997 and 4,573 thousand in 2005. In particular, the unemployment rate in eastern Germany was more severe than in western Germany. In 2000, the unemployment rate in West Germany was 7.8 percent, while in East Germany, it was 17.4 percent, more than twice that of western Germany. Besides, long-term unemployment for more than one year also increased significantly from 31.6 percent in 1991 to 51.5 percent in 2000(OECD Database 2020).

Since the German reunification, the high unemployment rate has led to worsening income inequality and increasing poverty, dealing with the financial burden on the government's social welfare. Increasing social welfare costs and fiscal deficits resulting from the reunification led to inflation in Germany. To curb it, the German government adopted a high-interest rate policy. However, it led to the inflow of foreign financial capital to Germany and the appreciation of the German mark. It then led to a slowdown in exportation and an increase in importation that ultimately resulted in a decline in Germany's economic growth potential. Therefore, Germany was once called the 'Sick man of Europe' with the falling employment rates, high unemployment rates, weaker distributions, increased demand for welfare, and lower economic growth potential.

Since 2001, the global economic bubble has resulted in plummeting economic growths. It sharply increased unemployment rates in Germany, so it faced structural problems and the weakness of its economic structure due to an economic downturn and fiscal deficits. The vulnerable factors of the export-oriented German economic structure at that time included: a rigid labor market, an over-stretched social security system, a complicated tax system, and high tax burden, government's market interventions and regulations on business activities, the side effect of the German unification, and constraints in its macro policy in the wake of the introduction of the euro currency. The problems of the German economy were the main cause of the Hartz reform of the Schröder government, which took office in 1998.

6.2.2 The Great Recession and the 2008 Economic Crisis

The 2008 global financial crisis, which began at the international financial center, Wall Street in the United States, impacted the German economy. The German economy experienced the most significant recession of an unprecedented degree in 2009. Its economic growth rate in 2009 was negative at 5.6 percent. Interestingly, however, its unemployment rate increased only slightly from 7.5 percent in 2008 to 7.7 percent in 2009. Despite the impact of the global economic crisis, the employment situation in Germany, unlike other EU countries, had not changed much. In 2009, the German labor market had lost only 70,000 jobs, despite a 5.6 percent drop in GDP (See Figure 6.1 above). Compared to the early 1990s when the labor market response to the recession showed a 5 percent decrease in GDP, which led to a cut of 1.5 million jobs, such unemployment indicators were very surprising (Anxo 2016, Geum 2012).

Compared with the other major EU countries, Germany performed very well in terms of the unemployment rate (see Table 6.1 below). As shown in Table 6.1, unemployment rates in the UK, France, and the US continued to increase from 2008 until 2012. However, the unemployment rate in Germany declined after reaching

7.7 percent in 2009, reaching 5.6 percent in 2012, which was lower than those before the financial crisis.

Table 6.1. Comparison of Unemployment Rates in Major EU Countries: 2006-2012

Year	2006	2007	2008	2009	2010	2011	2012
Germany	9.6	8.1	7.4	7.7	7.1	5.9	5.6
France	9.2	8.2	7.8	9.6	9.3	9.7	10.1
UK	5.5	5.2	6.3	7.8	7.9	8.0	8.1
US	4.4	4.8	6.9	10.0	9.6	8.9	8.2
EU	7.8	6.9	7.3	9.4	9.6	9.7	10.3

Source: Eurostat (2014)

Figure 6.2 illustrates well the assessment of Germany's employment status after the 2008 global economic crisis(Rinne & Zimmermann, 2012). When the employment rate was set at 100 as of 2008, the trend of German employment rates was different from other countries. While employment rates in Japan, the United Kingdom, and the United States declined, Germany continued to maintain it above 100. Germany's employment rate increased from 64 percent in 2004 to 70.1 percent in 2008 and 73.0 percent in 2012. The economic growth rates in Germany, excluding 2009 (negative 5.6 percent) just after the 2008 global financial crisis, recorded 4.1 percent in 2010 and 3.7 percent in 2011 (OECD 2013).

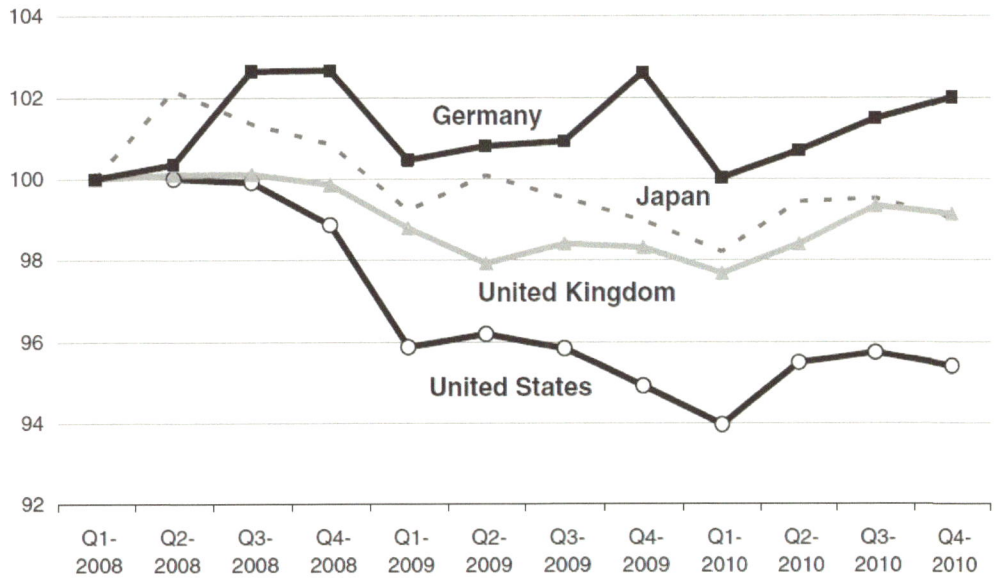

Note: The pre-recession peak in Q1-2008(employment at peak=100) for all countries except the United States, Q2-2008.
Source: OECD Database. Rinne & Zimmermann (2012) p. 4.

Figure 6.2. Comparison of Employment Rate Changes in Major OECD Countries

After the 2008 global financial crisis, Germany recovered its economy at the fastest speed among European countries. During the period of economic recovery, its economy and labor market went back to the normal state at the same time. For the German economic recovery, it took one and a half years. Above all, the phenomenon that the unemployment rate temporarily increases due to the economic recession and then fixates at a higher level even after the economic recovery disappeared. Until recently, Germany's economy has grown steadily and has emerged as an Economic Superstar (Dustmann et al., 2014).

As Germany has successfully overcome the 2008 global economic crisis at an early stage, it has attracted attention as an icon of economic success again, not the 'European Patient' in the 1990s. Therefore, it is necessary to analyze how German social actors have overcome the 2008 global economic crisis and created a system to cope with it, based on the historical perspective. In the next section, we will examine the response of major social actors such as the government, business, and labor to the 2008 global economic crisis.

6.3 Responses to the 2008 Economic Crisis

6.3.1 Political Responses

When the crisis hit Germany, the government invited the social partners to several meetings to find solutions. As Zagelmeyer (2010) notes, the representatives of the German government and labor and employer associations met to discuss the economic situation. They came up with the two stimulus packages and further measures. The German government took several steps in responding to the crisis relying upon labor unions and employer associations' expertise, and tried to secure their support in implementing measures.

In October 2008, the Financial Market Stabilization Act (Finanz market stabilisierungs Gesetz, FMStG) was passed, and the first and second rescue packages ensued in November 2008 and January 2009. The reforms took the general direction of stabilizing the German banking sector, ensuring credit supply, safeguarding economic stability, consumers' purchasing power, employment, and increasing public investment (Zagelmeyer 2010).

First Round of Measures (November 2008)

In November 2008, the German government announced its first response to the global financial crisis. The primary response was to strengthen employment and the social safety net as follows.

First, the German government tried to strengthen the job placement function of the Federal Employment Agency. In particular, the Merkel government wanted to expand the Job-to-Job-Placement Agency (Job-to-Job-Vermittlung) by adding 1,000 units to help the unemployed find their employment and strengthening job placement policies and vocational training.

Second, the German government reinforced the subsidy and extended its benefit period for reduced working hours. For instance, the Federal Employment Service has extended the period of entitlement to the allowance for workers for reduced working hours (Kurzarbeitergeld), which provided 60 to 67 percent of the corresponding employee's salary to enterprises retaining employment during the period of shortened working hours, from the 12 to 18 months. This change took effect on 1 January 2009. The shortening of working hours was a joint response by workers and enterprises to the economic crisis. Workers and the company agreed to shorten working hours for a certain period, and then workers remained employed. The company could reduce the expenditures so that it could respond to the crisis. When job adjustment was inevitable for management-related reasons, companies needed to reduce production rather than dismiss workers, thus reducing working hours so that as many workers as possible could remain in employment without losing their jobs. In this case, a government subsidy was provided. The Merkel government extended the period for the subsidy to prevent unemployment and prepare for future economic recovery. The German government could have a policy effect to reduce the financial burden for unemployment insurance due to the payment of unemployment insurance benefits.

Third, the German government has expanded special assistance programs for older and unskilled workers. Special education programs for unskilled and older workers aged 45 and over were developed to improve their job skills and prepare for unemployment in advance. To enhance their employment opportunities and reduce the shortage of skilled workers, the Federal Labor Administration has implemented programs to subsidize training costs, transportation costs, and accommodation costs, in addition to wages, for workplaces with 250 or fewer employees. Early retirement for middle and older workers was also extended in a phased manner. The system was expanded by reducing their working hours and subsidizing 70 percent of their contributions to old-age pensions. The unemployment benefit period became more generous than before.

Second Round of Measures (Jan. 2009)

The Merkel government announced further measures on January 13, 2019, following the first response to the economic crisis. A policy plan was prepared through the ongoing discussions at 'the 32-Member Economic and Labor Summit', which Merkel promised when the German parliament voted on the first response. If the German government's first response was to support the German banking system and strengthen the social safety net to protect individuals from unemployment due to the economic crisis, the second response included policy measures to help the labor market operate smoothly. Following its first rescue package issued in

2008, the federal government adopted a second rescue package (in German) on 27 January 2009 that stipulated further investments worth about €50 billion. It sought to achieve broader goals, including financial relief in the form of tax reduction schemes and reduced contributions to statutory health insurance schemes, support for enterprises, and further investments were to be made to secure future prosperity like improving infrastructure, education system, environment, and economy. To strengthen the support for enterprises, the German government expanded the flexible working system and short-term work allowance and legally and financially reinforced these institutions.

First, the German government strengthened support for companies reducing working hours (Kurzarbeit). There were three types of allowances for shortened working hours. Regardless of size or sector, any company was granted assistance for the temporary shortfall in orders (Konjunktur-Kurzarbeitergeld). Allowance for restructuring or plant closure (Transfer-Kurzarbeitergeld) was only paid if the affected employees were assigned to a transition company that participated in a continuous training program. Seasonal allowance (Saison-Kurzarbeitergeld) was restricted to companies and employees in the construction sector. These allowances were available only during the winter season from 1 December until 31 March. The allowances were granted if the weather conditions prevented any work from being carried out at construction sites or if the volume of new orders was not enough to maintain the employment level at a specific company. The government also supported 50 percent of social insurance payments in case of shortening working hours (Kurzarbeit) for companies and workers in 2009 and 2010. When workers of these companies completed the vocational training, the Federal Labor Administration (BA) supported

100 percent of the social insurance contributions.

The German government has actively worked to provide legal and financial supports for job retention and job-sharing measures. The introduction of the working hour account system helped to prevent the dismissal of other workers who performed the same job if there was time accumulated in the account among the workers so that the employment of part-time and fixed-term workers could sustain. The government also tried to prevent workers' living standards from falling by providing a salary equivalent to unemployment benefits as the working hours were reduced through the rules for reduction of working hours, applying for short-term work benefits, and extending the period of benefits. As a result, the number of people who benefited from short-term work allowances quadrupled to 1.5 million. Besides, to strengthen the job placement activities recommended in the first response plan, 5,000 employees in charge of job placement at the Federal Labor Service were added, and the financial scale to support special education programs had been expanded (A Kee Ku 2010). In general, the Merkel government sought and introduced new systems, such as reducing corporate tax burden (from 39 percent to less than 30 percent) and reducing unemployment insurance burden, while the German government continued to maintain Hartz labor reforms and policy stance and respond to the economic crisis with these policy measures.

6.3.2 Economic Responses

In the response to the 2008 economic crisis, German employers relied on the successfully functioning social partnership.[1] The social partners have successfully

---

[1] The Confederation of German Employers Association (BDA) emphasized the joint achievements

managed to mitigate the effects of the crisis. Their cooperative, solution-seeking behavior at the establishment and sectoral levels served to stabilize employment levels, particularly in the most crisis-hit industries. In this regard, employers and unions alike welcomed the new short-time working rules introduced by the federal government. At the same time, employers and unions asked the government to extend short-time work and stimulate domestic demand.

Companies have used a variety of measures aiming to tackle the crisis by cutting labor costs while avoiding layoffs. The most widespread measure was the use of the working hour account to reduce effective working time. In total, 30 percent of companies made use of the working hour account either in the form of reduced hours saved in an individual account or in the form of the working hour credit that will have to be worked in the future when business recovers. The second most widespread measure was the introduction of short-time work. Other measures included the internal posting of employees and adjusted schemes for paid leave and cuts in pay and benefits.

6.3.3 Labor Responses

In Germany, SMEs have a strong trust system with the workers' organization. This factor was also pointed out as a key factor in overcoming the global economic crisis. First, the German workers' organization had a 'workers council' in addition to trade unions organized by industry.[2] Thus, German workers were doubly guaranteed

---

of employers and unions during the crisis. The Employers' Associations for the Metal and Electrical Industry (Gesamtmetall) also stressed that the crisis of 2009~2010 was overcome by the close collaboration between employers, unions, work councils and policymakers. The BDA chair, Mr Dieter Hundt, pointed to the jointly pursued collective bargaining policy that helped maintain employment levels.

in their systems of realizing their interests, not only through the labor union but also through the employee council.

Based on the German Co-determination Act, German workers can participate in management on an equal basis with employers. The German union has taken on a strong role in every company. Companies have also recognized that unions are necessary for their operation. The advantage of the German unions was that they had worked very quietly in all aspects of society. The supervisory board, which consisted of an equal number of representatives of labor unions and stakeholders, had a role in overseeing the executive board as the highest decision-making body.

This union's high level of trust made Hartz's reforms and agreements possible, which would increase flexibility in the face of Germany's economic crisis. The right to management participation was guaranteed, and workers were able to participate in the adjustment of working hours. So, workers agreed to a flexible scheme: 'solidarity for work, preserving the jobs of the entire people.' In particular, it was noteworthy for Germany's flexibility policy that the employment was guaranteed, but the economic fluctuations had been dealt with through 'internal flexibility' such as shorter working hours and flexible work schedules.

A representative example of expanding internal flexibility was the 'working hour account system' (Daily Labor News, July 23, 2012). This was a kind of banking concept that puts working hours in an account as much as they worked more than standard working hours when there was a lot of work, and deducted working hours

---

[2] A workers' council can be established at workplaces with more than five employees, based on the voluntary will of the workers, with an aim of ensuring the participation of workers and the right to cooperation and co-determination (Jang, 2004).

as much as they worked less than standard working hours when the work was rare. Thanks to this system, during the economic downturn, companies were able to maintain employment without paying full wages and without dismissing skilled workers and help them to overcome the costs and time lags associated with hiring new workers when the economy recovered. Also, workers were designed to get the minimum earned income from their employers with no shorter or no less than regular work, and the government guaranteed more than 60 percent of the income gap.

In the case of working hours, there was a working hour account. This working hour account was not only unlimited in terms of duration but could be saved and used later, just as it saves money in the bank for production and overall working hours. In addition to this, there was a system for changing working hours, which was usually set in collective agreements. For example, in the case of metal trade unions, the working hours per week were 35 hours. However, depending on the situation, measures were taken so that they could be reduced by at least 30 hours and increased by up to 40 hours. It must be agreed to by the workers' council (Betriebsrat). To overcome the global economic crisis, the worker gave up certain rights and bonuses while the employer guaranteed their jobs. When the economy deteriorated, workers were guaranteed jobs without being laid off for three or five years.

German unions also participated in a series of negotiations on concessions during the crisis years and exercised wage restraint. For instance, Volkswagen made a 20 percent reduction of working hours from 36 hours per week and cut a 10 percent reduction of wage through labor-management compromise. In this regard, according to the analysis of pay increases agreed in sectoral collective agreements, collectively agreed wages rose by 2.9 percent in 2008, 2.6 percent in 2009, and 1.8 percent in 2010 (in comparison to the previous year). These slower wage rises reflect the impact of the crisis (The WSI's Annual Collective Bargaining Reports 2012).

These achievements were also due to the relative flexibility of the German industrial relation system, which allows for deviation from collectively agreed standards through opening clauses, and the wage restraints and concessions negotiated during collective bargaining rounds. Moreover, the reform measures taken by the federal government (such as prolonging the period for short-term work entitlements and introducing two rescue packages) set the right framework for the action of social partners.

6.4 Labor Policy for Job Creation

6.4.1 Policies for youth Job Creation

The German government's efforts to reduce youth unemployment in the face of the economic crisis were materialized in various policies, including the TFD program, JUMP and JUMP Plus program, Ausbildung Job-AQTIV law, and the Hartz bills.

TFD and JUMP program

The TFD(Teamarbeit für Deutschland) program, which started in June 2003 by the German Federal Ministry of Economy and Labor, was organized by various social actors, including citizens, organizations, and corporations that were interested in resolving unemployment in various regions by 2006. It held various events to promote the employment of young people.

The JUMP program was an emergency support plan for the youth that the German government had implemented with an annual expenditure of 2 billion marks from 1999 to 2003. The program was made of support projects for obtaining certifications or vocational training (such as apprentice technician support), employment promotion projects (wage subsidies), and job creation projects. Based on the experience of the United Kingdom and France, the program was part of a policy aimed at helping young people with future job prospects in the form of an extended active labor market policy. The number of young participants increased in monthly averages from 400,000 in 1998 to 500,000 in 1999 and 2000. As a result, the youth unemployment rate fell from 10.2 percent in 1997 to 8.4 percent in 2001. Therefore, the Jump program was evaluated as having a positive effect on youth unemployment (Lee, 2017). Since late 2003, JUMP Plus had been implemented by the end of 2004, with additional programs to support the social integration of the youth in the East German region. After the 2008 global economic crisis, the measures of the JUMP plus program were sustained within the Youth Guarantee program that the EU has pursued to resolve youth unemployment.

Vocational Training program: Ausbildung

Ausbildung is one of Germany's technical and vocational training programs, based on the traditional dual system, which started in 2004 with the Vocational Training Agreement (Ausbildungspakt) between German educational institutions, governments, and employers' organizations. According to the Vocational Training Agreement, the employer decided to provide 30,000 new training jobs each year for the next three years, and the federal government decided to provide 20 percent of the government's training jobs additionally. In the Ausbildung curriculum, more than half the students who had completed the first-level curriculum, including vocational schools and regular and general schools, had concluded a contract with employers and received more than three years of vocational education and training. Vocational training consisted of formal vocational training in vocational schools and field training in firms. The Ausbildung program currently offers more than 300 occupational pieces of training, which comprise 70 percent of on-the-job training and 30 percent of vocational training at vocational schools (Korean-German Chamber of Commerce and Industry). Completing this training program will allow them to enter the labor market with nationally recognized qualifications (Funk 2006, Lee 2017). The course is also a part of the Meister system. If students want to work as a Meister, they will receive a Meister certification after they complete the training for at least three years in the field and if they pass the assessment test.

Job-AQTIV Law and Youth Employment Policy

In 2001, the Schröder government embarked on various legislative changes, seeking active employment measures to combat mass unemployment. One important legislation at the time was the Job-AQTIV Act. As the Job-AQTIV Act stood for Activation, Qualification, Training, Investing, and Mediating, it aimed to support job search activities and enhance the employment capacity of individuals through skilled education, vocational training, and human investment. The slogan of the

Job-AQTIV Act was 'Promote and Demand (fördern und fordern)'. Among these legislations, measures for youth employment included emergency youth programs, subsidies for training within companies, mitigation of the acts on worker dispatch, the introduction of the circulatory job system, strengthening job placement and profiling. The Job-AQTIV Act was promoted by 'Alliance for Jobs (Bundnis fur Arbeit)' and had preceding characteristics of the Hartz Reform Acts, which was subsequently implemented (Brinkmann 2002, Lee Ho-Keun 2017).

6.4.2 Hartz Reforms: Welfare-to-Work Reforms in Germany

Gerhard Schröder, who defeated Prime Minister Helmut Kohl in the 1998 general elections, tried to reform the social system and labor market to overcome Germany's low economic growth, high unemployment, and fiscal deficits. The Agenda 2010, released in March 2003 by the Schroeder government, contained a very comprehensive set of policies on the labor market, social security and tax reforms, and economic revitalization, training, and innovation (see Table 6.2).

Table 6.2. Policies of Agenda 2010

Agenda	Contents of Reform
Improving Labor Market Flexibility	- Amendment of the Employment Security Act (Dismissal Regulation): Excluded SMEs with less than 5 employees → with less than 10 - Extension of new apprenticeship period: 6 months → 2 years - Shorter benefit period and reduced unemployment benefit: up to 32 months → 18 months - Integration of unemployment benefits and social security benefits - Job Center installation - Customer and competitiveness oriented Federal Labor Administration - Youth employment promotion in eastern Germany region

Social Welfare System Reform	- Pension age increase from 2011 onwards: 65 → 67 years old - Healthcare reform: Introducing high premium and decreasing optional services
Economic Revitalization	- Introduction of Craft Trades Act - Strengthen SME start-up support
Tax and Finance	- Expanding financial support for housing modernization and infrastructure investment in eastern Germany - Local financial reform
Training and Innovation	- Reform of law and system to promote vocational training in private companies - Enhance full-time school education - Strengthening preschool education

Source: Geum (2013). p.82

The Agenda 2010 was responsive to the challenges posed by globalization and an aging population in Germany, making the labor market more flexible, keeping social welfare contributions affordable, and lowering taxes for employees and companies. The Schröder government's Agenda 2010 reforms included measures for labor market flexibilization, such as easing layoff requirements, reducing unemployment benefits, tax cuts, health care and pension reform, and part-time jobs. It also included policy measures such as job creation, strengthening corporate investment capacities, investing in future growth engine industries, strengthening social welfare and health infrastructure, expanding education programs for the elderly and unskilled workers, and reducing unemployment and health insurance premiums. It aimed to improve the competitiveness of the export-driven German economy and create new jobs through a comprehensive social system and labor market reforms. Its labor market reforms, presented by Gerhard Schröder Social Democratic Government, reflected some of the neoliberal elements of 'Welfare to Work.'

At the core of the Agenda 2010 was labor market reforms. When the government's efforts to overcome the German economic situation did not pay off, Prime

Minister Schröder from the Social Democratic Party launched the 'Committee for Modern Services in the Labor Market' comprised of 15 experts. Named after Peter Hartz, chairperson of the committee in 2002, the Hartz Committee's most important goal was to establish fundamental measures to reduce the high unemployment rate in Germany. The Hartz Committee announced a labor market reform plan in four stages in August 2002, the Hartz Bill. The key driver of the Hartz Committee, which consisted of 15 labor and management and social experts from all areas of the society, was to revitalize the German economy through labor reform (Hartz, 2015).

Table 6.3. The Hartz Reforms

Act	Contents	Note
Hartz I	• Reform to expand new employment and create new jobs • Amendment of the Dispatch Worker Act: mitigation of fixed-term and dispatched work - Repeatable labor contracts can be concluded with the provision of 24 months dispatch period and the re-employment ban within 3 months - Possible to terminate dispatched work relations within the first six months - Establishment of the principle of equal treatment of dispatch workers - Start-up company: free employment of fixed-term workers for the first four years • Employment support for the elderly - Waiver of employers' contribution to employment insurance - Free labor contracts for those over 52 • Reorganization of job search system and employment support service • Reorganize the existing Federal Labor Office into employment offices and Personal Service Agencies (PSAs)	Effective January 01, 2003
Hartz II	• Tax benefits for low-wage work (Mini-Job, Midi-Job) - Mini Job: Abolished working hours less than 15 hours a week, raised income from 325 euro or less per month to 400 euro or less, and exempted social insurance and earned income tax - Midi job: Reduced social insurance premiums under € 400-800 per month	Effective January 1, 2003

	• Support for individual self-employment and livelihood start-up support of the unemployed: Salary during 3 years for one-person enterprise • Establishment of the Job Center to manage long-term unemployment	
Hartz III	• Reorganization of Federal Labor Office → Federal Labor Agency (Bundesagentur fur Arbeit, BA): customer-oriented and competitiveness-oriented perspective - Headquarters: Policy development and work for institutional improvement - Strengthening autonomy of local labor offices: a responsible management system for daily administrative work - Additional staff to reduce no. of the unemployed workers in charge per an official: 400 → 75 - Employment Office → Job Center • Reorganization of the unemployment benefit system and mitigation of conditions for the benefit	Effective January 1, 2004
Hartz IV	• Introduction of Unemployment Benefit II, which combines unemployment assistance and social assistance - Salary cuts for rejecting legally recruited jobs - Reduce unemployment benefits for long-term unemployed and abolish unemployment assistance - Mandatory active job search for long-term unemployed: mandatory to accept a 'one-euro job' that supports an additional income of one euro per hour	Effective January 1, 2005

The fundamental philosophy of the Hartz Reform starts from defining the criteria of four limits that the unemployed can endure: the regional, material, functional, and social welfare limits. Based on the criteria of four limits, the system was designed through discussion and consensus so that the unemployed could be connected to new jobs. Prime Minister Schröder promised to implement the content of these key policies agreed to by the Hartz Committee. The reforms proposed by the Hartz Committee were revised several times and finally implemented in the form of the Hartz Reforms I to IV (See Table 6.3).

Hartz I Act: Employment Flexibilization Measures and Welfare to Work

The core reforms of the Hartz I Act, the first legislation on modern services in the labor market, included key employment flexibilization measures and the system improvement to switch to 'Welfare to Work,' such as increased government support for employment, stronger conditions for receiving unemployment benefits, and the introduction of a personal service agency (PSA). In particular, the PSA had two functions of personal service and job placement: it hired unemployed workers to send them to companies and/or to arrange jobs. Also, the government has strengthened the obligations of the unemployed and created a provision to deprive workers of unemployment benefits if they did not accept a job that the PSA suggested during four months after unemployment or participation in job training.

With Hartz I, the existing Federal Labor Service was reorganized into an Employment Office (Agentur fur Arbeit, AA) and a PSA (Personal Service Agentur). In the case of a recruitment agency, it was a kind of service company in which the private sector participated, integrating worker dispatch, job introduction, and vocational education during the non-deployment period. At least one recruitment agency was set up in each employment office, and incentives were provided to the recruitment agencies based on their performance to improve the federal labor agency's job placement activities, which were not efficient before. For example, a recruitment agency was paid up to 2,000 Euros when it got an unemployed person a job working more than 15 hours per week. An additional 1,000 Euro was paid to it when the employment persisted for more than six weeks and another 1,000 Euro when it persisted for more than six months (Günther Schmid, 2008). However, the PSA was changed into an optional body rather than mandatory in January 2006 and then abolished in January 2009 due to its poor performance in the mid-term evaluation and criticism of unfair competition.

The Dispatch Worker Act (AUG) was also completely revised. The provision of a 24-month limit on dispatch and the prohibition of reemployment within three months were abolished, and a new principle of equal treatment for dispatched workers was established (Lee, 2013). Through this, the government tried to revitalize the dispatch worker system and secure the elasticity of the labor market. Hartz I Act strengthened the obligations of the unemployed. From the fourth month after being unemployed, they were obliged to work for a job placed by the employment service agency or participate in vocational training. Unless there were special reasons like health or family, they must accept the offer. Otherwise, they were temporarily deprived of their benefits (Geum 2013).

Employment support for older workers was also established. The policy of claiming wage preservation for reemployment of unemployed people aged 50 and older and the policy of temporarily exempting employment insurance contributions until 2006 were implemented. This aimed at activating the employment of older workers considering their relative weakness in the labor market. The payment requirements and criteria for employment insurance benefits and unemployment benefits were revised. By preventing unemployment benefits from rising in line with wage levels, it prevented the unemployed from relying on unemployment benefits. As a vocational training voucher system was introduced, individuals could make their own choices, unlike the traditional federal labor agency designated educational institutions.

Hartz II Act: Enhancement of New Job Creation through Establishment and Improvement of Midi Job system

The Hartz II Act introduced the system of mini-jobs, midi jobs, floater jobs, and 'one-person enterprise' (Ich-AG).[3] The Act sought to increase labor flexibility through mini and midi jobs while mitigating employment protection acts by introducing short-term jobs. The German federal government has invested about 4 billion euros in converting illegal laborers into mini-jobs. Mini jobs were applied to housework, which was often considered illegal labor. For example, at the time, workers such as cleaners, childcare givers, and caregivers for the elderly were engaged in unlawful labor without social insurance. However, with the introduction of the mini job system, the illegal laborer was all converted into legal workers. The 'one-person enterprise' system was designed to encourage start-ups, and about 4,000 one-person enterprises were established at that time. However, with the change of regime, the system was abolished for political reasons such as budget constraints, etc. (Hartz 2015).

The Hartz II Act also focused on the creation of small and medium-sized jobs, such as the improvement of the mini-job system and the establishment of the mid-job system. First, the Act sought to revitalize the creation of new jobs by improving the Mini-job system and establishing the Midi-job system. Before the Hartz II Act, mini-jobs were defined in German society as jobs with less than 15 hours of work a week and less than € 325 a month. Then, the government has exempted workers

---

[3] Mini-Job is a form of labor introduced by the German Schroeder government in 2003. It is a kind of employment that breaks down working hours and earns less than 400 euros a month. From 2013, it was raised to less than 450 euros per month. Midi-job, on the other hand, like mini-jobs, is a job with shorter working hours, with employment of less than € 401-800 per month. From 2013, it was raised to less than 451 ~ 850 euros per month. A floater job is a form of employment that moves from place to place where the service is needed without having a fixed position.

from social insurance premiums and earned income taxes. Instead, the employer was obliged to pay the reduced social insurance and taxes, such as 12 percent pension premium, 11 percent medical insurance, and 2 percent tax (currently 13 percent, 15 percent, and 2 percent, respectively) (Geum 2013, Kim 2013). This mini-job system was intended to promote the employment of long-term unemployed workers by providing low-wage jobs and eliminating labor with no taxes. Hartz II Act removed the standard of working hours for mini-jobs and raised the standard salary from € 325 per month to € 400 per month. Also, in the household sector, a minimum job of 500 euro per month was recognized as a mini-job regardless of working hours (Park 2016). As a result, even if a worker worked more than 15 hours a week, it was recognized as a mini job if he/she received a wage of less than 400 euro per month. Moreover, a worker earned more than 400 euro working shorter than two months or 50 days, it was regarded as a mini job.

At the same time, with the introduction of the Midi-job concept, social insurance tax cuts were granted according to salary levels for workers earning between 400 and 800 euros per month. Unlike mini-jobs, social insurance premiums and taxes were not exempt completely, but the exemption rules were designed to allow workers to pay taxes based on reduced income levels. However, employers paid premiums and taxes based on workers' gross income. As a result, workers often paid half of the social insurance premiums, while employers paid taxes at the same level as the case of regular workers. In short, the revision of the Hartz II Acts about the Mini-job system and the establishment of a Midi-job aimed at creating new jobs through flexibilization of the form of work.

The Hartz II Act also subsidized for a maximum of three years the salary of the one-person enterprises (Ich-AG) unless the beneficiary's annual income exceeds 25,000 euros (Günther Schmid, 2008). More specifically, in the first year of the start-up, 600 euro per month was subsidized, in the second year 360 euro, and in the third year 240 euros. Like general workers, they were also entitled to social insurance coverage.

Hartz III Act: Reorganization of the Unemployment Benefits System and the Dismissal Protection Law

The Hartz III Act was transforming into a modern service provider by turning the Federal Labor Office into a 'Federal Labor Agency' (Hartz 2015). To this end, the Federal Labor Office (Bundesanstalt für Arbeit) was converted to the Federal Labor Agency, and the division of work between headquarters and regional offices was carried out. The headquarters was responsible for policy development, institutional improvement, and intermediation for the unemployed, while the regional office was responsible for daily administrative tasks. A total of 180 regional offices introduced an independent management system and established a customer center to manage unemployed people into three groups of information, consultation, and protection (Kim, 2013). Also, the reorganization was carried out, such as renaming the Regional Labor Office (Arbeitsamt) to the Employment Support Center (Agentur für Arbeit).

Particularly, the target of intensive employment services in the new system was young people under 25. Since 2005, the youth should have their first consultation with a vocational counselor within one week and have to write a separate integration plan into the labor market within three weeks, and a specific program was provided to him/her within four weeks. On the other hand, more relaxed conditions were applied to adults, requiring the initial consultation within three weeks and a separate integration plan within eight weeks. For this purpose, the amount of work undertaken by individual counselors was set at 75 per person for the youth and 150 per person for adults.

Table 6.4. Reform of the Unemployment Benefit System

	Before reform	After reform	Note
Eligibility Requirements	Pay premiums for 12 months or more in the past 3 years	Pay premiums for 12 months or more in the past 2 years	30% reduction in salary if do not accept the job placement
Receipt Period	6 months ~ 32 months	6 months ~ 18 months	

Source: Geum (2013). p.81

Through the reorganization of the unemployment benefit system, the minimum period of unemployment insurance coverage for receiving benefits was reduced from three years to two years. However, the period of benefits was also shortened as the requirements of unemployment benefits were relaxed. In mass unemployment, the period of assistance was reduced from two years to one year.

The German government revised the Dismissal Protection Act to adjust its scope and changed the regulations on the selection of the targets of dismissal. The government recognized the right to claim compensation by workers who were laid off and expanded the scope of the dismissal-related lawsuits. The Act made small-sized workplaces an exception. The existing Act reckoned small businesses as workplaces with five or fewer employees. Still, it revised them to those with ten or fewer employees, allowing them to lay off employees for managerial reasons.[4]

In the case of managerial dismissals, the criteria for selecting targets for the dismissal were specified to protect socially underprivileged who were inferior in terms of the need for social protection (Kwon, 2007). In the process of selecting dismissal targets, disability, the number of dependents, years of service, and age were considered. If the employer did not select targets of dismissal according to the above criteria, the dismissal itself was invalid. Workers dismissed for managerial reasons were given the right to exercise compensation claims. Dismissed workers may file a dismissal lawsuit within three weeks after the dismissal, and when the claim was exercised, he/she may demand monetary compensation for the dismissal on the premise that he will not proceed with the lawsuit for dismissal. In this case, the compensation amount by the company was equivalent to one and a half months of salary per year of service. Besides, the areas where dismissed workers can file a dismissal lawsuit were extended. Previously, litigation could only be filed against the social justification of dismissal, but all dismissal-related litigation could be filed regardless of the cause.

The amendment of the Dismissal Protection Act was to realize the paradigm of the Dismissal Act harmoniously, which did not go against the tendency of labor flexibility but prioritized the guarantee of employment for workers as the socially underprivileged. It expanded the number of workplaces exempted from the application of the Dismissal Protection Act to ensure the interests of employers, adjusted the dispute-related regulations that may arise during the dismissal process, and guaranteed

---

[4] In Germany, small-sized workplaces were considered not to have sufficient management capacity to enforce the Dismissal Protection Act, and the relationship between workers and employers was so close that it was not justified to force state intervention (Kwon, 2007).

workers' rights. These all contributed to the labor reforms.

The Hartz III Act also deregulated the Short-term and Fixed-term Work Act (TzBfG) and the Work Hours Act (ArbZG). According to the Short-term and Fixed-term Work Act (TzBfG) before the Hartz III Act, employment of part-time workers was permitted when there were eight objective reasons, including 'temporary workforce demand' etc.(Jeong, 2013). However, even if there was no objective reason, fixed-term employment could be permitted. This was the case when a worker was over 58 years of age with fixed-term employment within two years. The Hartz III Act extended cases in which fixed-term employment was possible without objective reasons. In the case of new business establishments, temporary workers were allowed to be hired without objective reasons for four years after the establishment, and the ages of those subject to the exclusion of the Fixed-term Act were changed from 58 to 52 to promote employment of older workers. In Germany, conditions for fixed-term employment were strict. Although the maximum length of work was two years at the time of the contract, which was the same as that of Korea, only firms within four years of the establishment were allowed to hire fixed-term workers, and the targets of employment were limited to those over 52 years old or the long-term unemployed.

The Hartz III Act also provided 'one-time payment for entrepreneurs (bridge-crossing allowance or conversion benefit, Überbrückungsgeld)' for the self-employed who started the company. 300 euro per month was added to the existing unemployment benefits, and the period of payment was limited to six months (Günther Schmid, 2008). The mandatory payment of these subsidies had strengthened government support for startups. This policy was integrated with the funds for start-ups for livelihood in August 2006. At the same time, Hartz III Act strengthened job seekers' obligation for cooperation and mitigated regulations on job creation measures (ABM). Job creation measure (ABM) was to provide jobs from days to up to 12 months to unskilled workers through government assistance (LGERI 2010: 35). It was operated by local governments and social institutions based on the assistance provided by the government. However, this policy was abolished in 2009, according to criticism that the government subsidy distorted competition and motivated the unemployed to participate in vocational training less, rather than guaranteeing substantial and autonomous competitiveness in jobs.

Hartz IV Act: Reform of Unemployment Insurance System

The Hartz IV Act focused on the reform of the unemployment benefit and insurance system. The changes in unemployment benefits in the Hartz IV Act can be summarized into three points: First, the period for unemployment social benefits based on social insurance was shortened, and the level of benefits was adjusted (the name was changed to unemployment benefit I). Second, it was unified with the social aid which was the minimum income security of the unemployment aid amount linked to the past income. Third, the Unemployment Benefit II was created for unemployment benefit recipients and social assistance recipients with the ability to work. As a result, social assistance targeted only beneficiaries who could not work. Among recipients of social assistance, those who could work more than three days a week were newly included as the targets of the activation measures. The unemployment insurance system of the Hartz IV Act was divided into Unemployment Benefit I, Unemployment Benefit II, and Social Allowance. First, Unemployment

Benefit I is an unemployment benefit for the short-term unemployed. Unlike the previous unemployment benefits that were paid for three years after unemployment, its payment period was set differently according to the age and working period of the unemployed.

Table 6.5. Unemployment Benefits System Reform and Change

	Old System		New System
Unemployment Benefits	• Benefits from unemployment insurance, financing by contributions, and payments linked to past income levels over a certain period - Payment for 3 years after unemployment: 66% of salary before job loss	Unemploy-ment Benefit I	• Provide benefits link
Unemployment Assistancee	• Recipients are selected by unemployment assistance linked to income levels, tax procurement, and asset surveys • Provide unemployment assistance during the indefinite period for unemployed failed to re-employment within three years after unemployment • Paid to those who have completed receiving a period of unemployment benefits - the amount of payment is 53% or 57% (if dependent family) 12, 16, 20, and 24 months of work - 55 years old and over: unemployment benefits of 15 and 18 months for 30 and 36 months of work - Benefit: 60% of your salary pre-unemployment, 67% if you have dependent children	Unemploy-ment Benefit II Social Allowance	• Procurement of taxes • Provision of flat-rate benefits through asset surveys, and indefinite provision for job seekers with working ability after Unemployment Benefit I has been exhausted - The basic cost of living: € 331-345 per month - Reduction of salary (30 ~ 100%) for refusal of suggested jobs • Provided to children under the age of 15 in the household of unemployment Assistance II beneficiaries
Social Assistance	• Procurement by tax • providing indefinite benefits through asset surveys - Minimum livelihood guarantees for socially vulnerable groups with low income	New Social Assistance	• Provided to people over 65 who don't have working ability • Tax procurement • Fixed-term salary based on asset survey

Source: Konle-Seidl (2008). p.9 revised

Unemployed workers under the age of 55 received unemployment benefits for six, eight, ten, and twelve months, respectively, for 12, 16, 20, and 24 months of work. If he/she was 55 years of age or older, he/she was entitled to 15 months and 18 months of unemployment benefits for 30 and 36 months of work, respectively. The amount of payment depended on the presence of dependent children. If he/she has dependent children, he/she was paid 67 percent of pre-employment salary and 60 percent if you did not have one.

On the other hand, Unemployment Benefit II was the same as the previous unemployment subsidy. Still, the difference was that the payment was lowered to the level of basic living expenses. Specific targets of payment were those who were able to perform economic activities among those who were eligible for social aid and part of a living community. However, the unemployed whose spouses had a job could not apply it. Based on the evaluation of their property situation, the amount they needed to live on was paid. Specifically, it consisted of the standard support subsidy, housing, and heating expenses, etc. Those who had already received unemployment benefits could receive an additional subsidy for two years in addition to Unemployment Benefit II, of which the amount gradually decreased. Recipients of Unemployment Benefit II were subject to active job search activities instead of livelihood support. For example, if someone refused to accept a job properly arranged, 100 euro (30 percent) would be cut over three months, and his/her benefits would be shortened. Also, childcare services for re-employment, vocational education and training, psychological counseling programs were supported. Integrated services at job centers were also provided to encourage the long-term unemployed to get a job.

Social aid (Sozialgeld) was provided to those who were incapable of economic activity and made up the living community with at least one of the qualified recipients who could lead to economic activity. Suppose the Unemployment Benefit II was an allowance paid to those who were capable of economic activity, while social aid was given to those who could not expect earned income because economic activity was not possible at all. Being capable of economic activity amounted to that at least three hours of daily income activity was possible in the current labor market and under normal labor market conditions soon.

In short, the reform of the unemployment insurance system by the Hartz IV Act aimed to decrease the amount of unemployment support to reduce the state's financial burden and help the unemployed seek a job actively. In the case of unemployment benefit I, the unemployment benefits were set according to the age and working period of the unemployed, and the period of benefits was also reduced. Also, newly created unemployment benefits II for low-income families with working capacities significantly lowered the level of support for the basic cost of living and applied strict screening criteria.

6.4.3 Youth Guarantee and Job Training System

The policy target of the new employment service system following the Hartz reform was young people under the age of 25. After 2005, young people should have their first consultation with a vocational counselor within one week and have to write a separate integration plan into the labor market within three weeks, and then a specific program was provided within four weeks. The employment service system for the youth has maintained its reputation in the form of the 'Youth Guarantee' system that has been implemented at the EU level since the 2008 economic crisis. The German Youth Guarantee system is based on the dual vocational training system for the youth.

Due to early student selection based on ability in Germany, there are only a few pools for university admission. Instead, because of the industrial structure of manufacturing-oriented SMEs, many jobs requiring skilled workers are provided. Therefore, the enrollment rates for vocational schools remain high. In 2009, Germany's university enrollment rate was 40 percent, lower than 71 percent in Korea, and 59 percent in the OECD average (OECD 2015). On the other hand, more than 50 percent of students entered vocational high schools in 2009. It was very high compared to other countries. As of 2010, more than 500,000 companies offered vocational education and training courses, of which over 99 percent were SMEs with 500 or fewer employees. Companies usually hire people among those who completed their vocational education. Due to this vocational training system, the youth unemployment rate in Germany was kept very low compared to other countries. The vocational training system in Germany has several characteristics as follows.

First, it functions as a vocational education system that reduces mismatches between job openings and job search. Germany's vocational training system connects students with companies and trains them with the skills they need. Then, companies hire them directly through vocational training. Reducing job mismatches results in a lowering in the youth unemployment rate. It also promotes entrepreneurship. Students can receive a variety of vocational training through the dual vocational education system, and relevant certifications can be used effectively in the labor market. Also, after a period of work experience, they can choose a variety of courses to grow into a professional master (meister).

Second, the German vocational education and training system is based on social partnership, in which social partners are actively engaged. Social partners such as German companies, chambers of commerce, and workers' organizations are deeply involved in the design and implementation of vocational education and training. They participate in the development and revision of vocational training guidelines and determine wages for trainees through collective wage negotiations. Various chambers have a very important role in enforcing the regulations on vocational education and training as intermediaries between the government and corporations. Professional chambers regularly manage whether companies can provide adequate training following government regulations. Termination of training sessions is also done through tests administered by these chambers. The qualification test assesses whether the trainee has completed the training period and is qualified as a skilled technician. The assessment is made through an evaluation committee composed of employee representatives, employer representatives, and vocational school teachers. The company's active participation through the Chamber of Commerce and Industry gives the company a higher interest in and appreciation of the apprenticeship system and an opportunity to actively support it. Besides, the vocational education and training system in Germany has a sophisticated role-sharing, mutual check, and balance system among relevant institutions such as central and local governments, corporations, chambers of commerce, and industry. It is very rare that the educational and economic objectives of the system are distorted due to the short-term needs of companies.

Third, although most of the vocational and apprenticeship training is done by private companies, trainees need to be trained as skilled technicians in the future. Therefore, the government is interested in vocational education and training that educates appropriate skills and knowledge and supports it. In establishing regulations on vocational education and training, the government should revise them based on the consensus and agreement between employers and workers organizations. In this regard, the Federal Vocational Training and Training Institute builds a database, advises employers and workers organizations and the government, and provides a platform for vocational training and training planning and institutional improvement. The federal government is also responsible for the overall vocational education and training policy, and local governments are responsible for financial support for vocational schools such as teacher salaries, facilities, and equipment. In general, companies pay for training costs for trainees, usually supported by the fund raised by companies in the same sector. There is also a wide range of government support for trainees. Training costs are also provided to vocational school students who have difficulty in finding training companies and to companies employing immigrants or low-income students. Companies that hire interns for six to twelve months may be eligible for a subsidy in wages and other costs.

  The German government did not reduce financial support for vocational education and training in the face of the 2008 global financial crisis, and companies have continued to provide jobs for apprentices. This has greatly contributed to reducing the youth unemployment rate and securing a workforce that has been reduced by the shrinking population. The Vocational Training Bonus Program, implemented in August 2008, was a subsidy program for companies that accepted the youth seeking long-term employment as vocational trainees. As of 2010, more than half a million companies offered vocational training and training courses. They also benefited from the fact that they could immediately hire the required workforce from students who have completed vocational education.

6.4.4 Evaluations of the Hartz Reforms

The Hartz reforms under the Schröder government were the most comprehensive reforms of the social system and labor market to address the low economic growth, high unemployment, and the fiscal deficit. The Hartz reforms were based on the concept of 'Welfare to Work' to solve the high unemployment at the time. First, the core idea and principle of the Hartz Reforms begin to define the limits of what the unemployed can afford, including local, physical, functional, and social welfare limits, and propose jobs based on what they have expected (zumutbarkeit). In that sense, it was very different from those that have only considered the unemployed with the viewpoint of social structure. By defining the limits, the unemployed workers, including the long-term unemployed, were brought back to work.

In short, it was an effort to set an affordable limit for someone, based on 'what the unemployed have expected (zumutbarkeit),' and connect them with the job prospects (Hartz 2015). The Hartz reform contains a strategy for activating the unemployed in two ways: promotion and demanding (fördern und fordern). Here, 'fördern' means improvement of job placement services, including job placement and job promotion. On the other hand, the method of demanding involves tightening the rules for unemployed people to accept 'suitable' jobs and, if not, cut in their pay. The key points of labor market reform in the Hartz Acts are summarized as follows.

First, to expand new employment and create new jobs, the government mitigated fixed-term and dispatched work restrictions. At the same time, the government granted tax benefits to short-term and low-wage work such as mini-jobs and mid-jobs, thereby expanding the creation of small and medium-sized jobs and providing them with social insurance benefits. It resulted in a policy effect attracting non-regular workers outside the labor market into the institutionalized labor market framework.

Secondly, the Federal Labor Office was reorganized into headquarters responsible for policy development, institutional improvement, and unemployment intermediation. Regional labor offices in charge of daily administrative tasks were transformed into Job Centers to strengthen job placement and training. By setting up and operating a personal service agency, a kind of workforce recruitment company (PSA) within the regional labor office, the function of linking the unemployed to jobs was greatly strengthened. The PSA hired the unemployed and dispatched them to companies or conducted vocational training for employment. In this case, the unemployed had an obligation to accept a job offer or participate in vocational training. The duties and responsibilities of the unemployed have been strengthened. If they refused a reasonable job offer, their benefits were reduced (usually 70 percent or more of their wages). If they continued to decline it, it could reduce the total amount of unemployment benefit II. Besides, the government also supported unemployed start-ups such as 'one-person enterprises' and provided up to 50 percent of wages to employers when hiring the long-term unemployed. This program aimed to solve low motivation to work and the career management gap due to long-term unemployment.

Third, the government has actively tried to have the long-term unemployed go back to work by reorganizing the unemployment insurance and benefits system that reinforced the requirements for unemployment benefits. Unemployment benefit II was calculated by reflecting the income and wealth of the unemployed and was revised to the flat rate from the wage-linked system in the past to suppress the motive for maintaining unemployment among the middle class and high-income earners. Also, the government tried to solve the chronic long-term unemployment problem by reducing the payment period of basic unemployment benefit I from 32 months to 12 months and by reducing the unemployment benefits to long-term unemployed if they refused to take on a job offer properly arranged. After 2005, the German labor market began to show positive results with implementing the Hartz Reform Acts. As indicated above, the unemployment rate, which peaked at 11.2 percent in 2005, dropped to 7.5 percent just before the 2008 economic crisis and rose to 7.7 percent in 2009 when the aftermath of the global financial crisis began to take effect. After that, the unemployment rate continued to fall, falling to 4 percent in 2015. Given these indicators of the German labor market, Hartz Reforms had a positive policy effect in overcoming the 2008 global economic crisis faster than other OECD countries. They had a meaning as preemptive reforms in response to the financial crisis.

 Despite the positive performance of the Hartz Reforms in the German economy and labor market, there were problems that they raised in the labor market. As for the German labor market policy following the Hartz reforms, measures of labor market flexibilization were at the core. They have inevitably resulted in social inequalities due to the increase in non-regular work and the expansion of low-wage jobs(See Table 6.6).

Table 6.6. Percentage of part-time workers in Germany (%)

Year	2000	2005	2006	2007	2008	2009	2010	2011	2012
Germany	17.6	21.5	21.8	22.0	21.8	21.9	21.7	22.1	22.1
OECD	11.9	15.2	15.2	15.4	15.6	16.4	166.6	16.5	16.9

Source: OECD (2014)

The biggest problem with the Hartz reforms in the German labor market was the rapid increase in the number of non-regular workers. The proportion of non-regular workers in the German labor market, such as mini-jobs and mid-jobs, part-time work, dispatched work, and fixed-term work, has increased significantly since the 2008 global economic crisis.

The share of non-regular workers in Germany was one-fifth in the early 1990s but increased to more than one-third after the financial crisis. As more than 80 percent of all part-time workers were women, the recent rapid increase in the female employment rate was in line with the rise in part-time work. Another problem that the Hartz Reforms caused was the expansion of the low-wage workers due to the increase in non-regular work. In 2010, 20.6 percent of low-wage workers earned less than two-thirds of the median income of all German workers. In particular, women's rate of low-wage work was 27 percent, which was about 10 percent point higher than that of the low-wage work by men. Accordingly, criticism has continued that the Merkel government's employment policy was simply achieved through the quantitative expansion of jobs. Also, there was another problem in the German labor markets, such as the problem of increased instability in the German labor market due to the expansion of non-regular and low-wage workers, the reduction of real income of workers, and the disparity of income distribution and social bi-polarization.

The problems in the process of institutionalization of the Hartz reforms cannot be overlooked. If the delivery system and financing method are not adequately designed, the institutions may be distorted. For example, when Unemployment Benefit II was created for unemployed workers and social aid recipients in line with working capacity, more than 90 percent of them were determined to be Unemployment Benefit II recipients. Then, this was because the local government, which had the authority to classify recipients, classified existing social aid recipients as policy targets of Unemployment Benefit II of the Federal government in consideration of the financial burden because the Federal government shouldered a significant proportion of the cost.

The German case also shows that a more prudent policy approach is needed to outsource employment services to the private sector. The German government has attempted to entrust employment services to the private sector since 1998 and actively introduced private entrustment of the employment services through the Hartz reforms. Still, the actual results were far below expectations.

6.4.5 Trends and Changes of ALMPs

The unification in 1990 resulted in a significant change in the German economy and society. A severe economic downturn was caused by the collapse of the foundation of the East German economy and the cost of the unification. Increasing social welfare costs and fiscal deficits resulting from the reunification led to inflation in Germany. To curb it, the German government adopted a high-interest rate policy. However, it led to the inflow of foreign financial capital to Germany and the appreciation of the German Mark and then led to a slowdown in exportation and an increase in importation that ultimately resulted in a decline in Germany's economic growth. In such a severe economic recession, the German government relied on unemployment supports rather than the ALMPs to resolve the high unemployment rate in the East German areas.

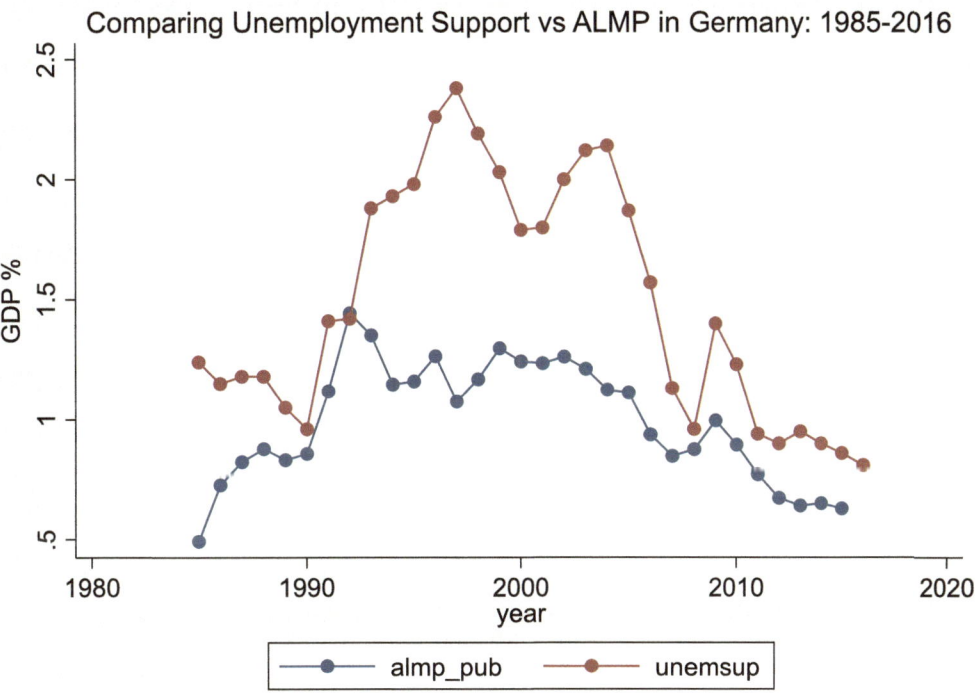

Figure 6.3. Comparing Expenditure of Unemployment Support and ALMPs in Germany: 1985-2016

As shown in Figure 6.3, the expenditure of unemployment support surged shortly after German unification. Since 2001, the collapse of the global economic bubble also caused a sharp decline in economic growth and sharply increased Germany's unemployment rates. Therefore, spending on unemployment assistance also soared again.

In response to the economic crisis, the German government has generally preferred passive labor market policies such as unemployment support rather than active labor market policies. As a result, expenditures of unemployment support in Germany have consistently exceeded the spending of ALMPs (See Figure 6.3). Under the pressures of fiscal discipline, which have been high since the early 1990s, introducing new programs such as AMLPs was difficult because they may require resource redistribution from traditional welfare schemes (Armingeon 2007). Like in France, therefore, the development of ALMPs was also delayed in Germany. Above all, the social insurance system and its governance structure have acted as an obstacle to the development of ALMPs in Germany (Clasen 2000, Eichhorst et al. 2008). Social actors such as labor unions and employer associations also opposed the reduction of the welfare system and responded passively to the introduction of active labor market policies.

However, the trends and types of ALMPs spending had changed over time. Like Sweden, vocational training, a representative policy of ALMPs in Germany, had been used as an important policy measure in the economic crisis after the unification. Germany, which has a relatively strong manufacturing industry compared to other OECD countries, has developed a dual vocational training system that offers on-the-job training at vocational school(Berufsschule) and work experience at a company. For this, a large portion of the expenditure of ALMPs was spent on vocational training compared to other ALMPs' measures. Since 2003, however, the spending on training has been continuously declining except in 2009, shortly after the 2008 economic crisis.

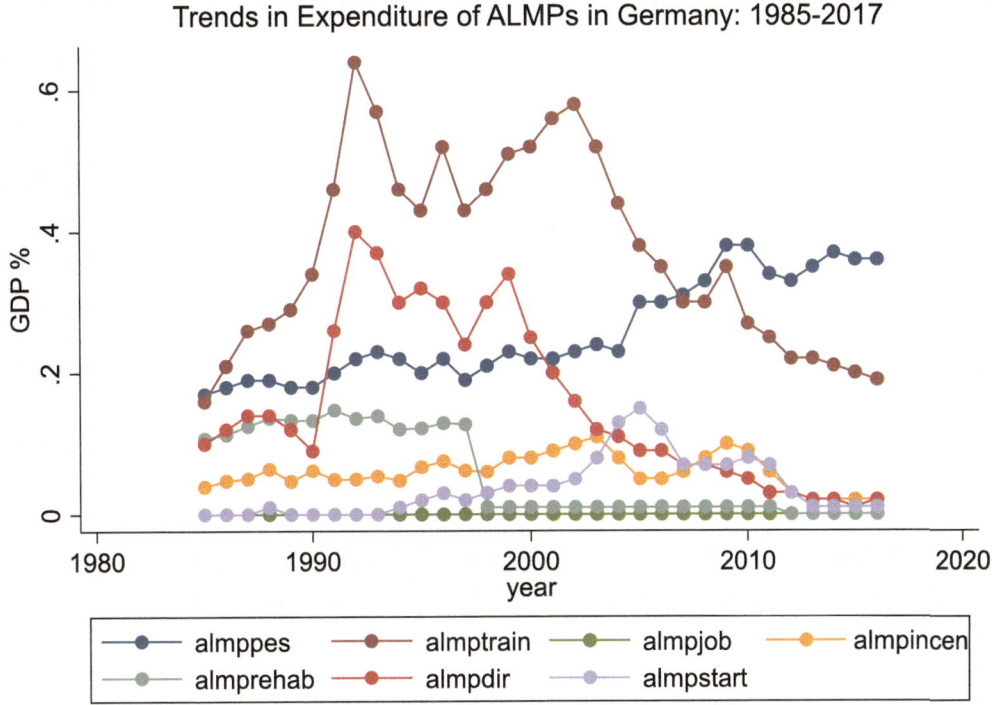

Figure 6.4. **Trends in Expenditure of ALMPs in Germany: 1985-2017**

As a result, the spending on vocational training conceded first place to the expenditure on PES in 2007. This change in the expenditure of ALMPs was a major change in Germany, where the government has consistently emphasized vocation training. The spending on direct job creation also shows the same trajectory. After the unification, the German government relied heavily on direct job creation policies to overcome unemployment. However, since 2000, spending on direct job creation has declined sharply. On the other hand, PES expenditure has increased significantly after the Hartz reforms and the 2008 economic crisis, overtaking spending on vocational training.

The reasons why it has been changed in trends and types of ALMPs spending in Germany include the following points. First, the reason that PES spending has increased significantly since the mid-2000s can be found in the Hartz reform. The German government reorganized the Federal Labor Office into a 'Federal Labor Agency' through the Hartz III Act. It also transformed the local labor offices into a modern service provider, renaming the Regional Labor Office (Arbeitsamt) to the Labor Agency as a local employment support center (Agentur für Arbeit). The employment support centers provided intensive employment services to the unemployed and young people under 25. Therefore, job placement and matching services under the new system have greatly strengthened, and then the expenditure of PES has also increased.

In Germany, the direct job creation policy was one of the major ALMPs policies to address the unemployment crisis in the 1990s. However, the expenditure on direct job creation policy has sharply decreased. This change in the spending of direct job creation resulted from research findings that direct job creation policies have not achieved the desired policy results for continuing and stable jobs (Kluve and Schmit 2002).

Overall, the Hartz reforms were based on the concept of 'Welfare to Work' to solve the high unemployment at the time. Therefore, ALMPs in Germany have focused on the strategies for activating the unemployed, including job placement services and the expansion of part-time such as mini-jobs and midi-jobs.

6.5 Summary

The Schröder government has developed the most comprehensive social system in the history of Germany to solve the problems of the German economy, which was once a European patient, including the low economic growth rate, high unemployment rate, and the fiscal deficit resulting from increased social welfare burden. The Hartz reforms which were a radical change in labor market policy based on the idea of 'Welfare to Work' have positively impacted the unemployment rate and the increases in employment rates since 2005. In particular, the achievements of German economic indicators during the 2008 global economic crisis highlighted the significance of the preemptive Hartz reforms.

There is generally no disagreement that the positive effects of the Hartz reforms in the German labor market have played a decisive role in preventing the downturn in the labor market due to economic slowdown during the 2008 global economic crisis. Indeed, in the context of the global economic crisis, Germany was one of the fastest recovering economies among European countries, thanks to its job-oriented economic policy. In November 2008, the Merkel government strengthened the job placement function of the Federal Employment Agency, provided subsidies for curtailment of working hours, and extended special worker support programs with an emphasis on employment and social safety nets. In January 2009, the 2nd response was to provide legal and financial support to the business through the support for short-run enterprises, the working hours' account system, and the introduction of the short-time work allowance to overcome unemployment and stabilize employment. As an extension of the first response plan, the government also strengthened job placement activities and provided additional funding for special education programs. In this process, the German government met closely and consulted with the employers' associations and labor unions through the 32-person Economic Labor Summit. With the social partnership to overcome the economic crisis, labor and management also actively responded to and cooperated with the government's job policies.

The tripartite social partnership was also maintained during the discussion of the Hartz Reform Bills. The German Trade Union Confederation (DGB) that participated in the Hartz Committee engaged in the whole process discussion for the reform acts. Despite the strong opposition to reforming the unemployment benefits in the Hartz Act IV, DGB generally agreed with labor market reform measures of flexibilization, based on the 'Welfare to Work' idea. During the 2008 economic crisis, the social partnership between labor and management remained at the individual company level. In particular, the tradition of labor-management co-determination at the corporate level worked positively to overcome the unemployment crisis caused by the 2008 global economic crisis, keeping cooperative labor-management relations over the reduction of working hours, the system of working hours account, and the introduction of short-time work allowances.

The Hartz reforms are evaluated as a successful policy that energized the German labor market. However, there are also negative sides to the achievements of the Hartz reforms. In particular, mini-jobs and mid-jobs have made achievements in improving the quantitative indicators of the labor market through the flexibilization of the labor market and the creation of jobs, but they have problems in terms of job quality, such as the expansion of low-wage workers and the exclusion from social security systems.

The reorganization of unemployment benefits and social assistance, which are the core contents of the Hartz IV Act, aims to secure the fiscal soundness of social insurance and strengthen the conditions for receiving unemployment benefits, leading people back to work. The change in the unemployment benefits system was positive in terms of the quantitative improvement of the labor market. However, it is criticized that the quality of the labor market has deteriorated in terms of the substantial reduction of unemployment benefits and work-related welfare (Hwang, 2014). In particular, criticisms over unemployment benefits, reorganization of the social aid, and reduction of benefits, which are the core of the Hartz IV Act, have come from the labor unions and the employers' associations, including the DGB. Critical evaluations of the Hartz reforms mostly focus on discussions on the quality of employment. In short, the evaluation of the Hartz reform can be summarized by the quantitative improvement of the employment indicators and the qualitative deterioration of employment. In particular, the expansion of part-time employment contributed to reducing the unemployment rate by promoting low-wage work. However, the growth in non-regular workers has been evaluated to have a negligible effect on the reentry of the unemployed into the regular labor market. The employment protection indicator for temporary workers is high when excluding the Netherlands and English-speaking European countries but differs significantly from other continental countries in Europe. Recently, the German government has introduced measures, including the introduction of the statutory minimum wage system and strengthened regulations on dispatch work.

In short, the reason that PES spending has significantly increased since the mid-2000s resulted from the Hartz reforms. The Hartz reforms were based on the concept of 'Welfare to Work' to solve the high unemployment at the time. Therefore, ALMPs in Germany have focused on the strategies for activating the unemployed, including job placement and matching services. Then the expenditure of PES rapidly increased after the 2008 economic crisis.

Chapter 7

KOREA: ECONOMIC CRISIS AND JOB CREATION Policies

7.1 Introduction

The 1997 financial crisis was a major shock to the Korean economy and society. The IMF crisis was a historical event and critical conjuncture that demarcated Korean society before and after the crisis (Lee 2002). Korea has achieved amazing double-digit economic growths since starting an export-oriented industrialization policy through the five-year economic development plan in the early 1960s. However, the IMF crisis that was triggered by the foreign exchange crisis in Asian financial markets, including Thailand, Indonesia, and Malaysia, collapsed the Korean economy at once.

The Korean economy recorded negative growth, and the unemployment rate nearly quadrupled from 2 to 8 percent, while almost 1.8 million people became unemployed. Numerous banks and corporations were in danger of bankruptcy, and poverty and social inequalities have increased due to a decline in household incomes in the wake of unemployment. The Kim Dae-Jung administration, which had succeeded in seizing power with the horizontal regime change amid the IMF economic crisis, could not find any other policy alternative except accepting the IMF bailout. At the time, the IMF asked the Korean government to execute structural reforms in the four sectors of finance, corporation, public domain, and labor as preconditions for the bailout (Lee 2002), among which opening of the capital market, corporate restructuring, and measures for labor market flexibility was called for as key reform tasks. In particular, the measures for labor market flexibility that the IMF demanded to the Korean government aimed to enable layoffs as a key measure for structural reform.

The IMF economic crisis and neoliberal reforms fundamentally changed the structure of the Korean labor market. Full-time regular employment up to that time had been replaced by non-regular employment, and non-regular labor had greatly expanded due to an increase in outsourcing by enterprises. The corporate employment culture also shifted to career-based employment rather than recruitment after the IMF economic crisis. Voluntary retirement and layoffs became commonplace where the concept of a lifetime job disappeared. As a result, unemployment of the youth who are faced with narrowed entry paths to the labor market became a major social problem, and most of the new recruitments were filled with non-regular workers. The dual labor market structure divided into regular and non-regular workers resulted in a deepening social bi-polarization and inequality structure.

The biggest political agenda in Korean society after the IMF crisis has been job creation. The government's macro-economic response to the IMF crisis has led to an escape from it, but employment and job problems, including jobless growth, have continued. The 2008 global economic crisis brought about another unemployment crisis in Korean society. The Korean government's rapid response to it, thanks to the experience of the IMF crisis, has made it possible to quickly ward off the crisis, but job problems such as youth unemployment, remain.

This chapter explores a few points, focusing on how Korea has overcome the 1997 IMF crisis and the 2008 global economic crisis. First, how have the major social actors responded to the two economic crises? Second, it also analyzes how Korea's job policies have changed during the two economic crises. Third, it examines what kinds of specific job policies have been taken to overcome the unemployment crisis in the two economic crises. Then, it will try to look at the reasons why a specific policy has been chosen and continued.

7.2 Economic Crises in Korea: Causes and Progress

7.2.1 The 1997 IMF Economic Crisis

Since the beginning of industrialization in the early 1960s, the Korean economy has achieved economic growths of at least 6-7 percent every year except for the temporary recession caused by the military coup in December 1980. However, the 1997 IMF crisis was a radically different form of economic shock from the historical institutional perspective. It was a critical conjuncture in which the 1997 IMF crisis fundamentally changed Korean society, including the dual labor market structure, deepening of social bi-polarization and social inequality, etc. (Lee 2002).

The 1997 economic crisis in Korea was caused by a combination of factors. The 1997 financial crisis began with the Asian financial crisis in Thailand, Indonesia, and Malaysia. Still, it can be attributed to the management relying on short-term foreign debt borrowing by the Korean economy and enterprises, which adopted the accession to the OECD and the logic of globalized economy. The government failed in properly managing fiscal and financial policies. In particular, the Asian economic crisis, triggered by the Thai Baht collapse in July 1997, drove the Korean economy which had relatively decent macroeconomic indicators into instability.

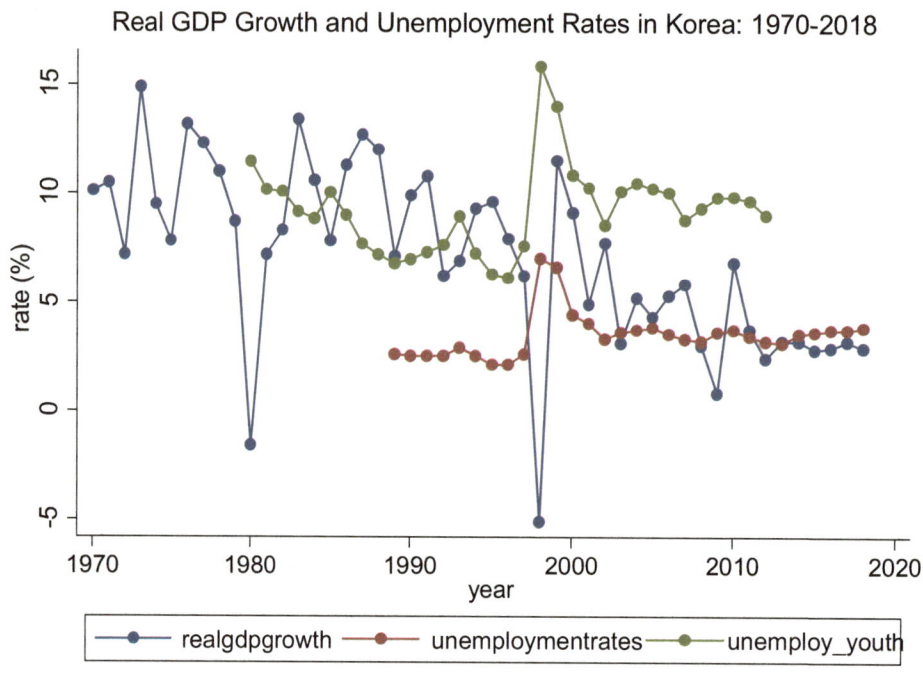

Figure 7.1 Real Growth & Unemployment rate in Korea: 1970 – 2012

The 1997 economic crisis began with the foreign exchange crisis and expanded to fiscal, financial, and corporate crises. As the foreign exchange rate rose significantly, the foreign currency plunged out of Korea's financial market, causing a series of bankruptcies of financial institutions. Consequently, the Korean economy was on the verge of collapse, as the corporate sector that depended on a high level of debt was also forced to go bankrupt.

In November 1997, the Korean government agreed to accept the bailout of the IMF, and the IMF asked the Korean government to undertake structural reforms in the four sectors of finance, corporation, public domain, and labor and presented strict guidelines in return (Lee, 2002). As soon as the IMF's demands for the bailout were announced, the exchange rate per US dollar soared to 1,965 won, and foreign reserves plummeted to 3.9 billion dollars from 63.4 billion dollars in 1995 (IMF International Financial Statistics). In 1998, real GDP registered a negative growth of 6.8 percent. The unemployment rate, which remained at 2 percent before the crisis, soared to 8 percent at the end of 1998, and the unemployed reached 1.8 million (Statistics Korea 2009).

It can be said that the direct cause of the 1997 economic crisis was the government's failure in the foreign exchange market. It failed not only in managing the liquidity of foreign exchange but also in monitoring financial institutions. With the introduction of the foreign exchange liberalization policy, foreign debt increased by more than 30 percent annually between 1994 and 1996. In particular, short-term liabilities accounted for a large portion of the total foreign debt, thereby raising the possibility of a foreign exchange liquidity crisis. The rapid decline in foreign exchange liquidity in 1997 was due to the government's offering foreign currency to related institutions to prevent the withdrawal of international lenders and bankruptcy of commercial banks.

7.2.2 The 2008 Global Economic Crisis

The 2008 economic crisis started with the subprime mortgage insolvency in the United States and expanded into the global financial market, leading to a series of the bankruptcy of global financial institutions that resulted in a simultaneous global economic recession. The 2008 global financial crisis that originated from Wall Street also hit the Korean economy. Financial market instability such as interest rates, stock prices, and foreign exchange rates have greatly expanded, and the real economy has slumped rapidly.

Domestic financial markets were left in a state of shock due to the global financial crisis. Interest rates, stock prices, and exchange rates all fluctuated, and the credit crisis worsened. In the foreign exchange market, the rate of won to dollar fell 38.9 percent for three months from August to November 2008, reaching 1,513 won on November 24. Exchange rate fluctuations also intensified significantly. Thereafter instability in the foreign exchange market was aggravated. The KOSPI index hit its lowest on November 24th. The stock prices tumbled from 1,888 in May to 938.7 in October 2008, recording the steepest nosedive.

Short-term market interest rates rose sharply, mainly on bank bonds and corporate bonds. Financial institutions had avoided the provision of credit to under-valued households and businesses, resulting in a credit crisis in the financial markets. The instability of financial markets had a big impact on the real economy. Retail sales fell 1.8 percent in September 2008 and 3.3 percent in October 2008, while facility investment fell 2.4 percent compared to the previous month. In November 2008, exports fell 15.6 percent, while manufacturing output fell 14.2 percent, and service production decreased 0.9 percent. As a result, the GDP growth rate in 2008 was 2.8 percent, a large scale of the drop from 5.5 percent in 2007, and the GDP growth rate in 2009 was 0.7 percent, further dropping from the previous year. Such economic growth rates are the lowest levels since the growth rate of negative 5.7% in 1998 (Statistics Korea 2009).

Employment and wage levels also deteriorated significantly. In August 2008, the number of newly recruited employees increased by 160,000 year-on-year but decreased by 10,000 in December. Real wage growth fell 2.7% in the third quarter and 6.4% in the fourth quarter. In the fourth quarter of 2008, the economic growth rate was negative 3.4 percent, and sharp contraction of the real economy also affected employment, leading to a negative employment situation in which the number of jobs in the labor market decreased since December 2008. Employment declined by 103,000 in January 2009, 142,000 in February, and 195,000 in March year on year, and the number of unemployed persons increased by more than 900,000 since February. Fortunately, the job market stabilized after the number of unemployed people peaked at 960,000 in June 2019 and eased off afterward (Statistics Korea 2009, Jeong 2012: 33).

After the global economic crisis in 2008, Korea's unemployment rate rose from 3.6 percent in 2009 to 3.7 percent in 2010. Since then, it has calmed down to 3.4 percent in 2011, further down to 3.1 percent in 2013, but has rebounded to 3.8 percent in 2018. However, these employment indicators are relatively low compared to the unemployment rates of 7.0 percent, 6.3 percent, and 4.4 percent in 1998, 1999, and 2000 respectively, at the time of the 1997 IMF crisis. After the 2008 global economic crisis, Korea's economic growth rate of 0.7 percent in 2009 was relatively less severe than the economic growth rate of negative 5.8 percent in 1998 during the IMF crisis (Figure 7.1. above, Statistics Korea 2009). However, the socio-economic shocks and trauma that Korean society experienced during the 1997 financial crisis brought about the Korean government's rapid response to the 2008 global economic crisis.

7.3 Responses to the Economic Crisis

7.3.1 Political Responses

The 1997 financial crisis brought about a major change in the political landscape. For the first time since the 1987 democratization movement, horizontal regime change took place. To overcome the IMF economic crisis, the Kim Dae-Jung administration adopted four major structural reforms, which were prerequisites for the IMF bailout, and embarked on full-scale reforms. The Kim Dae-Jung government and the IMF agreed to fiscal austerity policies, close-downs of financial institutions, the introduction of a strict financial monitoring system, and expansion of labor market flexibility as preconditions for the bailout (Lee 2002).

The Kim Dae-Jung administration promised to open capital markets and to carry out economic restructuring. It tried to hammer out a social consensus for the sharing of pain among the tripartite actors of the economy, following the reform measures proposed by the IMF for the implementation of the IMF Agreement and economic restructuring. It launched the Korean Tripartite Commission (KTC) on January 15, 1998, and hammered out the social compact to overcome the economic crisis in February 1998. The so-called 'Feb. 2 Social Pact' consisted of 90 items in ten sectors (Jeong 2012, Lee 2002). In line with the pacts, the Labor Relations Act was amended to introduce a layoff and dispatched work system. The government expanded the scope of employment insurance benefits to a greater extent to cope with the unemployment crisis caused by the permission of layoffs and decided to invest 10 trillion won in the measures to prevent unemployment. Following the agreement by the Tripartite Commission, the government promoted structural reforms in the four sectors of finance, corporation, public domain, and labor and economic restructuring to strengthen the free market economic system (Hur 2002, Lee 2002). Facilitating greater flexibility in the labor market was a very urgent policy issue for the Kim Dae-Jung administration to propel the restructuring of the financial and corporate sectors successfully. If the legislation about flexible labor market policies couldn't proceed, the IMF's requirements for the structural reform policy would be impossible to meet.

Table 7.1. Comparing the 2008 Economic Crisis with 1997 IMF Economic Crisis

	IMF Economic Crisis (1997)	Global Economic Crisis (2008)
Crisis Symptoms	Excessive Lending by Financial Institutions and Rise in Asset Prices Credit Crunch and Instability in Financial System Rapid Drop in Stocks Prices and Soaring of Foreign Exchange Rates	Excessive Lending by Financia
Nature of the Crisis 1 Institutions and Rise in Asset Prices	Combination of Monetary and Financial Crises	Global Financial Crisis
Cause of Crisis	Deepened Insolvency of Domestic Enterprises Lack of Risk Management in Financial Institutions Contraction in Domestic Investment and Sales of Domestic Stocks by Foreign Capitals	Collapse of US Asset Bubble Lack of Risk Management in International Financial Institutions Recovery of Investment Funds from Emerging Market Countries (preferring safe assets like US bonds)
Economic Conditions	Favorable Global Economic Conditions Economic Slowdown (1995 ~) High Debt Burden Too Small Foreign Reserves Surge in Domestic Interest Rates	Simultaneous Global Economic Recession Gradual Rise in Economic Growth Rate (2004 ~) Low External Debt Burden Increase in Foreign Exchange Reserves Downward Trends in Domestic and Foreign Interest Rates
Social Dialogue	Tripartite Commission	Emergency Meeting among Labor, Management, Civic Group, and the Government
Social Pacts	Feb·6 Social Pacts	Four-party Agreement to Overcome the Economic Crisis

Policy Responses	IMF-led Tight Fiscal and Monetary Policies Export-led Economic Recovery Reforms in 4 Sectors of Corporation, Finance, Public Domain, and Labor Measures for Labor Market Flexibility	Expansionary Fiscal and Monetary policies Domestic Demand-led Economic Recovery Policy Corporate Reform Centered on Financial Institutions Active Labor Market Policy

Source: Jeong (2012). P. 27. Revised.

The launch of the Korean Tripartite Commission (Jan. 15, 1998) and the Feb.6 Social Pacts for Overcoming the Economic Crisis (Feb. 6, 1998) had a primary purpose of improving the labor market's flexibility when it came to the revision of labor laws. The 'Feb.6 Social Pacts' included several flexibility measures that allowed for layoffs, which labor organizations strongly opposed at that time. It was a cataclysmic moment for the structure of Korea's labor market.

Table 7.2. Structural Reforms of Four Sectors after IMF Economic Crisis

	Financial Reform	Corporate Reform	Public Reform	Labor Reform
Target	•Strengthening the competitiveness of financial institutions •Enhanced financial supervision	•Business competitiveness •Centralization of enterprises in key areas	•Slimmer administration organizations •Privatization •Dereg	•Creating a flexible labor market •Advanced labor relations •Economic reform by social consensusulation
Primary Challenges	•Banning insolvent financial institutions •Liquidation of insolvent bonds •BIS ratio compliance •Establishment of the Financial Supervisory Commission	•Improvement of corporate governance •Reducing cross-debt guarantees •Lowering the debt ratio to 200% •Big deals and Workouts •Establishing corporate responsibility	•Government reorganization •Establishing privatization plans •Various regulatory reforms	•Introducing layoffs and dispatched workers •Installing the Korean Tripartite Commission •Preparing a social safety net
Remarks	•Credit crunch persists •More bad bonds raised	•55 insolvent companies banned	•Delay due to the confusion of government functions	•Increase in unemployment

Source: Ministry of Finance and Economy (1998) & Lee (2002).

The structural reform of the Kim Dae-Jung administration, based on the Memorandum of Understanding with the IMF, was a comprehensive economic reform that consisted of reforms in four sectors, including finance, corporation, public domain, and labor, that would be conducive to these reforms (See Table 7.2). However, Kim Dae-Jung administration's structural reforms were immediately beset by the IMF's stringent conditions rather than the administration's selective autonomy. The IMF's key policy requirements were based on neo-liberal policies like the fully opening of the capital and financial markets and the introduction of labor market-related institutions for greater flexibility.

The Kim Dae-Jung administration's structural reforms were conducted in a two-step process, without exception in the financial, corporate, and public sectors, which was the key to the restructuring based on quantitative flexibility. The restructuring in the financial sector was very quickly promoted by the Financial Supervisory Commission which virtually led the whole process. Besides, the restructuring of insolvent companies was done by the major banks, which was also encouraged by the Financial Supervisory Commission. The structural reforms in the public sector were done by a plan which was suggested by the Ministry of Planning and Budget, including management reforms, budgeting guidelines, and privatization of public enterprises. The structural reforms of all these sectors have in common that they were promoted not by exploring rational alternatives through agreement and coordination among economic actors but by the administration's aggressive intervention.

The Kim Dae-Jung administration's structural reform after the IMF economic crisis was the opening of capital markets, financial reforms, restructuring of insolvent firms, and labor market flexibilization measures to support them. It has actively promoted labor market policies to provide a basic social security system for the unemployed and to provide jobs for the unemployed. In March 1998, the 'Comprehensive Unemployment Measures' was announced, and the budget for employment incentives and job training significantly increased. To provide short-term jobs for the poor, a great deal of budget was allocated to public job programs: 9,252 billion won in 1998, 2.3 trillion won in 1999, and 1.5 trillion won in 2000. Especially, the government has replaced the Livelihood Protection Act with the Act on National Basic Livelihood to expand the guarantee for welfare recipients and welfare benefits and to strengthen the provision of welfare and duty to work.

Meanwhile, the Korean government's response to the 2008 global economic crisis was very rapid. In response to the crisis, the Blue House has shifted to an emergency economic system at the pan-government level. If the Kim Dae-Jung administration's initial response to the 1997 IMF economic crisis was characterized by a comprehensive policy of emergency prescriptions to cope with the crisis, the Lee Myung-Bak administration's policy to respond to the 2008 global economic crisis can be called an expansionary fiscal policy. Unlike the tightening fiscal policy chosen by the Kim Dae-Jung administration during the 1997 IMF crisis, the Lee Myung-Bak administration implemented an expansionary fiscal policy in 2008, including monetary policies, interest rate cuts, increased fiscal spending, and tax support. In particular, the President organized the Labor-Management-Civic Group-Government Emergency Economic Conference, which included representatives from labor unions, enterprises, private organizations, and the government, to actively respond to the economic, financial, and unemployment crisis caused by the 2008 global economic crisis. Starting with the first 'Emergency Economic Conference' on January 8, 2009, it gathered opinions from the fields and adopted the 'Labor-Management-Civic Group-Government Agreement on Overcoming the Economic Crisis' on February 23, 2009, for pain and job sharing.

The agreement included that labor and management were committed to maintaining and sharing jobs through pain sharing. The government actively supported such efforts by labor and management, pursued price stabilization and expansion of a social safety net, and arranged protective measures for the underprivileged poor. It also included that the government shall make an effort to prepare a framework for sustainable development through bold investments in future growth industries (Labor-Management-Civic Group-Government Emergency Economic Conference, 2009). The Lee Myung-Bak government drafted a revised supplementary budget of KRW 10 trillion on November 10, 2008, and another one of KRW 28.9 trillion in April 2009 and used them to create and maintain jobs and stabilize the livelihood of low-income people.[1]

In detail, the first supplementary budget in the wake of the 2008 global economic crisis allocated 4.6 trillion won for the expansion of SOC programs, 3.4 trillion won for the support of SMEs, and 1.0 trillion won for emergency support for the livelihood of low-income people. For the second supplementary budget in 2009, more than 12 trillion won was used for public job creation, and livelihood support, including 4.2 trillion won for stabilization of the livelihood of low-income families, 3.5 trillion won for creation and retention and expansion of jobs, and

---

[1] The Lee Myung-Bak administration planned to provide a total of 800,000 public jobs to vulnerable and unemployed people, including 166,000 social welfare jobs and 250,000 jobs in the name of 'Hope Work Project' for low-income people through the supplementary budgets.

4.5 trillion won for the support of SMEs and self-employed people.

In particular, the 'Task Force for Employment and Social Safety Net' was installed in the Prime Minister's Office for the systematic management of job measures in December 2008. In 2010, the government tried actively to address job problems, beginning with the '2010 Employment Recovery Project'. The government also tried to revitalize the economy by implementing tax reforms to reduce the tax burden. In 2008, the government lowered the compound income tax rate by 2 percent to stabilize the livelihoods of low- and middle-income families and promote domestic consumption. It also reduced the corporate income tax rate and expanded the targets of tax breaks to SMEs to boost investment. At the same time, the government prepared 'Emergency People's Livelihood Stabilization Measures' (March 12, 2009) and 'Cost of Living Stabilization Measures' (September 10, 2009) to prevent the contraction of consumption and investment sentiments due to the global economic crisis and to stabilize prices and the livelihood of ordinary people.

7.3.2 Economic Responses

The IMF economic crisis of 1997 had a tremendous impact on the financial industry and enterprises. To overcome the IMF economic crisis, the business circle also acted following the government's policy stance in line with the structural reform guidelines proposed by the IMF. The economic response to the IMF crisis was largely achieved through financial and corporate restructuring.

The purpose of the financial reform was to restore the capital intermediation function of financial institutions and resolve financial markets' instability. In particular, the government tried to prevent the domino bankruptcy effect of the financial market by insolvent financial institutions and remove the financial market instability by getting rid of financial institutions and bonds in bad shape. For the structural reform of the financial sector, the Kim Dae-Jung government established a 'Restructuring Planning Board' under the Financial Supervisory Service in May 1998 to promote structural reform in financial institutions. As a result, it liquidated five commercial banks, which are considered less likely to normalize, out of 12 commercial banks with a BIS ratio of less than 8% by transferring their assets and liabilities to healthy commercial banks. The remaining seven commercial banks were required to conduct strong self-help efforts, including reducing capital and personnel. Also, many non-bank financial institutions were liquidated (Lee 2002).

On the other hand, restructuring in the corporate sector focused on reducing market instability through the liquidation of insolvent enterprises and improved corporate governance, based on credit banks' evaluation of enterprises. Large enterprises agreed with the government to reduce their corporate debt ratio to 200% through a capital increase, separation of affiliates, and sale of assets to prevent bankruptcy (Kim 2014).

Table 7.3. Liquidation Plan of Insolvent Large Enterprises in June 1999

	Target companies	Existence	Work-out	Liquidation
Affiliates of 15 conglomerates	248	12	38	198 (78)
Medium-sized conglomerates	106	17	38	51 (17)
Total	354	29	76	249 (96)

Note: (   ) refers to the number of companies liquidated by June 1999
Source: Financial Supervisory Commission (1999) & Kim (2014)

According to the evaluation of credit banks, the liquidation of insolvent companies in the 2008 global economic crisis took two kinds of paths. In the case of recoverable companies, they went through a workout process, but unrecoverable companies went through a merger, sale, and liquidation process. From July 1998 to June 1999, 76 recoverable companies out of 325 insolvent companies classified as large enterprises and those of middle standing were subject to work-out process through the sale of assets, capital increase, and the debt for equity swap on the premise of self-help efforts including the donation of private property. The remaining 249 companies were liquidated through sale, merger, liquidation, and court receivership (see Table 7.3, Kim 2014).

Companies responded to the global economic crisis in 2008 in two ways. One was corporate restructuring due to the economic crisis, and the other was self-help efforts through the reduction in labor costs. The corporate restructuring was led by creditors centered on the principal transaction bank. However, this was done with government intervention too. The government provided effective directions for business restructuring with financial institutions in relation to corporate restructuring and supervised them to play a pivotal role in the process of corporate restructuring. To this end, in November 2008, the government established a support team for business restructuring and made it set up the overall direction of corporate restructuring and act as a control tower for relevant ministries. The creditors that were led by creditor banks categorized these companies into four groups through credit risk assessments of the companies and promoted the restructuring of low-grade insolvent companies such as workout, liquidation, etc. Creditor-led corporate restructuring focused on sectors sensitive to the economic downturn, such as the construction and shipping industries. Besides, in the case of large enterprises, the arrangement of self-help measures was recommended under a restructuring agreement with creditors to improve their financial structure. In the case of SMEs, creditors selected restructuring targets through separate credit risk assessments. The government implemented the 'SME Fast-Track Program (FTP)' to help resolve SMEs' temporary liquidity problems in the wake of bankruptcy.[2]

In response to the global economic crisis in 2008, companies tried to overcome it by cutting and freezing wages. Most companies had tried to cut wages or freeze them after the crisis.

7.3.3 Labor Responses

Facing the IMF economic crisis in 1997 and the global economic crisis in 2008, the labor circle's response was focused on stopping layoffs and retaining jobs. During the IMF crisis, the leadership of the Korean Confederation of Trade Unions, who proposed to establish the Tripartite Committee as a social dialogue body, recognized in the earlier stage of the crisis that the restructuring movements, including layoffs, were unavoidable and tried to deter layoffs or minimize the damage with the participation in the Tripartite Commission. Finally, on January 15, 1998, the Tripartite Commission, in which labor, management, and the government, as well as political parties, participated, was launched. On February 6, the very first tripartite compromise was hammered

---

[2] The SME Fest-Track Program supported the repayment deferral, cut in interest rates, and support of new funds for approximately 7,100 companies that experienced a temporary liquidity crisis according to credit risk assessment up to July 2016 since its introduction in 2008. As a result, 3,400 companies (48%) had succeeded in normalizing and the program was evaluated as being a useful temporary support tool for SMEs (Financial Supervisory Commission, Press Release Feb 27, 2016).

out, including specific action plans for the top ten policy agendas such as corporate restructuring, unemployment measures, expansion of social security system, basic labor rights, labor market flexibility, etc. In particular, the 'Feb·6 Social Pacts' were not limited to the agendas concerning labor market and industrial relations, but included a broader agenda across the national economy, including macroeconomic policy, price stabilization, corporate management, expansion of social security system, etc. Thus, it could be understood as a 'political exchange' among labor, management, and the government (Tripartite Commission, 1998).

While the government has implemented amendments to the Employment Adjustment Act and the introduction of a worker dispatch system, which were agreed with the IMF, the labor circle secured funds for unemployment measures (5 trillion won), guarantee for the right of association of government employees and teachers, political activities of labor unions, eligibility of the unemployed as union members, the elimination of the Public Fund Management Act, the consolidation of medical insurance and its expanded application, and the transfer of labor administration affairs of regional labor employment offices to local governments. As such, the 'Feb·6 Social Pacts', which was based on the introduction of layoffs and the dispatch work system and the expansion of the basic labor rights, was the result of the first tripartite compromise in Korean history where labor, management, and the government agreed to overcome the economic crisis by pain sharing (Lee 2002, Park 2005).

However, the evaluation of the 'Feb·6 Social Pacts' by the organized labor was different between the FKTU and the KCTU. The FKTU expressed satisfaction in general. It came out with a self-evaluation that it had achieved the basic strategic goal of maintaining a cooperative relationship with the new government, acting as an arbitrator for the KCTU, and taking a leading in the Tripartite Commission. In contrast, the KCTU faced strong internal opposition and criticism that the leadership failed in judging the outcome of the tripartite agreement, taking things easy. The central point of the internal criticism was that the leaders of the KCTU approved the legislation of dismissal and instead focused on the benefits in return, thus invalidating the fruits of the 1996 general strike struggle. Such evaluation later resulted in an organizational split like a crack between the leadership and fields, thus weakening internal executive power. Taking responsibility for the 'Feb·6 Social Pacts', the KCTU leadership voluntarily resigned. Thereafter, the KCTU went ahead with withdrawal from the Tripartite Commission and a general strike struggle in protest of the government's unilateral restructuring of the public sector and the financial industry.

Despite the withdrawal of the KCTU, the Tripartite Commission's activities during the IMF crisis had made certain contributions to resolving large-scale labor disputes in the restructuring process of banks, public and private enterprises. It was a very important achievement to avoid the catastrophic situation by arbitrating the strike at Hyundai Motors, which occurred in the process of large-scale reduction of employees through layoffs in 1998. The Tripartite Commission, however, became very unstable as the government unilaterally pushed for the restructuring of the financial industry and the public sector.

The government delayed the implementation of the agreements with the labor and unilaterally pursued restructuring without prior negotiations. Organized labor, even in the face of the unilateral structural reforms by the government and capital, may have a defensive mobilization of labor but failed in carrying their political position and interest within the political system. Thus, during the regular session of the National Assembly in 1998, where the tripartite agreements, including the legislation of the teachers' union and legislation of the subscription to the union by the unemployed, emerged as major issues, the relevant government ministries took a passive stance or showed strong opposition toward them. Then the KCTU withdrew from the Tripartite Commission.

The government did not go through sufficient consultation with the union breaking the agreement at the time of the 1st General Strike of the Financial Industry (2000.7.11) that "there would be no compulsory merger by the government and as for the organizational and personnel reduction of financial institutions, the government would respect collective agreements between labor unions and management." When the merger between Kook-Min Bank and the Housing Bank was pursued by the government, the Financial Industry Union launched its second round of a general strike in the financial industry with the participation of 10,000 members from December 22 to 28, 2000. The second general strike, which was triggered by the government's unilateral destruction of the tripartite agreement, had a decisive blow to the Tripartite Commission, which had been in a difficult situation amid the official abstention of the KCTU.

In Korea, the politics of social pacts have brought about institutional changes that partially embraced demands of organized labor on the labor market democratization, such as the establishment of a new policy consultation framework called the Tripartite Commission and the expansion of basic labor rights through the guarantee of the right to organize. The policy consultation through the Tripartite Commission contributed to the democratization of the Korean labor market by providing a path for the organized labor and enterprises to participate in the decision-making process the government had monopolized. The Tripartite Commission played not only a role to minimize social conflicts caused by the restructuring during the IMF economic crisis through democratic principles of dialogue and compromise, but also a role as an institutional device for stabilizing labor-management relations, such as overcoming the IMF economic crisis and realizing policy participation by labor and management.

Meanwhile, labor's response to the 2008 global economic crisis was somewhat different from the 1997 economic crisis. Even though the 1997 financial crisis was triggered by the Asian financial crisis, it originated from a problem directly related to the inside of the Korean economy. However, the 2008 global economic crisis was caused by an external shock that started in Wall Street, called the world's economic and financial center. The labor response to the economic crisis was, therefore, different from that of the IMF crisis. The labor also joined the meeting to overcome the crisis in the face of a serious economic crisis such as a sharp decline in exports and a contraction in domestic demand due to the global economic crisis in 2008, which led to negative growth in the Korean economy and a sharp decline in employment. Through the 'Labor-Management-Civic Group-Government Agreement on Overcoming the Economic Crisis' (Feb. 23, 2009), the government demanded the participation and cooperation of labor, management, and civic groups together with policy efforts for co-existence, such as job retention and sharing, rather than restructuring or layoffs during the economic crisis. Afterward, the labor circle also took part in efforts to freeze and reduce wages.

7.4 Labor Policies for Job Creation

7.4.1 IMF Economic Crisis and Expansion of Employment Insurance System

The biggest change brought about by the 1997 financial crisis in the labor market system is the expansion of the employment insurance system to support the securement of the social safety net following an unemployment crisis (Hur and Kim 2002). Korea's employment insurance system was introduced in 1995 as an institutional mechanism to promote the re-employment of the unemployed and prevent side effects of unemployment benefits by combining unemployment benefits and active labor market policies in preparation for an era of low growth and high unemployment as experienced in Europe. Since then, Korea's employment insurance system has greatly expanded its role as a social safety net to cope with mass layoffs and unemployment following the 1997 economic crisis. [3]

Table 7.4. Status and System of Employment Security Project: 2014

(735.6 billion won in total)

Project Name	Detailed Support Measures	Note (Won)
Employment adjustment support (50 billion won)	• Employment Retention Subsidy - Temporary closure of business, leave of absence, training • Support for unpaid workers during the temporary closure of business and leave of absence	44.8 billion 5.2 billion
Job creation project (134.2 billion won)	• Job Sharing • Part-time job creation • Employment environment improvement • Promising start-up company • Professional workforce recruitment	78.3 billion 22.8 billion 25.8 billion 3.6 billion 3.8 billion

---

[3] Since its launch in 1995, it began to cover workplaces with 30 or more employees and expanded to all workplaces with one or more employees in October 1998. After January 2004, the application criteria was changed from 18 to 15 hours a week for not only daily workers but also part-time workers. The application was extended to those aged 60 and over (under 65). As a result, as of the end of 2014, the number of those who subscribed to the employment insurance counted about 11.1 million, about 64% of the total wage workers (about 18.7 million) (Bang Ha-Nam and Nam Jae-Wook 2016).

Employment promotion support (173.2 billion won)	• Employment promotion subsidy • Elderly employment extension subsidy - Retirement extension subsidy, subsidy for re-employment support for retirees • Employment subsidy for seniors over 60 • Wage peak system subsidy - Retirement extension type, re-employment type, working hour reduction type • Employment security subsidy for childbirth and childcare period - Reemployment of non-regular workers, a grant of maternity leave, support for replacement workers, regional employment promotion subsidy	30.5 billion 57.7 billion 29.1 billion 55.1 billion 800 million
Employment promotion facility support (79.8 billion won)	• Support for the operation of workplace childcare facilities • Loan support for employment environment improvement	79 billion 800 million
Other employment security projects (321 billion won)	• Support for self-employed people's job transfer • Youth internship at SMEs • Internship for the employment of the prime-aged • Regionally customized job creation support project	140 million 201.2 billion 39.5 billion 80.2 billion

Source: Ministry of Employment and Labor (2014), Reconfigured from the 'Status and Future Plan of Employment Security Project'

Korea's employment insurance system included major projects such as unemployment benefits, employment security, vocational skills development project, maternity protection, etc. Therefore, it includes not only unemployment benefits that allowed the unemployed to make a living in the labor market but also an active labor market policy that provided for vocational education and training and job opportunities so that they can return to the labor market (see Table 7.5).

Korea's employment insurance system requires at least 180 days of the insured period to prevent recurrent unemployment and provide incentives to find a job. When unemployment benefits have already been provided, a new 180-day insured period is required to receive benefits again. The unemployed must report their status to the job center and receive recognition for unemployment for every one to four weeks. Unemployed persons who do not have a just cause and/or their reasons do not qualify for unemployment benefits. Also, the voluntary unemployed who do not have a just cause and the unemployed persons due to the causes attributable to themselves do not qualify for unemployment benefits. In particular, the number of days for unemployment benefits is set relatively short compared to other OECD countries to curtail long-term unemployment. An employment promotion allowance system is arranged to encourage the early employment of the unemployed. As shown in Figure 7.2, the employment insurance system contributed to a greater extent to overcoming the economic and unemployment crises through livelihood security and employment security of the unemployed through unemployment benefits, training for the unemployed utilizing vocational skills development, employment retention, public jobs creation, and employment promotion project in the phases of the 1997 IMF crisis and 2008 global economic crisis. (Yoo 2012).

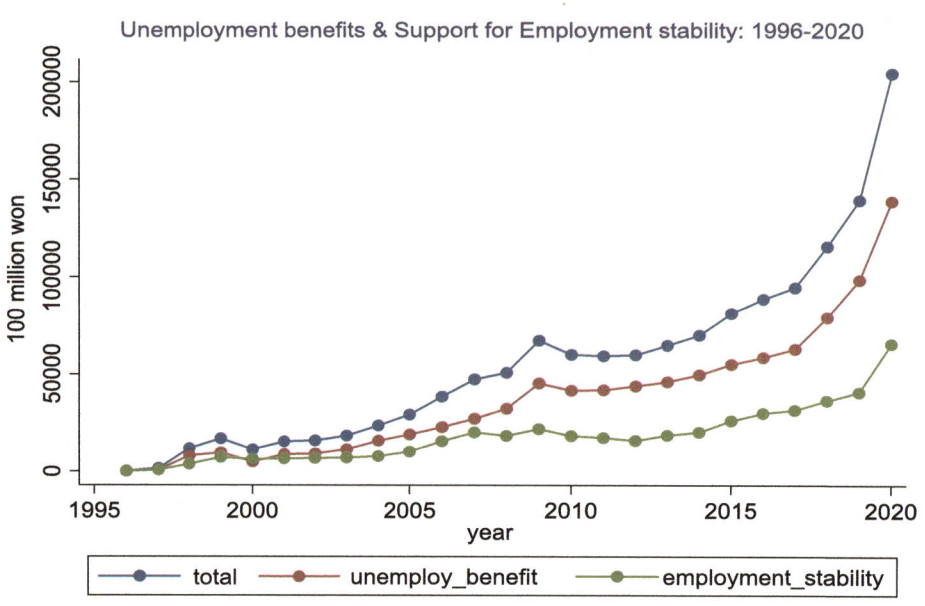

Source: Employment Insurance DB (2020)

Figure 7.2. Trends of Unemployment Benefits and Support for Employment stability & Vocational competency development

Table 7.5. Types and Causes of Blind Spots in Employment Insurance

Classification				Limitations in Social Insurance	Peculiarity of Korean Labor Market	Limitations of Korean Employment Insurance
Blind Spots in Application	Economically Active	Wage Workers Population	Legal Exclusion: Special Occupations, 65 years old or older, Ultra-Short Hours, Special Employment, Housework			O O O O O
			Practical Exclusion		O	
		Non-Wage Workers	Self-employed	O	O	
			Unpaid Family Worker	O	O	
	Economically Inactive Population	Potential Job Seekers among the Youth		O		
		Career-interrupted Women		O		
Requirements for Benefit Payment	Dissatisfactory Unit Period Insured Dissatisfactory Reasons for Job Transfers			O	O	O
Expiration of Benefit Payment Period						O

Source: Bang & Nam (2016). p. 71

During the IMF economic crisis, the Kim Dae-Jung administration increased the number of public job security facilities, including job centers, from 53 in 1997 to 191 in 2001 to establish an employment service delivery system for employment stabilization. Nationally distributed job centers played an important role as a conveyor belt of employment services, in which unemployment benefits, vocational skills training, and job placement were organically linked with each other.

In short, the Korean employment insurance system has a kind of nature as workfare that minimizes the side effects of unemployment benefits and induces incentives for jobs through the combination of unemployment benefits, which is one of passive labor market policies, and active labor market policies. At the same time, it had brought changes to the vocational skills development system and public employment services. Capitalizing on this opportunity, job centers were expanded across the nation and the former vocational training system that was focused on skilled workers in manufacturing to a lifelong vocational skills development system.

However, employment insurance covers workers in the formal labor market as its main protection target. Thus there are certain limitations on the employment security of vulnerable workers in its blind spot. These include, for example, workers of small businesses, special employment workers, small business owners, and unpaid family workers, and the youth who are about to enter the labor market, and career-interrupted women (see Table 7.5). As a result, during the 2008 global economic crisis, the government implemented various job projects based on general account resources for vulnerable workers in the labor market (Yoo 2012).

7.4.2 The 2008 Global Economic Crisis and Changes in Job Policy

The two administrations' job policies, which emerged in the course of responding to the 1997 IMF economic crisis and the 2008 global economic crisis, show commonalities and differences. The common and different points of these job policies can be attributed to the following. First, in the economic crisis, the government was forced to respond quickly because of the inevitability of labor restructuring and unemployment. The two economic crises also show differences in their causes and progress. For example, the main causes for the 1997 financial crisis were the instability in the financial market due to the management relying on excessive short-term debt borrowing and a high ratio of debt. In the 2008 global economic crisis, external factors caused by the collapse of the international financial market played a significant role while the domestic financial market was relatively stabilized.

Table 7.6. Comparing the Job Policies in the Economic Crises

Measures	IMF Economic Crisis (1997)	Global Economic Crisis (2008)

Job Retention	• Support for layoff evasion effort
	  - Work-sharing
	  - Support for the temporary closure of business
	  - Workforce relocation support
	  - Support for employment retention training
	• Credit guarantee expansion
	• Housing construction support
	• Maturity extension for loans in foreign currency
		• Job sharing and retention
		  - Reduction of working hours
		  - Expanded introduction of the wage peak system
		  - Introduction of the unpaid sabbatical year
		  - Workforce relocation
		• Support for a wage freeze and saving
		• Expanded targets for employment retention subsidy
		• SME employment promotion

Job Creation	• Early execution of public investment projects
	• Expanded public work projects
	• Support for export and venture start-ups
	• Attracting foreign investment
	• Expansion of investment in KEPCO transmission and distribution facility
	• Expansion of major SOC investment
	• Regional economy revitalization
		• Hope Work Project
		• Expanding youth internship at SMEs
		• Expanding social service jobs
		  - Afforestation, child caregivers
		  - Internship teacher for learning support
		  - Employment of college graduates as TA
		  - Expansion of jobs for the elderly

Job Training & Job Placement	• Vocational training for the jobless
	  - Unemployment reemployment training
	  - New Unemployment Vocational Training
	• In-service training
	• Strengthening job search linkage system
	• Highly Educated Unemployed Support
	• Strengthening Women's Training and Employment Support
		• Expanding vocational training for the jobless
		• Expanding support for the development of unemployed and unemployed college graduates: Support for opening educational programs in universities
		• Expanding packaged programs in connection with counseling, training, and job placement
		• Provision of vocational training programs specialized for daily workers such as construction

Social Security	• Expansion of all workplaces covered by Employment Insurance • Expansion of benefits during the benefit period • Job Security and Loan for Housing • Low-income earner protection • Daily worker measures • Unemployed Child Tuition Support	• Eliminating blind spots in social insurance • Unemployment benefit payments expanded • Supporting livelihoods for jobless people and expanding loans • Reduction and support of some low-income health insurance premiums • Low-Income Child Support • Expanding financial aid for unemployed children

Source: '2.6 Social Pacts' & 'Labor-Management-Civil-Government Agreement for Overcoming Economic Crisis'

The differences in the causes of these two economic crises led to differences in social impacts. The 1997 IMF financial crisis directly affected regular workers in the face of a massive restructuring. However, the 2008 global economic crisis had more impact on the number of non-regular and vulnerable workers that massively increased after the IMF crisis. As a result, there were differences in the job policy coping with the two economic crises. Such differences took a more advanced form based on job policy experiences and assessments in response to the 1997 IMF economic crisis (Lee 2009).

In response to two unemployment crises caused by the two economic crises, including the 1997 IMF economic crisis and the 2008 global economic crisis, the Kim Dae-Jung and Lee Myung-Bak administrations had adopted very similar job policy measures such as providing public work jobs, sharing jobs, expanding job training, and supporting the livelihood of the unemployed. (See Table 7.6, Lee 2009). This was because much of the job policy was supported by the employment insurance support project discussed above.

The way of dealing with job problems was very similar in that it provided comprehensive unemployment measures at the pan-government level. However, a comparison between the detailed contents of the job policy and the procedures revealed differences. Such a difference was derived from the fact that the job policy in the 1997 IMF crisis mainly targeted the unemployed who were in the official labor market. Instead, the job policy in the 2008 global economic crisis was targeting vulnerable groups and the youth who were left out of the formal labor market and difficult to make a comeback.

First, it was the job creation policy that played an important role as the two administrations' policies on unemployment during the economic crises. The public work project in the period of economic crises took the form of short-time work providing temporary support for livelihoods in return for simple labor like maintenance of road and river facilities and environmental beautification with the socially vulnerable groups that were capable of working, including the unemployed who had been pushed out of the labor market and the self-employed who temporarily or terminally closed businesses. However, unlike simple public work in the IMF economic crisis, the Hope Work Project at the time of the global economic crisis in 2008 paid part of wages in the form of gift certificates (coupons or vouchers) to induce rapid consumption and to support small business owners like those from traditional markets and neighborhood business districts. However, the public work had been criticized for being ineffective as a long-term job policy, as it was a short-term project to improve employment indicators, including the high unemployment rate, and the sustainability of jobs was not guaranteed. For this reason, Germany and France, which relied on direct job creation in the public sector during the economic crisis of the 1990s, have recently eliminated or drastically reduced their expenditures on such policies (OECD 2017, Bonoli 2010).

Differences in the policy of direct job creation between the 1997 IMF economic crisis and the 2008 global economic crisis were also revealed. While the Kim Dae-Jung administration expanded its investment in major SOC projects such as Korea Electric Power Corporation (KEPCO) transmission and investment facilities to directly create public jobs during the 1997 IMF crisis, but the Lee Myung-Bak administration focused on job creation in the social service sector such as child caregivers, learning assistant teachers, research assistants, etc. in 2008.

The way in which vocational training was operated also changed. During the 1997 IMF crisis, vocational training mainly focused on jobless training for unemployed people or incumbent employees. However, the vocational training for the unemployed after the 2008 global economic crisis has been transformed into a package of policies in which counseling, education, and job placement are interlinked. Therefore, the vocational training under the Lee Myung-Bak administration took a dispersed form of individualized vocational training rather than one of intensive training for unemployed people. Such trends of vocational training focus on non-regular workers who were more likely to become unemployed than regular workers. Accordingly, since 2009, the Lee Myung-bak administration had introduced a personal learning account system that allowed non-regular workers to access educational programs more easily and autonomously select programs.

The problem of high youth unemployment in the wake of the expansion of non-regular work brought on by labor market flexibility measures after the IMF economic crisis in1997 has become a key issue in the Korean government's job policy. This was because the youth became unemployed or fell into the trap of non-regular work, unable to enter the regular labor market immediately after graduating from school.[4] As the youth unemployment problem became more serious, the Roh Moo Hyun administration, so-called Participatory Administration (2003-2007), enacted the 'Special Act on Resolution of Youth Unemployment in June and arranged comprehensive measures at the central and local government level to resolve the

---

[4] Since the 1997 economic crisis, the youth unemployment has grown, and many neologisms have been coined in a sarcastic manner. Starting from the '880 thousand won generation' symbolizing the low wages of non-regular workers, Lee Tae Baek (meaning that most of people in their 20s are unemployed), 3 Give-ups (romance, marriage, and childbirth), 5 Give-ups (3 give-ups + home ownership and human relations), 7 Give-ups (5 give-ups + dream and hopeful job), even N-Give-up Generation, etc. are a few examples.

unemployment of the youth. It recommended that 3% of the public sector's personnel quota be filled with new youth hires (changed to be a mandatory provision since January 1, 2014). When the youth unemployment became more severe due to the 2008 global economic crisis, the Lee Myung-Bak administration amended the act aforementioned to the Special Act on Youth Employment Promotion. It established the Special Committee on Youth Employment Promotion. Through this, employment support services were provided to young people who had difficulty finding employment, while the youth internship program was expanded, and a global talent cultivation project was implemented.[5]

Expanding and Systemizing Public Employment Services

The changes in the labor market system brought about by the 1997 financial crisis and the 2008 global economic crisis were the expansion and institutionalization of public employment services. The massive restructuring immediately following the 1997 economic crisis led to the necessity of public institutions that could smoothly carry out employment security projects such as job retention and creation, employment promotion, etc., as well as the project of unemployment benefits. As a result, the Kim Dae-Jung Administration expanded job centers and related agencies from just 53 in 1997 to 191 in 2001. However, it was not until 2005 that facilities for public

---

[5] Representative examples of the 'global talent cultivation project' were the projects of 'Global Youth Leader Training Plan' and '100 thousand Youth Leader Training for Future Industries'. The Lee Myung-Bak administration presented the 'Global Youth Leader Training Plan' as one of the national tasks and promoted overseas employment support, overseas internship, and overseas volunteering projects. In addition, for the 100 thousand Youth Leader Training for Future Industries' 1 trillion won was to be invested between 2009 and 2013 to foster 12,800 youth leaders in the green industry sector such as new renewable energy and environmental service research on climate change and in the knowledge-based service sector including financial design, etc.

employment services were expanded in full scale and operated more systematically. The Roh Moo-hyun Administration (Participatory Administration) expanded the role and status of the public employment service center by enacting the 'Special Act on Resolution of Youth Unemployment' and arranging comprehensive youth unemployment measures to solve the problem of high youth unemployment. To this end, the government newly recruited 620 job center employees nationwide from 2006 to 2007 (Hur 2013).

Table 7.7. Employment Services with Activation Programs

	Employment Success Package program	New Job Finding Program	YES program (New Start Project)
Target Group	Low-Income Jobseekers at All Ages • Those belonging to the households with earnings less than 150% of the minimum costs of living or beneficiaries of "National Basic Livelihood Security" who are capable of working • The homeless, North Korean refugees, the youth in troubled families, and handicapped jobseekers	Middle- and Old- Job Seekers Aged 40-64 • Those belonging to the households with earnings less than 200% of the minimum costs of living • The unemployed for more than one month since receiving final unemployment benefits • The unemployed that have subscribed to employment insurance in the past but do not yet qualify for benefits • Jobseekers unemployed for the past six months or more	Youths Aged 15-29 • Unemployed high school graduates • Unemployed college or university graduates who have not found a job for more than six months since graduation
Services	Stage 1: Diagnosis and career path-setting (three weeks to one month) • Participants receive intensive individual counseling from JobCentre counselors (job consultants), and an assessment of their job capacities, desire, and techniques. • In accordance with the results of the evaluation, an Individual Action Plan is established, which includes services provided after the second stage. Stage 2: Improvement in vocational skills (max. 8 months; max. 6 months*) • Vocational training, jobs for experienced people, start-up programs, youth internship programs.		

	Stage 3: Intensive job placement (max. 3 months; max. 2 months*) ● Job center counselors accompany program participants to their job interviews and provide support. ● Group interview sessions are held by participants and recruiting companies.	
Allowance	Stage 1: 200,000 won per month Stage 2: 200,000 won per month, and 116,000 won when participating in vocational training	
Allowance Payment Period	A maximum of 6 months	
Support for Training Costs	Up to 3 million won via the training voucher system	Up to 2 million won via the training voucher system
Incentives upon Successful Job Finding	Up to 1 million won as a successful job finding allowance	None

Note: * Stage-2 and Stage-3 services are given up to eight months and three months in the Employment Success Package program, and up to six months and two months for the YES program and New Job Searching program, respectively, while the allowance payment period is up to six months in all the three programs.
Source: Hur (2013). p.41

After the financial crisis, the Korean government made efforts to expand facilities for public employment services and systemize public employment services. As the unemployment problem remained a major social issue even after the IMF crisis ended, Roh Moo-Hyun Administration (Participatory Administration) took steps to strengthen consumer-oriented public employment services in 2006 through the 'Customized One-Stop Employment Service Program.' The program provided phased employment services to job seekers by evaluating job applicants' capabilities and establishing an individual action plan through intensive counseling with job counselors. In 2006, the government introduced the customized "YES (Youth Employment Service)" program for young people.

During the 2008 global economic crisis, the Lee Myung-Bak Administration strengthened public employment services. It provided differentiated employment service programs suiting policy targets such as the youth, the middle- and prime-aged, and women (see Table 7.7).

The 'Employment Success Package Program' was introduced in 2009 to promote employment for the low-educated and low-paid people. The 'Employment Success Package Program' was a step-by-step, integrated plan for up to one year's work period for individuals benefiting from the basic living security system, workers with lower incomes (60% or less), and the youth and middle-aged workers. It included measures to promote employment and escape from poverty and provide employment assistance programs by paying employment success allowances when employed. The Employment Success Package Program was divided into Type I and II according to the policy subjects. Participants in the Program went through the situation diagnosis, motivation, and individual job-seeking activity plan (IAP) in the first stage. In the second stage, education programs were provided to the participants (vocational training, vocational skills development account system, workplace experience programs, youth internships, stepping-stone jobs, etc.). In the third stage, for participants who had completed both stages, a job placement service was provided. Besides, in the case of successful employment, an incentive equivalent to one million won was given as a success allowance.

As Table 7.8 shows, in the global economic crisis of 2008, the Employment Success Package Program has achieved certain results in the number of participants and employment rate (Hur 2013). In 2012, the Lee Myung-Bak administration introduced the 'New Employment Program' for the youth and middle-aged (40 to

64-year-olds) based on the experience of the 'Employment Success Package Program.' The new start project, a customized employment support program for young people, was implemented, expanding the YES program introduced in 2006.

Table 7.8. The Number of Participants and Employment Success Rate by Employment Success Package

Year	2009	2010	2011
Number of Participants	9,831	25,132	63,728
Job finding rate	54.1	60.4	65.2

Note: Job finding rate is defined as a rate of success within tewlve months with is the maximum duration of 'Package' program per participant.
Source: Ministry of Employment and Labor (2012)

The Youth Employment Service Program (New Start Project) was designed for individuals who have difficulty finding jobs (15 to 29-year-olds or younger than 31 when military service was completed) as a total employment service that supported young people in a whole process from individual career counseling to job placement. However, participants must not receive unemployment benefits, and the beneficiaries of the basic living security (as participants in the employment success package program) and business registrants were excluded. In the first stage (diagnosis, path setting), the IAP was established through individual counseling, vocational and psychological test, and career guidance program. The second stage (motivation, skills improvement) included the vocational training and vocational skills development account system (2 million won limit), working life experience program (500,000 won per month), youth internship, and stepping-stone job experience.

The third stage (intensive job placement) concentrated on the job placement for participants through visits to enterprises, active employment support, a resume and self-introduction clinic, and interview guides, and they were accompanied to job interviews by counselors when necessary. The characteristic of this program was to provide employment support services through one-on-one personalized counseling management by operating a personal advisor system and to provide support for job-seeking skills, information provision, and permanent job placement through various job fairs, accompanied interviews, etc. for up to one year until the participants succeeded in employment.[6]

The Lee Myung-Bak Administration actively supported youth's overseas employment through customized training programs and working holiday programs under the plan to nurture 100,000 global talents. Also, the government developed a work-life balance job model such as part-time work, work at home, etc., to encourage and support women's economic activities. To promote the employment of the elderly, it promoted the wage peak system, extension of retirement age, a subsidy for continuous employment system, activation of jobs suitable for the elderly, and strengthening of the outplacement service (Hur 2013, Jeong 2012).

In particular, the three employment support services presented in Table 7.6 were driven by the general accounting budget, not the employment insurance fund during the 2008 global economic crisis. Though, the job center (PES) played an important role in the operation and coordination of the actual program. However,

---

[6] Since 2011, the Employment Success Package Program, Youth News Start Project, and the Elderly New Start Program have been integrated into the Employment Success Package Support Program along with the Stepping-stone Job Project (Chang Hong Geun 2011).

as the number of participants in the employment support services increased significantly, the government utilized private employment service companies and non-profit organizations through insourcing and outsourcing of employment services but faced criticism that outsourcing services were not properly managed (Jeong 2012).

Measures of Direct Job Creation

The active labor market policy that the Korean government had relied on during the 1997 financial crisis and the 2008 global economic crisis was direct job creation. Representative policy measures in the field of direct job creation were public work (Hope Work) and youth internship programs. There was a positive aspect that the two programs functioned as a social safety net through temporary improvement in employment indicators and support for livelihood in the phase of an economic crisis. However, there had been continued criticism in the aspect of the sustainability of jobs. The social job program was proposed as an alternative to the issue of sustainability of public jobs.

Hope Work Project

The Hope Work Project was another version of the public work program implemented during the 1997 IMF crisis. During the 2008 global economic crisis, the Lee Myung-Bak Administration implemented it as a project to support the livelihoods of the vulnerable people through jobs and to support local small-sized merchants. It was a temporary livelihood support project for socially vulnerable groups (the unemployed, the self-employed in the case of temporary or permanent closure of business, etc.) who were capable of working during the 2008 economic crisis. It also had a purpose to induce quick consumption and to support small business owners such as traditional markets and neighborhood business districts in the region by paying some of the wages in the form of gift certificates. The Hope Work Project was carried out to create 250,000 jobs by local governments with an investment of a total of 1.7 trillion won from June to November 2009. In this project, the largest proportion of manpower (43.6%) was devoted to the environment maintenance project in which simple labor was provided, and the place where the most money was invested was informatization and data research in order (Han 2010).

During the two economic crises, public work programs have stabilized employment indicators to lower the unemployment rate by creating a large number of jobs in the public sector and contributed to the protection of livelihoods for low-income people. But it was a temporary program to cope with the economic crises, and the issue of job sustainability remained an issue to tackle.

Youth Internship Program

The youth internship program was implemented for 174,000 people over the seven years from 1999 to 2005 (total project cost of 393.6 billion won) after the 1997 financial crisis.

Table 7.9. Types of Youth Internship

Classification	Public Sector Internship		Youth Internship at SMEs
	Administrative agencies	Public institutions	
Ministry in Charge	Ministry of Public Administration and Security (including local governments)	Ministry of Planning and Finance	Ministry of Employment and Labor
Age and	Graduates (graduates-to-be) who are	Unemployed who are aged between 18 and 29	Unemployed who are aged between 15 and 29

	aged between 18 and 29 Educational Requirements		
Workplaces	Administrative agencies	Public corporations, public institutions	SMEs
Working Hours and Salary Level	Less than 1 Yea	Less than 1 year Being different by organization Four major social insurances Unemployment benefit payment for involuntary retirement in the case of those who worked more than 6 monthsr 40 hours approximately, 1 million won Four major social insurance Unemployment benefit payment for involuntary retirement in the case of those who worked more than 6 months	Within 6 months Over minimum wage (KRW 1.2 -1.6 million) Four major social insurances Unemployment benefit payment for involuntary retirement in the case of those who worked more than 6 months
Task to Perform	Depends on the nature of the institution but mainly auxiliary work	Depends on the nature of the institution	Not different from regular workers
Guarantee for Employment	Employment not guaranteed Letter of recommendation issued to excellent participants When employed as a government employee of Grade 9, 50% of the working period is recognized in the calculation of service years	Not guaranteed employment Letter of recommendation issued to excellent participants Some organizations provide added points at the job interview for recruitment as full-time employees	Very high possibility for the company's direct recruitment When employed as a regular employee, 50% of the salary is additionally subsidized (six months).

Source: Han (2010). P. 22

Table 7.10. State of Youth Internship at SMEs: 2009 ~ 2015

Year	Budget (million won)	No. of Participants	No, of completions	No. of Participating Companies	No. of Conversions to Regular Employees	Rate of Conversion to Regular Employees (%, based on no. of participants)
2009	159,059	31,150	20,537	14,875	17,659	56.7
2010	176,481	29,554	20,481	12,9	18,46263	62.5

2011	171,092	32,079	22,088	12,479	20,164	62.9
2012	201,305	36,415	25,658	13,879	23,188	63.7
2013	242,915	43,560	32,262	16,444	29,001	66.6
2014	201,143	37,023	18,554	15,688	-	64.4
2015	183,003	35,000	-	0	-	-

Source: Ministry of Employment and Labor, Internal Data (2015)

Then, the government suspended the program in 2006 in the wake of the improvement of the employment situation following the economic recovery and the overlapping of programs due to the introduction of the subsidy for promotion of new recruitment of the youth. As part of the unemployment measures, it was promoted again to create public jobs and provide employment support through work experience and training (Lee 2009).

After the 2008 global economic crisis, it was further subdivided into the internship in administrative agencies, an internship in public institutions in the public sector, and a youth internship at SMEs in the private sector (see Table 7.9). The Lee Myung-Bak Administration invested 159 billion won in 2009 to support the youth internship at SMEs and provided an internship to more than 31,150 youths (see Table 7.10).

The SME Youth Internship had helped the unemployed youth to gain experience through internships and settling into SMEs as regular workers. However, it also had some problems. The dropout rate was about 30 percent, and the rate of conversion to regular workers was about 60 percent. As it was pointed out that the employer-centered support method had limitations in inducing young people to find jobs at quality in SMEs and to work for a long time, it was required to find ways to help them to settle down in SMEs with support for early conversion to full-time employment and long-term service. For this, in 2015, the government reduced the internship period from six months to three months, increased the number of targets and the amount of employment support subsidies, and reorganized it into a system to induce long-term service (Ministry of Employment and Labor 2015).

Social Job Project (Social Service Job Project)

After the 1997 IMF crisis, the social job project was first launched in 2003 with the government's supplementary budget to create jobs for the vulnerable and provide social services that were socially useful but not available in the market due to profitability. The social job project was renamed a social service job project after 2007 to emphasize the policy implications of preemptive investment in the social service industry (Kim Hye-Won 2009).

Table 7.11. Process of Social Service Job Projects: 2003-2009

Year	2003	2006	2009
Classification	Social Jobs	Social Jobs	Social Service Jobs
Participating Ministries (Number of Projects)	Ministry of Labor	8 Ministries (21 Projects)	8 Ministries (46 Projects)
Budget (100 million won)	73	3,039	15,757
Number of People	2000	133,509	164,589

Note: Unification of the terms related social jobs into 'social service jobs' in July 2009.
Source: Kim (2009). P. 21.

Social service jobs have expanded significantly since the 2008 global economic crisis. The budget for social job project, which amounted to only 30.3 billion won in 2006, increased fivefold in 2009 after the global economic crisis. After the global economic crisis in 2008, while jobs in the manufacturing sector had been stagnant, the social service job project became a new job provider for the vulnerable. As of 2016, a total of 1423,000 social service jobs were created through 58 social service projects in nine government ministries, and 95,000 new jobs were created in 2016. Therefore, the government has been gradually expanding social service job projects and actively making institutional arrangements to support them.

Recently, the social service job projects have caught more and more social attention from the viewpoint of increasing demand for social services and new job creation in the wake of the low birthrate and aging society. Indeed, while social service jobs have been steadily increasing due to government policies and efforts, the quality of social service jobs and the activation of the social service industry and market are still lower than expected due to government budget constraints. Therefore, as a policy alternative, it is needed to introduce social service insurance and to establish a public social service corporation to raise the quality of life of the people (Yoo, 2017).

Other Measures of Job Sharing

In contrast to the 1997 IMF crisis, the government had been active in supporting employee retention and job sharing during the 2008 global economic crisis. In other words, labor market flexibility and layoffs were issues during the 1997 economic crisis, while employment retention and job sharing were the main issues during the 2008 global economic crisis. Since then, the government began to pay attention to job retention and sharing.

Table 7.12. Status of Participation in Job Sharing (as of October 31, 2009)

Participating Companies			Wage Adjustment				Work Type Adjustment				Hybrid* (Wage adjustment + Work type adjustment) (B+C-A)
Total (A)	Employment Retention	Job Creation	Sub Total (B)	Wage Freeze	Wage Return	Wage reduction (Cut)	Sub Total (C)	Reduction of Working Hours (Overtime)	Suspension of business	Others	
1,965	1,629	336	1,665	1,300	274	250	601	135	329	236	301

Note: Concession bargaining and labor-management harmony declaration workplaces with 100 or more employees counted 2,008 (98.8% increase compared to the previous year). Total workplaces with 100 or more employees counted 6,781.
Source: Cho (2009). p. 66.

Job-sharing was a policy aimed at preventing job losses in the private sector by shortening working hours rather than carrying out layoffs when companies face employment adjustments due to reduced sales and growing deficits. These job-sharing projects include measures to maintain and create employment through not only wage freezes, returns, and reductions, but also reductions in working hours, suspension of business, and a wage peak system to create youth jobs and continued employment for older people. It also included the activation of a part-time job for regular employees through job sharing (see Figure 7.12).

During the 2008 global economic crisis, the Lee Myung-Bak Administration formulated and implemented job-sharing policies by forming a regional labor-management-civic group-local government partnership council for each region. As a result, individual private companies practiced job-sharing according to the company's situation by adjusting their work types such as wage adjustment and shift system, relocation, etc., and the government-subsidized accompanying costs. As shown in Table 7.11, as of the end of October 2009, all workplaces with 100 or more employees totaled 6,781, and 1,965 companies participated in the job sharing, representing 29 percent of the participation rate. Besides, the number of workplaces that executed wage freezes and cuts was the largest since the 1997 financial crisis, while the wage growth rate through collective agreements in 2009 was 1.5%, the lowest since the 1997 economic crisis. However, those who shortened working hours for job sharing counted only 135, accounting for only 1.9 percent of the 6,781 workplaces.[7] In short, in the face of the economic crisis, labor and management were more likely to prefer temporary wage freezes, returns, and reductions rather than shortened working hours to retain and share jobs.

7.4.3 Trends and Changes of ALMPs

Figure 7.4 shows active labor market policy trends during the 1997 IMF and 2008 global economic crises. The most active labor market policy used to resolve unemployment during the two economic crises was direct job creation. When looking at the budget for job protection during the 2008 global crisis, direct job creation in the public sector was the most common, except for unemployment benefits, followed by education and training, job

---

[7] Cho Seong-Jae (2009) evaluated the Lee Myung-Bak administration's job-sharing policy in response to the 2008 global economic crisis. Success factors include: (1) the government quickly setting policy directions and establishing a comprehensive plan for job sharing (2009.1.29), (2) creating a social atmosphere on pain sharing through labor-management-civic group-government agreements (2.23), and spreading it to the regions and industrial complexes. (3) the institutional basis of the employment retention subsidies, and (4) the normalization of management faster than expected, especially in large manufacturing enterprises.

promotion, and job retention (See Table 7.13).

Direct job creation policies such as public work projects and the Hope Work Project had positive effects on improving employment indicators and stabilizing the livelihoods of vulnerable workers as short-term and temporary measures.

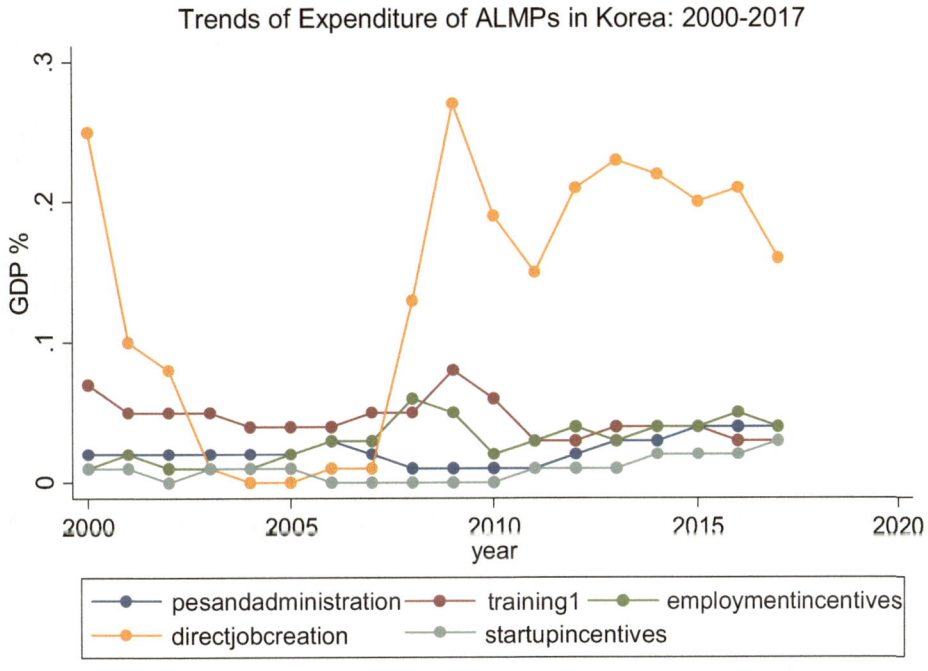

Figure 7.3. Expenditure of ALMPs in Korea: 2000-2012

However, most direct jobs in the public sector were not only low-quality and low wages but also short-term jobs that disappeared when the economic crisis subsided. Because of these problems with direct job creation policies, some countries in Europe, such as Germany and France, have recently been decreasing their budgets for direct job creation. Nevertheless, in the case of Korea, the most preferred policy during the two economic crises was the direct job policy.

Table 7.13. Budget for Job Policies for 2008-2010

(Unit: 100 million won)

Year	Job Creation (direct job)	Employment Retention	Employment Promotion (excluding unemployment benefits)	Education and Training	Total
2008	21,131	381	33,701 (8,966)	11,464	66,677
2009	47,073	5,938	53,129 (8,457)	15,059	121,199
2010	35,883	1,142	38,	13,015988 (5,328)	89,028
Total	104,087	7,461	125,818 (22,751)	39,538	

Source: Ministry of Strategy and Finance (2010)

The share of education and vocational training was also relatively high compared to other types of active labor market policies. In vocational training, financial support was mostly provided to vocational training for the unemployed and the training for those in the workplace during the 1997 IMF crisis. In the case of the existing vocational training, support for incumbent workers was the focus. In the 1997 IMF crisis, it was also operated in a supplier-centered delivery system for the unemployed. However, this type of vocational training had been evaluated as not adequately reflecting the skills and demand for the workforce from industrial sites in the course of the development of training courses and the implementation of training (Chang 2011).

Therefore, after the 2008 global economic crisis, the Vocational Skills Development Account System (Tomorrow's Learning Card System) and job package program were invented to provide a selection and training opportunity for training courses based on the needs of those who have met the requirements to participate in training, instead of the existing supplier-centered vocational training methods. A good example was the 'Employment Success Package Project,' a package training method that combined in-depth work and training consultation, individual activation plan (IAP), vocational training, job placement assistance, livelihood support, etc. After the 2008 global economic crisis, support for incentives for job retention and new hires had also increased. Typical employment retention measures included support for labor costs in the wake of the suspension of business, leave of absence, and additional hires.

7.5 Summary

The job policies of the Kim Dae-Jung Administration and the Lee Myung-Bak Administration responding to unemployment crises during the 1997 IMF economic crisis and the 2008 global economic crisis can be characterized as government (bureaucrat)-led policies. Both governments responded quickly to the unemployment crises at the government level. In the process, the employment insurance system introduced in 1995 played a very important role in overcoming the crises, including unemployment benefits, direct job creation, employment retention, and job training, job promotion, and livelihood support for the vulnerable.

However, the role of social dialogue organizations, including the Tripartite Commission (1998-2007) in the phase of the IMF economic crisis and the Economic and Social Development Tripartite Commission (2007-2018) during the 2008 global economic crisis, played an important role in the earlier overcoming of the economic crises, through the 'Feb·6 Social Pacts' and the reduction of confrontations caused by the introduction of labor market flexibility measures. Despite the positive role of the Tripartite Commission, including the 'Social Pacts for Job Creation' (February

10, 2004) and 'the Labor-Management-Government Agreement on Overcoming the Economic Crisis' (February 23, 2009), many problems were exposed due to the labor-government confrontation due to the crisis in the representative nature of the organized labor and the destruction of the agreement, and the lack of social trust among labor, management, and the government.

In general, the response to the unemployment crises in both the IMF and 2008 global economic crises shows that both governments relied heavily on direct public job creation such as public work projects (Hope Work Project), youth internships, and social service jobs. In particular, to overcome the 2008 global economic crisis, the Lee Myung-Bak administration focused on youth unemployment measures centered on the New Start Project (activation of experiencing life at work, providing short-term jobs, activating overseas employment and internship, strengthening youth job training, expanding youth employment infrastructure, and recruiting people for idle jobs at SMEs) and social job support projects (social service job support projects). At the background of the Lee Myung-Bak administration's growing interest in youth employment policies and social job policies targeting vulnerable groups, there was the fact that the low-income vulnerable groups, including the youth, women, and non-regular workers, were suffering more during the 2008 global economic crisis.

Another characteristic of the change in job policies during the two economic crises was the introduction of the employment package-type vocational training based on the needs of consumers and the vocational training account system to support it. In particular, the employment success package program consisted of three stages: individual interview, career aptitude test, and individual activity plan (IAP); education and vocational training; and job placement. Compared to the previous public employment service program, the employment success package program meant a step further from the previous program, such as providing employment allowance upon successful employment.

In 2008, the Lee Myung-Bak administration's job-sharing campaign to minimize job losses in the private sector as compared with the Kim Dae-Jung administration, which responded to the unemployment issue caused by layoffs during the IMF crisis. To cope with the unemployment issue caused by the 2008 economic crisis, Lee Myung-Bak administration had promoted job retention and sharing the campaign, and there had been several economic factors, such as the huge proportion of non-regular workers already produced through the IMF economic crisis and excessive income inequality due to social bi-polarization. There was a sense of social crisis that the government should no longer allow job losses in the private sector.

Though, the Lee Myung Bak administration continued to pursue labor market flexibility measures in the spirit of neo-liberalism, which included flexible working system, wage peak system, and performance-based wage system as long-term job measures, and expanded incentives for employers such as tax reduction benefits for SMEs practicing new hires and the employment of older workers. The government also introduced programs to support short-term working schemes and support career-interrupted women for work-life balance.

In sum, while there was concern about the rapid recession of the global economy, the government's job policy during the global economic crisis in 2008 was driven by the participation and cooperation of major social actors, including wage freezes and cuts and job-sharing campaigns. On the other hand, reform measures based on the notion of the neoliberal economies, such as wage peak system and performance-based wage system, caused opposition from labor unions, as they were unilaterally processed at workers' sacrifice. Moreover, the extensive dependence on excessive direct job creation policies during the unemployment crisis created mostly low-quality, short-term jobs that were to disappear as soon as the economic crisis was over. Therefore, it resulted in the issue of sustainability and the necessity of 'decent jobs.' At the same time, the problems of inefficiency and moral hazard in the execution of such job creation projects can be pointed out, including the dispersion and waste of budgetary resources, which was manifested in the diversity and redundancy of job policies.

Nonetheless, the reason that the Korean government has relied on the direct job creations in the phase of the IMF economic crisis and 2008 global economic crisis is that these policy measures have functioned as a kind of social safety net in Korea, where the social welfare system was not properly established. Public-work programs have stabilized employment indicators to lower the unemployment rate by creating many short-time jobs in the public sector and contributed to the protection of livelihoods for low-income people. As mentioned above, however, it was a temporary program to cope with the economic crises, and the issue of job sustainability remained an issue to tackle.

Overall, the Korean government's job policies in the two economic crises played a positive role in overcoming the unemployment crises caused by the recession. However, even after getting out of the crises, labor market instability continued to exist, centering on the socially vulnerable groups such as the youth, women, and irregular workers. The problem of income inequality and social polarization remained unresolved.

Chapter 8

CONCLUSION

Sustainable growth and new job creation are the core policy issues facing OECD countries. In particular, unemployment and job problems during the economic crisis are significant challenges for politicians and policymakers. For this reason, ALMPs have been advocated by social democratic and conservative politicians and liberal economists as an effective policy tool to decrease unemployment rates. However, the spending and types of ALMPs are different between welfare regimes and OCED countries. This study examines why the expenditure and types of ALMPs, attracting attention as policies for unemployment and new job creation, appear differently between welfare systems and OECD countries. At the same time, this study tried to explore what determinant factors resulted in the difference if there is a difference in the expenditure or type of ALMPs between welfare regimes or among OECD countries.

This study also examines how and why these countries chose particular ALMPs in response to the 2008 economic crisis. It tried to compare and analyze the changes and recent trends of ALMPs in OECD countries and explain the politics of job creation in response to the 2008 financial crisis. This regard examines how three countries with different socioeconomic institutions and systems, such as Sweden,

Germany, and Korea, have responded to the unemployment during the economic crisis. In particular, this study focuses on what job creation policies these countries have pursued and which strategies and institutions have been formed by prominent social actors in the process of economic crises. Another main puzzle in this study was about the pathways of job creation before and after the 2008 economic crisis. This study tried to implore that the recent trend of type of ALMP in the OECD countries is headed to the high-road or low-road because digital transformation and the advent of the 4th industrial revolution era has been gradually producing a few decent jobs and a lot of low-quality jobs with the dark prospect of the end of labor. In the following, the research results of this study are summarized, and their theoretical implications are examined.

8.1 Analytic Results of Trends and Changes on ALMPs

The analysis of OECD datasets on ALMPs in this study attempted to examine the characteristics of trends and changes in the expenditure of ALMPs and job creation policies in OECD countries. The findings based on descriptive statistical analysis can be summarized as follows. First, there were still differences in the total spending for ALMPs among welfare state types. The ALMP expenditures of SMCs as a percentage of GDP are generally higher than those of CMCs and LMCs, while the spending of ALMP has a relationship with the economic downturns and crises (*Hypothesis 1*). Second, the expenditure on training has gradually decreased except for the recent economic crisis among OECD countries. Although the spending of training in CMCs does not reach the level of SMCs, however, they have remained constant. Third, while the overall expenditures on training have decreased, the spending on PES and subsidies such as the employment incentives and subsidized employment have been growing after the 2008 economic crisis. Fourth, in an economic crisis, countries in LMCs, particularly the Korean government, have considerably relied on direct job creation, unlike countries in SMCs and CMCs. Fifth, the average expenditure on startup incentives in CMCs has been much higher than SMCs and LMCs since the early 2000s. In short, the total expenditure and the type of ALMPs were different for each welfare regime. In other words, it can be said that the type of welfare regime and its characteristics are the decisive factors to explain the difference in the total expenditure of ALMPs. Although each welfare regime shows different total expenditures, the types of ALMPs tend to increase spending on PES or employment incentives rather than vocational training.

Why do different welfare regimes show different total expenditures and types of ALMPs? In this study, regression analysis was performed using the pooled cross-sectional OECD panel datasets (1985-2017) to analyze determinant factors resulting in the differences in ALMPs among OECD countries. Based on the estimation results using the Fixed effects model and Random-effects model through the Hausman test, the findings can be summarized in the following points.

The cabinet composition (Schmidt-Index) (gov_party) also shows a positive direction to the expenditures of ALMPs. It means that the left party or left-wing government has positively affected the expenditure of ALMPs(Hypothesis 2). It is also confirmed that institutional factors such as union density rate and wage-setting coordination system positively correlate with ALMPs' expenditure (Hypothesis 3). However, the effects of neoliberal ideology on the spending of ALMPs are also mixed. It showed a positive relationship under CMCs, but it was not significant. Instead, it showed a negative relationship at the 0.05 level in SMCs. It means that the effect of neoliberal ideology on ALMPs expenditure depends on domestic institutional conditions. Lastly, the analysis results for dummy variables show that the ALMPs spending has significantly changed only under SMCs, but it was not significant in CMCs and LMCs. It is confirmed that the ALMPs expenditure still shows a difference according to the type of welfare regimes. In short, it was found that the political party, union organization rate, and wage-determining structure of each welfare system were related to the change and difference in the total expenditure of ALMPs. Although the effects of neoliberal ideology on the total expenditure of ALMPs are also mixed, neoliberal ideology has influenced the types of ALMPs. In recent ALMPs spending patterns, the increase in short-term, pro-market-oriented PES and employment incentives spending in each welfare system was due to the influence of neoliberal economic ideology. It is confirmed that the relationship between neoliberal economic ideology and ALMPs expenditure differed depending on the welfare state system and politics.

On the other hand, in relation to the trend and change of ALMPs within the welfare system, Sweden, Germany, and Korea showed different characteristics, each as follows. First, in the case of SMCs, the expenditure of ALPMs was in the order of Training, PES, Employment Incentives, and Direct Job creation. The expenditures of Training in SMCs have occupied the highest proportion of ALMPs over the entire period. Sweden was similar until the early 2000s, but after the mid-2000s, employment incentive spending increased, and training spending fell significantly (Puzzle 1). Second, In CMCs, the expenditure of ALPMs was in the order of PES, Training, Employment Incentives, and Direct Job creation. Likewise, in Germany, training spending has occupied the highest proportion among the types of ALMPs. However, the expenditure of PES has recently outpaced the spending on vocational training in Germany, which has a strong vocational training system traditionally (Puzzle 2). Third, in LMCs, the expenditure of ALPMs was in the order of PES, Training, Direct Job creation, and Employment Incentives. The expenditure of PES in LMCs has outpaced vocational training spending since the mid-1990s. However, the Korean government has been highly dependent on direct job creation in the 1997 and 2008 economic crises (Puzzle 3). A more in-depth analysis of these countries is required to answer this research puzzle. These research puzzles that were shown in statistical analyses but did not answer were examined through case studies.

8.2 Findings of Case Studies on the Research Puzzle

There were differences in the types of detailed policies of ALMPs among different welfare states. The expenditures of ALMPs in Sweden have traditionally focused on vocational training until the 1990s and early 2000s, but since the mid-2000s, budget spending on employment incentives and PES has been increasing while spending on vocational training is being reduced. After the recent center-right government took office, the budget expenditure on vocational training has significantly decreased from 1% of GDP in the early 1990s to 0.1%. Such a sharp decrease in public budgetary spending on vocational training in Sweden was closely related to the labor market reform policies of the right-wing government, which has taken power twice since 2006.

The Swedish government emphasized the supply side of the labor market based on the neo-liberal policies and cut off the 'Plus Job' policy, some employment subsidies, and unemployment benefits. The recent increase in employment incentives spending in Sweden can also be a strategic choice in terms of responding to neoliberal influences. Even after the Social Democratic Party's government took power in 2014, the budget for vocational training has not increased. It is also analyzed that the changes in the industrial structure according to the 4th Industrial Revolution make the existing vocational training not valid. According to the decrease in employment in the manufacturing sector and the shift to the service sector-led industry structure, an emphasis on higher education and intensive use of budgets on it instead of traditional vocational training are also analyzed as being related to the situation. In particular, jobs in service economies are typically organized around very simple or narrow tasks, often highly routinized. In this case, the countries are more likely to rely on short-term and temporary ALMPs, such as job-matching services and employment incentives, rather than vocational training that takes money and time. The Swedish government and labor and management also reduced the budget demand for vocational training by gradually changing their functional flexibility response instead of quantitative restructuring flexibility during the 2008 global economic crisis.

In the case of Germany's ALMPs, budget expenditures on the job training and direct job creation had prevailed until the early 2000s. Still, after the 2008 economic crisis, the expenditure of PES has significantly increased. The changes in ALMPs spending resulted from the Hartz reforms. The German government has implemented the Hartz reform, a labor market deregulation measure, for job creation to increase employment flexibility and competitiveness in the labor market and to allow for mid-jobs and mini-jobs, and increase wage subsidies and tax cuts for these non-regular jobs. After the Hartz reforms, ALMPs in Germany have focused on strengthening the public employment system and job strategies for activating the unemployed, including job placement and matching services. At the same time, in Germany during the 2008 economic crisis, support for individual self-employment and start-ups has greatly increased through the enterprise foundation support system for individual proprietors and start-ups, which had provided unemployment allowances in the form of start-up subsidies for three years to single-person enterprises and family companies (OECD datasets). On the other hand, the German government has significantly reduced its budget for direct job creation in the 2000s, according to the results of research showing that the policy did not affect continuous job creation.

In general, these countries in CMCs have seen a decrease in spending on traditional vocational training but an increase in expenditures on the public employment system and employment by incentives and subsidies. Unlike the OECD and EU policy proposals, the overall trend of ALMPs shows short-term, pro-market characteristics such as PES, employment incentives, and subsidies, rather than vocational training upskilling focused on human resource development. The overall change in ALMPs and budgetary spending is closely related to the impact of neoliberal economic ideology, which emphasizes competition among countries and economic efficiency in a global labor market environment that has strengthened since 2000.

What was unusual about the three countries, however, is that, except in

Korea, spending on direct job creation, such as public work, has rapidly decreased. In Germany and France, even in the 1990s, the direct job creation policy like public work in the economic crises was regarded as a major ALMPs. However, it is shown that the expenditure on direct job creation has sharply decreased since the 2000s. In short, the Hartz reforms resulted in the radical change of labor market policy, including reorganization of Federal Labor Office(Federal Labor Agency), Job Center installation, amendment of the Dispatch Worker Act, and Tax benefits for low-wage work(Mini-job, Midi-job), based on the idea of 'Welfare to Work' reforms (Agenda 2010). In 2008, the Merkel government strengthened the job placement function of the Federal Labor Agency, provided subsidies for curtailment of working hours, and extended worker support programs with an emphasis on employment.

In Korea, on the other hand, the job policy in the two economic crises has still relied on direct job creation like public work. In the period of economic crises, the Korean government's direct job creation policy was a short-term job policy to improve temporary employment indicators, which was far from the stability and sustainability of jobs in the long term. There are reasons why the Korean government has relied on direct job creations. First, these policy measures have functioned as a kind of social safety net in Korea, where the social welfare system was not properly established. It contributed to the protection of livelihoods for low-income people. Second, public-work programs have stabilized employment indicators to lower the unemployment rate by creating many short-time jobs in the public sector.

However, it was a temporary program to cope with the economic crises, and the issue of job sustainability remained an issue to tackle. Therefore, labor market instability in Korea has continued to exist, centering on the socially vulnerable groups such as the youth, women, and irregular workers. The problem of income inequality and social polarization remained unresolved. The case studies explain why different countries spend different types of ALMPs. This can be said to be a more specific and conditional difference in the spending of ALMPs in OECD countries in each country's job politics.

8.3 Comparing Analysis of Job Policies in the 2008 Economic Crisis

The case studies have analyzed how social actors have responded in the context of the economic crises and what policy measures have been taken to address job problems to see where the trend, changes, and differences in ALMPs of the three countries come from. Policy choices have been analyzed from the social actors' point of view. In this context, the welfare systems and job policies of the three countries have shown different historical and institutional paths.

Sweden is a representative social democratic welfare state in northern Europe that has sought typical universal welfare majorly led by the Social Democratic Party since the 1938 Saltsjöbaden Convention, while Germany has formed a conservative welfare state regime, based on the Protestant and family-centered culture, in which the role of the state in the capitalist market has been emphasized (Asping-Andersen 1990). South Korea is a country that has achieved rapid economic development through late industrial development since the 1960s, and successful industrialization and democratization through the democratization movement in 1987 and began to pursue market-oriented logic and selective welfare through neo-liberal reforms after the 1997 economic crisis. It belongs to the Anglo-American liberal welfare state system (See Table 8.1).

Despite different types of social welfare regimes, three countries have successfully achieved economic growth and social development. In the 2008 global economic crisis, they all have overcome it in a shorter period than other countries by successfully responding to it.

Table 8.1. Job Policies and Comparison of Three Countries (Summary)

Institutional Factors	Sweden	Germany	Korea
Welfare Regime	Social Democracy (SMC)	Conservativism (CMC)	Liberalism (LMC)
Ruling Party (2008-2016)	Right-wing	Right-wing	Right-wing
State	Weak	Medium	Strong
Unionization Rate	High	Medium	Low
Employer Organization	Strong	Medium	Low
Tr	Social Partnershipipartite Commission	Corporatism	Government-led
Collective Bargaining by Industry	Yes	Yes	No
Vocational Training	Strong	Strong	Weak
Higher Education	High	Medium	High
Child Care	High	Low	Low
Financial Crisis(negative) after 2008	None	None	None
Unemployment Benefit(Generosity)	High	Mediu	Lowm
Employment Strictness	High	Medium	Low
Labor and Management Cooperation	High	Medium	Low

Labor Market Issues	Refugees & Youth unemployment	High & Long-term unemployment	Irregular Workers & Youth unemployment
Major ALMPs after the 2008 economic crisis	Employment Incentives, PES	PES, Job Training, Mini-Job & Midi-Job, Working Time Individual Account	Direct Job Creation Public Work, Youth Intern

These countries have a few things in common. First of all, they have both similar export-oriented economic structures and manufacturing-oriented industrial structures. They all have a relatively high share of manufacturing in the economy compared to other OECD countries. As Katzenstein pointed out, they have developed economically through exports through manufacturing competition in the global economic environment. Therefore, they had been vulnerable to the oil shock in the 1970s, the economic crises in the 1990s, and the global economic crises in 2008 (Katzenstein 1985). Because of the dominant share of manufacturing in GDP in three countries, the new job creation in the sector has become a very important policy issue. Therefore, they have commonalities in which the job policy has become one of the core social policies by recognizing the crisis of unemployment centered on manufacturing during the economic crises as a big social problem.

However, the response of the major social actors to the economic crisis in the three countries shows a different picture. First, Sweden which had already experienced the economic crisis in 1991-1993 has attempted to cope with the 2008 economic crisis through a rapid fiscal expansion policy. Sweden's fiscal policy differed from other countries. When bank liquidity was a problem, the Swedish government has directly intervened and acquired banks and then reopened these banks when the economy recovered, thereby pursuing financial stability. Then, the Swedish government could recover more than what it had invested through a public offering. It was also noted that during the conservative right-wing government, despite the pursuit of institutional reforms based on neoliberal ideas, it did not break the traditional framework of bilateral labor-management relations and social partnership in Sweden.

As discussed in the previous chapter, the crisis pact by the IF Metall (Industrifacket Metall) and the Association of Swedish Engineering Industries (Teknikföretagen) in 2008 was a good example (see Chapter 5). At that time, based on social partnership, the labor union and employers' association signed a framework agreement that focused on retaining jobs through reducing working hours and wages instead of collective layoffs and employers' shouldering a part of the costs for wage cuts. In 2014, they also proposed a tripartite social agreement to the right-wing government, which led to a crisis pact preparing for the next economic crisis in 2014. As such, the framework of social dialogue in Sweden is characterized by bilateral relations at the industry/individual enterprise level. In labor-management relations, the government takes a role to support smooth social dialogue and collective bargaining rather than direct intervention. Such characteristics of the Swedish labor-management relations make a distinction between Germany and Korea.

Germany overcame the 2008 global economic crisis smoothly, and unlike other European countries, its job indicators look good at present. In particular, the youth unemployment rate has decreased, unlike Sweden or Korea, showing a very different pattern. Some scholars have argued that the main factor in overcoming the German economic crisis was the policy effect of preemptive Hartz reform (Dustman et al. 2013, Rinne & Zimmermann, 2013). The Hartz reform includes deregulation of the labor market aimed at streamlining the labor market policy, promoting job search through strengthening job seekers' responsibilities, and creating jobs through labor market flexibility and competitiveness (Hartz 2001). Scholars who pay attention to the employment performance of the Hartz reforms, such as the continued decline in the German unemployment rates and increase in employment rates, regard the recent German labor market situation as a 'miracle of employment.' In short, the Hartz reform that had focused on the deregulation of the labor market policy implies a new type of active labor market policy restructuring the German economic system.

Based on it, Germany tried to overcome the job crisis during the 2008 economic crisis by sharing jobs through reducing working hours. Mini-jobs and mid-jobs have made German labor market indicators relatively sound compared to other countries. However, these mid-jobs and mini-jobs have also contributed to the proliferation of non-regular workers and the creation of short-term and low-wage jobs, intensifying the labor market instability and increasing social inequality and bi-polarization (Keller & Seifert 2011, Lee 2019). After the Hartz reform, regular employment in the German labor market has weakened, and the spread of non-regular workers has led to an increase in short-term low-wage jobs and a widening wage gap by employment type.

On the other hand, in the case of Korea, the framework of the social dialogue was set up through the establishment of the Tripartite Commission which was a device for institutional and structural reform to introduce labor market flexibility measures in the 1997 financial crisis. Criticisms have been raised about the imbalance in labor-management relations and social dialogue on slanted playgrounds (Lee 2002, Park 2005). Both the labor union and employers had very low organizing rates, which resulted in a problem of representation. The lack of representation and autonomy of labor and management representatives in social dialogue resulted in a repetitive pattern of participation in the social dialogue body and withdrawal from it due to inexperience in the social dialogue process and lack of social trust. As a result, structural reforms and labor market flexibility measures imposed in the wake of the 1997 IMF economic crisis have given birth to the problems of massive irregular workers and social inequality and by-polarization.

As soon as the global economic crisis arrived in 2008, the Korean government organized the pan-government 'Emergency Economic Meeting' and tried to address the crisis through rapid national intervention, including fiscal and financial policies. At the same time, the government expended the expenditure for direct job creation, such as 'public work' and youth internships. The direct job creation policy through the financial support of the Korean government was a different policy response from Germany and Sweden. This direct job creation policy was a very short-term policy measure in the period of an economic crisis and a temporary one to avoid an unemployment crisis, irrespective of job security and continuity. Most of all, the youth unemployment problem has become more serious since the 2008 global economic crisis, which demanded a policy response. However, no clear solution has been found. Recently, with the introduction of the 'Youth Guarantee' system in Europe targeting the unemployed youth, policy experiments on youth dividends are underway.

8.4 Politics of Job Creation and Policymaking

The study paid analytical attention to the role of industrial relations and social actors with job creation policies in the phase of economic crises. The social pacts between labor and management were very important in Swedish job policymaking. Although the unionization rate of Swedish trade unions has recently declined since the 2008 economic crisis, it remains as high as 70% compared to other OECD countries. Above all, the Swedish Employer Association's organizing rate is 90%, higher than the unionization rate. Such high organizing rates of unions and employers' organizations are the basis for maintaining the validity of collective bargaining and social agreements in which they guarantee the representativeness of each organization. Overall, the Swedish government has also shown respect for social dialogue between labor and management rather than directly intervening in the process of making social agreements. Sweden's social dialogue framework on job creation policy has been characterized by bilateral relations at the industry level and individual enterprise level, and the role of the government in this process has been only to support smooth social dialogue and collective bargaining. However, the major changes in Swedish industrial relations and job creation policies after the global economic crisis have gradually reduced working hours and wages, as indicated by the crisis pact between IF Metal and the Association of Swedish Engineerig Industries after the 2008 global economic crisis. In other words, the strategy has been shifting from the existing external quantity flexibility to internal functional flexibility, as shown in the pursuit of employment retention through the reduction of working hours and wage cuts.

In Germany, the unionization rate is 17% as of 2018, much lower than 70% in Sweden, but the influence of labor unions is still very strong. The coverage rate of collective bargaining agreements on industries reaches 90%. Also, the mechanisms of union participation in management, such as the joint decision-making system and the operation of the supervisory board, have served as important systems for representing workers' interests. In particular, during the global economic crisis of 2008, the German unions refrained from demanding drastic shortening of real working hours and excessive wage hikes to create youth jobs and maintain employment. The government has implemented employment subsidies and tax breaks for businesses to maintain employment. German companies have also provided tens of thousands of apprenticeships positions each year through a national pact and made efforts to raise their funds without relying on government funding.

On the other hand, in the case of Korea, the Kim Dae-Jung government, which succeeded in the horizontal regime change after the 1997 economic crisis, accepted the neo-liberal structural reform requirements of the IMF as a prerequisite for bailouts, thereby helping Korean society move toward a neoliberal economic system. In particular, the Lee Myung-Bak and Park Geun-Hye administrations, which came to power after the Roh Moo-Hyun administration, made the neoliberal and pro-market labor policy more explicit. The unionization rate in Korea was very low, 11.8%, as of 2018, and collective bargaining took place at an individual enterprise level. Also, the working class was excluded from social dialogue and labor market policymaking. Regular layoffs during the two economic crises have heightened employment insecurity, and the Korean government's job policy to cope with unemployment has also relied on short-term public work. Korea's job creation policy was qualitatively different from that of Sweden that has focused on the job training and social security. And it also showed a difference from the German job creation policy, which has focused on employee retention and job sharing through shorter working hours and wage cuts.

8.5 Theoretical Implications

The active labor market policy has become the main policy solution for solving the unemployment problem in an economic crisis. However, before and after the 2008 global economic crisis, its application was different from country to country. As Gourevitch(1986) argues, such a difference could be attributed to the formation of national labor market institutions, economic conditions, and policy choices by social actors. After the 2008 global economic crisis, the active labor policy has gradually emphasized the role and importance of PES and employment incentives, breaking away from the emphasis on vocational training in the previous period. This change in the active labor market policy implies a shift to the short-term and pro-market policy.

The change in trends is analyzed as being influenced by the neoliberal economic ideology that has strengthened since the 2000s. Sweden, which has traditionally spent a large number of public expenditures on vocational training among the active labor market policies, has spent more on employment incentives and public employment services since 2003. A similar change occurred in Germany. Since 2005, when the Hartz reform was in full swing, the budget for public employment services has exceeded that for vocational training. On the other hand, Korea's active labor market policy has heavily relied on public work.

The 2008 global economic crisis has also brought about major changes in the active labor market policy. In the pre-2008 global economic crisis, the response to the economic crisis largely took on the pattern of restructuring based on external quantitative flexibility, vocational training for the unemployed, and a social safety net for them. However, after the 2008 global economic crisis, Sweden and Germany have responded to them based on internal functional flexibility, such as shorter working hours and wage cuts. In short, it can be seen that the active labor market policy of the governments has actively focused on promoting the employment incentive policies to compensate for reduced working hours and wage cuts and a public employment service system for unemployment management.

Unlike in Germany, however, job sharing and shorter working hours were less noticeable in Sweden. Sweden had tried to respond to the previous economic crisis based on external quantitative flexibility in the manufacturing sector and the active labor market policy (Anxo 2015). The economic crisis did not also lead to an increase in non-standard forms of employment in Sweden. In contrast to Germany, it did not experience the development of either mini-jobs or zero-hours contracts. However, after the 2008 global economic crisis, the crisis pact between IF Metal and the Association of Swedish Engineering Industries showed a shift from the external quantity flexibility to the internal functional flexibility by pursuing an employment retention strategy through shorter working hours and wage cuts.

The way of responding to neoliberal ideology, institutional changes, and policy measures also differed across countries. Sweden has pursued a so-called flexicurity model to minimize the wage gap among the industrial sectors while emphasizing flexibility in employment and the labor market through active labor market and universal welfare policies. The Swedish government has focused on providing more efficient and better social services to citizens by taking advantage of the core values of marketization rather than reducing public social services and privatizing them in full. For example, it allowed private companies to participate in education and medical services to expand their choices and improve service quality through competition. In the process of deregulation of the labor market, the virtuous cycle of growth, employment, and welfare has continued in Sweden. Sweden's social consensus model has relied heavily on its social democratic system that has early pursued community solidarity and regulation of the market. It still has the attributes of a social democracy that is qualitatively different from that of liberal democracy. Eventually, the governance of job politics in Sweden has become more of a coordinating mechanism for negotiation and compromise for social and economic sustainability.

Germany has successfully overcome the 2008 economic crisis thanks to the Hartz reform, which was based on the deregulation of labor market policy. However, the deregulation of the labor market system has increased the labor market instability and weakened institutional guarantee mechanisms such as collective agreement, dismissal protection, and social insurance. After the global economic crisis in 2008, unstable jobs such as dispatch work, mini-jobs and midi-jobs have expanded significantly. There were also negative aspects, such as a widening wage gap between regular and non-regular workers. As a result, the German government has recently introduced minimum legal regulations for short-term employment and dispatch work, expanded anti-discrimination and equal treatment principles, and introduced the statutory minimum wage (Lee 2019)

On the other hand, Korea's labor market policy in the IMF economic crisis was 'deregulation of the labor market.' It aimed to create a flexible labor market by introducing layoffs and allowing dispatched workers. It expanded the neoliberal market relations that emerged in a liberal economic model such as the U.K and the U.S.A. During the 2008 global financial crisis, there were no significant changes in the labor market policy. In Korea, job creation policies depended on short-term public work, and social inequality was greatly exacerbated by expanding non-regular work. However, the politics of job creation during the two economic crises were marked by the exclusion of labor and unilateral neoliberal reforms by the government.

In sum, during the 2008 global economic crisis, job politics has shown both similarities and differences within active labor market policies. In response to the 2008 financial crisis, many OECD countries have recently increased expenditures on public employment services (PES) and employment incentives rather than spending on job training. Most countries have recently preferred short-term and pro-market-oriented job creation measures instead of long-term based human resource development policies. The shift to public employment services and short-term employment incentives has been seen in all three countries instead of long-term human resource development policies. In this regard, the significant factors can be pointed out in the change in the spending patterns of ALMPs as follows. First, this clearly shows that neoliberal economic ideology has a major impact on the expenditures and types of ALMPs in OECD countries. Under the neoliberal economic system, governments and corporations have emphasized flexibility and efficiency within the labor market. Therefore, they prefer short-term education and job matching rather than vocational training, which requires a certain amount of time and social cost. Second, another important reason why the proportion of vocational training spending in ALMPs has decreased significantly seems to be a change in the industrial structure. The transition from manufacturing to service economies has largely affected the expenditure of training in OECD countries. Jobs in service economies are typically organized around very simple or narrow tasks, often highly routinized. In this case, the countries are more likely to rely on short-term and temporary ALMPs, such as job-matching services and employment incentives, rather than vocational training that takes money and time.

As the industrial structure changes from traditional manufacturing to the service industry, the types of ALMP in many OECD countries are shifting to financial spending on short-term employment services and employment incentives rather than on financial expenditure on vocational training. As Bengtsson argues, "up-skilling might not have the same effect today as it did in the mid-20th century" (Bengtsson 2014, 67). Because upskilling in the knowledge-based economies needs more cost and time consuming than job training in the period of post-war industrial development. As a result, most OECD countries recently are favoring short-term job placement and job-matching rather than longer-term-based job training that requires more policy attention and spending. Though, short-term and pro-market-oriented policy measures such as job matching and employment incentives have produced negative consequences such as low-wage job creation, job instability, and social inequality.

At the same time, the study shows that there are still differences in the expenditure of ALMPs according to the welfare system. The case study shows differences in the expenditures and types of ALMPs that three countries adopted in response to the economic crisis. Variations on ALMPs' spending in these OECD countries were more specific and conditional per the politics of job creation in each country. As the case study shows, it can also be seen that the types of job policies differ slightly by country. These differences in job creation policies are due to the institutional conditions of each country, their domestic politics, and the strategic choices of social actors surrounding job policies. Sweden's social concertation model based on the social democratic system has not changed significantly after the 2008 global economic crisis. As a result, there has been no sharp increase in non-standard work and severe income inequality, unlike the other two countries. Instead, the Hartz reform in Germany has increased job insecurity and social inequality. The politics of job creation in Korea has been driven by the exclusion of labor and unilateral neoliberal reform. In particular, the expansion of low-wage work and deepening social inequality reflects the limitation of short-term prescriptions for a job crisis. Therefore, as a policy alternative, there will be an urgent need for investment in a social policy that integrates social and economic policies such as higher education, income inequality, and protection of non-regular workers. In short, this study suggests that the differences and divergence in ALMPs among three countries are more specific and conditional on their domestic politics and social actors' policy choices.

Lastly, based on the results, OECD countries may be more likely to enter the pathway of the low-road instead of the high-road. High-skilled jobs require workers to perform analytical and cognitively demanding tasks, while low-skilled jobs demand workers to perform routine and simple tasks. Therefore, the countries headed to the 'high-road' are more likely to adopt ALMPs directed towards skill-upgrading and human capital development through lifetime training and higher education. Instead, jobs on the 'low-road' are mainly replaced through short-term training provided by the employer for the narrow tasks in that specific firm. As discussed above, the OECD countries have recently relied on short-term and temporary ALMPs, such as job-matching services and employment incentives rather than up-skilling. In particular, as the polarization of jobs divided into high-tech jobs and gigs or platform jobs intensifies with digital transformation, most OECD countries are likely to pursue such short-term, pro-market job policies. These recent trends of ALMP are more likely to increase and reproduce job insecurity and income inequality in the OECD countries.

In the era of digital transformation and the 4th industrial revolution, investment in high-tech technology from a long-term perspective is essential to create new high-quality jobs. However, high education and life-long training for new skills to go to high-road require a lot of time and sizeable social expenditure. Therefore, the responsibility and role of the state in job creation policy are essential, and job policy governance and decision-making through the participation of main social actors are vital. At the same time, ALMP needs to be supported by social investment policies targeted towards higher education, child care, amelioration of social inequality, and protection of increasing atypical labor.

In addition, the limitations of this study can be pointed out as follows. First, this study attempts various statistical analysis methods such as the fixed effects and random effects models based on the pooled cross-sectional panel datasets. Nevertheless, it is somewhat insufficient in terms of analytical methodology. It needs to be supplemented through follow-up studies. Second, public spending on traditional ALMPs' policies, such as vocational training, is declining. This study assumes that one of the reasons is the transition to the service industry structure. Though the explanation of the relationship between the two is somewhat lacking, and ongoing research is needed. Third, this study uses secondary literature and data sets without on-the-spot investigations of major overseas cases and direct interviews with internal policymakers. These limitations should be improved through succeeding research.

APPENDIX A
Summary of Variables

Variable Name	Obs	Mean	SD	Min	Max
Social expenditure on ALMP (soex_almp)	459	0.61	0.417	.036	2.261
Cabinet composition (gov_party)	459	2.40	1.493	1	5
Left party seats (leftcum)	434	20.09	13.062	0	53.86
Union density rate (ud_1)	412	35.18	21.991	8.500297	92.56619
Adjusted barga	316	58.68	29.302	11.22241	100
Coordination of wage setting (coord)	500	2.92	1.255	1	5
Index for the degree of openness (kaopen_1)	413	2.33	0.181	.7785647	2.45573
Civilian employment in industry (emp_ind)	458	4161.06	6493.693	23.125	315
Civilian employment in services (emp_serv)	45700	13298.66	23600.584	97.908	124034.7
PES and administration (pesandadministration)	445	0.16	0.097	.01	.54
Training (training1)	470	0.20	0.165	0	.94
Employment incentives (employmentincentives)	470	0.11	0.125	0	.65
Direct job creation (directjobcreation)	467	0.07	0.090	0	.5
Real GDP growth rate (realgdpgrowth)	525	2.19	2.708	-9.132494	25.1764
Employment rates (employmentrates)	350	68.63	6.676	52.2	85.7
Unemployment rates (unemploymentrates)	472	7.06	3.929	1.9	27.46715
dummy	525	0.52	0.500	0	1

APPENDIX B
OECD Classification of Labor Market Programs

Type	Code	Note
1. Public employment services and administration	1.1 Placement and related services 1.2 Benefit administration 1.3 Other	Active Measures (ALMP)
2. Training	2.1 Institutional training 2.2 Workplace training 2.3 Alternate training 2.4 Special support for apprenticeship	ALMP
3. Job	3.1 Job rotation 3.2 Job sharing rotation and job sharing	ALMP
4. Employment incentives	4.1 Recruitment incentives 4.2 Employment maintenance incentives	ALMP
5. Supported employment and rehabilitation	5.1 Supported employment 5.2 Rehabilitation	ALMP
6. Direct job creation	6.1 Direct job	ALMP
7. Start-up incentivescreation	7.1 Start-up incentives	ALMP
8. Out-of-work income maintenance and support	8.1 Full unemployment benefits 8.1.1. Unemployment insurance 8.1.2. Unemployment assistance 8.2 Partial unemployment benefits 8.3 Part-time unemployment benefits 8.4 Redundancy compensation 8.5 Bankruptcy compensation	Passive measures (Unemployment Benefits)
9. Early retirement	9.1 Conditional 9.2 Unconditional	Passive measures (Early Retirement)

Sources: OECD (2013)

REFERENCES

A, Kee-Ku. 2010. "Global Economic Crisis and German Economic and Social Policy against the crisis." *Korean Social Policy Review*. Vol. 16, No. 2. 93-129.

Agell, J., Lindh, T., and Ohlsson, H. 1997. "Growth and the public sector: A critical review essay." *European Journal of Political Economy* 13, 33–52.

Ahn, Jae-heung. 2007. "The Swedish General Election Results in 2006: Characteristics of the Swedish Model and Irony of 'New Politics'. *Future Strategy*. No. 4. Future Foundation.

Armingeon, Klaus. 2007. "Active Labour Market Policy, International Organizations and Domestic Politics," *Journal of European Public Policy* 14, no. 6: 905–32.

Bang, Ha-Nam and Nam, Jae-Wook. 2016. "The Exclusion from the Employment Insurance System and Policy Issues: Focused on Unemployment Benefit." *Social Welfare Policy Review* 43(1): 51-79.

Barbier, Jean-Claude. 2004. "Systems of Social Protection in Europe: Two Contrasted Paths to Activation, and Maybe a Third," in *Labour and Employment Regulation in Europe*, ed. J. Lind, H. Knudsen, and H. Jørgensen. Brussels, Belgium: Peter Lang.

Barro, R. 1990. "Government spending in a simple model of endogenous growth." *Journal of Political Economy* 98: S103–S125.

Barro, R. 1991. "Economic growth in a cross-section of countries." *Quarterly Journal of Economics* 106: 407–443.

Becker, Uwe (ed.). 2011. *The Changing Political Economies of Small West European Countries*. Amsterdam University Press.

Bengtsson, M. 2014. "Towards standby-ability: Swedish and Danish activation policies in flux." *International Journal of Social Welfare* Vol. 23: S54-S70.

Bengtsson, M. and Berglund, T. 2012. "Labour Market Policies in Transition: From Social Engineering to Stand-by Ability." In B. Larsson, M. Letell and H. Thörn (eds.) *Transformations of the Swedish Welfare State: From Social Engineering to Governance?* pp. 86-103. Houndmills,

Basingstoke: Palgrave Macmillan.

Berry, F. Strokes and William D. Berry. 2007. "Innovation and Diffusion Models in Policy Research." In Paul A. Sabatier (eds.) *Theories of the Policy Process*: 223–260.

Bonoli, Giuliano and David Natali. 2012. *The politics of the new welfare states*. Oxford University Press.

Bonoli, Giuliano. 2010. "The political Economy of Active Labor Market Policy." *Politics & Society* 38(4): 435-457.

Boone, J., and van Ours, J. 2009. "Bringing unemployed back to work: Effective active labor market policies." De Economist 157(3): 293-313.

Bradley, David H., and John D. Stephens. 2007. Employment Performance in OECD Countries A Test of Neoliberal and Institutionalist Hypotheses. *Comparative Political Studies* Volume 40 Number 12 (December 2007): 1486-1510.

Brinkmann, C. 2002. *Das Job-AQTIV-Gesetz: Evaluation zwischen Handlungszwängen und solidem Handwerk*. IAB, 21. März 2002.

Calmfors, L., A. Forslund, and M. Hemström, 2002, Does Active Labour Market Policy Work? Lessons from the Swedish Experiences, *Swedish Economic Policy Review* 7.

Calmfors, Lars and John Driffill. 1988. "Bargaining Structure, Corporatism, and Macroeconomic Performance," *Economic Policy* (6): 14–61.

Card, D., Jochen Kluve, and Andrea Weber. 2010. "Active labour market policy evaluations: A meta-analysis. *Economic Journal* 120(548): F452-F477.

Castles, F. G. (1994). "Is expenditure enough? On the nature of the dependent variable in comparative public policy analysis." *Journal of Commonwealth and Comparative Politics* 33(3): 349–63.

Castles, F. G. 1995. "Welfare state development in Southern Europe." *West European Politics* 18(2): 291–313.

Castles, F. G. 1998. *Comparative Public Policy: Patterns of Post-war Transformation* Cheltenham: Edward Elgar.

Castles, F. G. 2002. "Developing new measures of welfare state change and reform." *European Journal of Political Research* 41: 613–41.

Castles, F. G. 2004. *The Future of the Welfare State* Oxford: Oxford University Press.

Castles, F. G. 2006. "The growth of the post-war public expenditure state: long-term trajectories and recent trends." Tran-State Working Paper No 35. Bremen University.

Castles, F. G., and Obinger, H. 2007. "Social expenditure and the politics of redistribution." *Journal of European Social Policy* 17(3): 206–22.

Castles. 2008. "What Welfare States Do: A Disaggregated Expenditure Approach." *Journal of Social Policy* 38(1): 45–62.

Chang, Hong Geun. 2011. Evaluation of Job Training Programs: Training of the Unemployed. *Monthly Labor Review* (Issue No. 78, September 2011). Pp. 18-35. Korea Labor Institute.

Cho, Seong-Jae. 2009. "Work-Sharing Program: Evaluation and Future Challenges." *Monthly Labor Review* (Issue 58, October-December 2009). Pp. 64-82. Korea Labor Institute.

Clasen, Jochen. 2000. "Motives, Means and Opportunities: Reforming Unemployment Compensation in the 1990s." *West European Politics* 23(2): 89–112.

Creswell, J. W. 2007. *Qualitative inquiry and research design: Choosing among five traditions* (2nd Ed.). Thousand Oaks, CA: Sage.

Dar, A. A., & AmirKhalkhali, S. 2002. "Government size, factor accumulation, and economic growth: Evidence from OECD countries." *Journal of Policy Modeling* 24: 679–692.

Deyo, Frederick (ed.). 1987. *The Political Economy of the New Asian Industrialism.* Ithaca: Cornell University Press.

Dustmann et al. 2014. "From Sick Man of Europe to Economic Superstar: Germany's Resurgent Economy." Journal of Economic Perspectives. Vol 28(1): 167-188.

Eichhorst, Werner, Maria Grienberger-Zingerle, and Regina Konle-Seidl. 2008. "Activation Policies in Germany: From Status Protection to Basic Income Support." in *Bringing the Jobless into Work? Experiences with Activation in Europe and the US*, ed. W. Eichhorst, O. Kaufmann, and R. Konle-Seidl. Berlin, Germany: Springer.

Erhel, Christine, and Charlotte Levionnois. 2013. Labour Market Policies in Times of Crisis: A Comparison of the 1992-1993 and 2008-2010 Recessions. Documents de travail du Centre d'Economie de la Sorbonne.

Esping-Andersen, Gøsta. 1990. *The Three Worlds of Welfare Capitalism.* Cambridge: Polity Press.

Estevez-Abe, M., Iversen, T. and Soskice, D. 2001. "Social Protection and the Formation of Skills:

A Reinterpretation of the Welfare State." In Hall, P. A. and Soskice, D. (eds.) *Varieties of Capitalism: The Institutional Foundations of Comparative Advantage* New York: Oxford University Press, pp. 145–183.

Evans, Peter. 1995. *Embedded Autonomy: States and Industrial Transformation*. Princeton: Princeton University Press.

Fölster, Stefan and Magnus Henrekson. 1999. "Growth and the public sector: a critique of the critics." *European Journal of Political Economy* 15: 337-358.

Fölster, Stefan and Magnus Henrekson. 2001. "Growth Effects of Government Expenditure and Taxation in Rich Countries." *European Economic Review* 45 (8): 1501–1520

Friedman, Milton. 2002. *Capitalism and Freedom*. Chicago: University of Chicago.

Gerschenkron. 1962. "Economic Backwardness in Historical Perspective." in his *Economic Backwardness in Historical Perspective*. New York: Praeger, 5-30.

Geum, Jae-Ho. 2013. "What to learn from the German labor market?" *Monthly Labor Review* (June 2018): 75-88, Korea Labor Institute.

Glassner and Keune. 2010. Negotiating the crisis? Collective bargaining in Europe during the economic downturn. ILO.

Gourevitch. 1986. *Politics in Hard Times: Comparative Responses to International Economic Crisis*. Ithaca and London: Cornell University Press.

Graziano, Paolo R. 2011. Europeanization and Domestic Employment Policy Change: Conceptual and Methodological Background. *Governance: An International Journal of Policy, Administration, and Institutions*, Vol. 24(3): 583–605.

Graziano, Paolo R. 2012. Converging worlds of activation? Activation policies and governance in Europe and the role of the EU. *International Journal of Sociology and Social Policy* Vol. 32 No. 5/6, pp. 312-326.

Hall, P. 1997. "The role of interests, institutions, and ideas in the comparative political economic of the industrial nations," In Mark Irving Lichbach and Alan S. Zuckerman (Eds.), *Comparative Politics: Rationality, Culture, and Structure*. Cambridge University Press.

Hall, P. 1999. The political economy of Europe in an era of interdependence, In H. Kitschelt, P. Lange, G. Marks, & J. Stephens (Eds.), *Continuity and change in contemporary capitalism*(pp.

135-163). New York: Cambridge University Press.

Hall, Peter A. and David Soskice. 2001. An introduction to varieties of capitalism. In Peter A. Hall & David Soskice (Eds.), *Varieties of capitalism: The institutional foundations of comparative advantage* (pp. 1-68). Oxford: Oxford University Press.

Han, In-Sang. 2010. *Achievements of Job creation since the inauguration of the Lee Myung-Bak administration*. Seoul: National Assembly Research Service.

Hansson, P., and Henrekson, M. 1994. "A new framework for testing the effect of government spending on growth and productivity." *Public Choice* 81: 381–401.

Hartz. 2015. "Implications for the German Hartz Labor Reform and Korea." KITA Global Trade Forum Special Lectures.

Hay, C. and Wincott, D. 2013. The Political Economy of European Welfare Capitalism London: Palgrave Macmillan.

Hemerijck, Anton. 2013. *Changing Welfare States*. Oxford University Press.

Hetschko et al. 2020. Income support, employment transitions and well-being. *Labour Economics* 66.

Hicks, A. 1994. Introduction to pooling. In A. Hicks & T. Janoski (Eds.), *The comparative political economy of the welfare state* (pp. 169-188). New York: Cambridge University Press.

Hirschman 1968. "The Political Economy of ISI in Latin America." *The Quarterly Journal of Economics* 81(1): 1-32.

Huber, E. and John D. Stephens. 2001. *Development and Crisis of the Welfare State: Parties and Politics in Global Markets*. Chicago: University of Chicago Press.

Huh, Jae-Sung and Yoo, Hye-Mee. 2002. *An Evaluation of Financial and Business Restructuring after the Foreign Exchange Crisis*. Seoul: the Bank of Korea.

Huo, Jingjing and John D. Stephens. 2015. "From Industrial Corporatism to the Social Investment State." *Oxford Handbook on Transformation of the State*. P.p. 410-425. Oxford University Press.

Huo, Jingjing, Moira Nelson, and John D. Stephens. 2008. Decommodification and activation in social democratic policy: resolving the paradox *Journal of European Social Policy*. Vol. 18(1): 5-20.

Hur, Jae-Joon. 2013. *Korea's Active Labor Market Policy: Its Birth, Establishment, and Development.* Korea Labor Institute.

Hur, Jai-Joon and Kim, Ho-Kyung. 2002. "Employment Insurance and Work Injury Compensation as a Social Safety Net." In Won-duck Lee (ed.) *Labor in Korea.* Seoul: Korea Labor Institute.

Hüther, M. 2014. "The Hartz Reform and the German Miracle." *International Labor Brief* 12(7): 4-17. Korea Labor Institute.

Hwang, Gi-don. 2014. "10 Jahre Hartz-Reformen: Ein halber Erfolg." *Koreanische Zeitschrift fuer Wirtschaftswissenschaften* (KZfW) 32(2): 41-60. Koreanisch-Deutsche Gesellschaft Fuer Wirtschaftswissenschaften.

IMF. 2012. Fiscal Policy and Employment in Advanced and Emerging Economies.

Iversen, T. and Soskice, D. 2011. "Dualism and Political Coalitions: Inclusionary versus Exclusionary Reforms in Age of Rising Inequality." Working Paper, Harvard University and LSE.

Iversen, T. and Stephens, J.D. 2008. Partisan Politics, the Welfare State, and Three Worlds of Human Capital Formation *Comparative Political Studies* Volume 41 Number 4/5 April/May 2008: 600-637.

Iversen, T. and Wren, A. 1998. Equality, Employment, and Budgetary Restraint: The Trilemma of the Service Economy. *World Politics* 50 (4): 507-546.

Iversen, Torben. 2005. *Capitalism, democracy, and welfare.* Cambridge: Cambridge University Press.

Jang, Eun-Suk. 2004. 2004. "Predecessor system in the German union and employee council." *International Labor Brief*(September-October 2004) Vol. 2 No. 5: 45-50. Korea Labor Institute.

Jeong, In-Soo. 2012. "Evaluation of employment policy performance after the financial crisis and future tasks: Changes in the MB government's employment policy." Seoul: KDI Graduate School of International Policy.

Jeong, Won-Ho. 2013. " Mechanism of the German Employment Miracle: Interactions between Job Creation and Job Retention." *Monthly Labor Review*(Issue No.99, June 2013). Pp. 35-46. Korea Labor Institute.

Katzenstein, Peter J. 1985. *Small States in World Markets. Industrial Policy in Europe* Ithaca, NY: Cornell University Press.

Keller & Seifert 2011 Atypical employment in Germany. Forms, development, patterns. *Transfer* 19(4): 457-474.

Kim, Hye-Won 2009. "Evaluation of Social Services Job Program." *Monthly Labor Review* (Issue 58, October-December 2009). pp. 20-36. Korea Labor Institute.

Kim, Soon-Yang. 2014. "South Korea's Responses to Global Economic Crisis." Proceedings of the First Middle East Conference on Global Business, Economics, Finance and Banking. Dubai.

Kim, Tae-Ki and Cheon, Byung-You. 2002. "Restructuring and Labor Relations," a paper presented at the 2002 Korean Economic Association Conference.

Kim, Young-Mi. 2013. "Content and evaluation of legal reform related to employment promotion in Germany's hartz reform?." *Journal of Labor Law* (28): 173-217.

King, Desmond. 1995. *Actively Seeking Work? The Politics of Unemployment and Welfare Policy in the United States and Great Britain* Chicago, IL: University of Chicago Press.

Kingdon, John W. 2002. "The Policy Window, and Joining the Streams." *Agendas, Alternatives and Public Policies* 2nd edition, 165-95.

Kluve, J. 2007. "The effectiveness of European ALMP's." in Kluve, J. et al. *Active Labor Market Policies in Europe: Performance and Perspectives.* Berlin and Heidelberg, Springer, 153–203.

Kluve, J. and C.M. Schmidt. 2002. "Can training and employment subsidies combat European unemployment?" *Economic Policy* 35: 411-448.

Korpi, Walter. 1983. *The Democratic Class Struggle*. London Routledge & Kegan Paul.

Korpi, Walter. 1985. "Economic growth and the welfare state: leaky bucket or irrigation system?" *European Sociological Review*, 1(2): 97-118.

Korpi, Walter. 1989. Power, politics, and state autonomy in the development of social citizenship: Social rights during sickness in eighteen OECD countries since 1930 *American sociological review* 54(3): 309-328.

Korpi, Walter. 1998. "The Iceberg of Power below the Surface: A preface to Power Resources Theory," in O'Connor and Olsen(ed.) Power Resource Theory and the Welfare State: A Critical Approach. University of Toronto Press.

Kwon, Hyuk. 2007. "The contents of the 2003 German Dismissal Protection Act (KSchG) amended and its implications for flexible labor market." *Law Studies*. 48 (1): 1325-1348.

Layard, Richard, and Stephen J. Nickell. 2011. *Combatting Unemployment*. Oxford University Press.

Lee, Jong Sun. 2002. "The Neoliberal Economic Restructuring and the Change of Labor Market in South Korea: Paradox of Flexibility." Korean Journal of Sociology 36(3): 25-45. Korean Sociological Association.

Lee, Jong Sun. 2002. DJ government's Restructuring and Labor Market. Seoul: Baeksan Seodang.

Lee, Ho-Geun. 2017. "Youth Unemployment and Employment Policy in Germany." *Korean social policy Review*. 24(3): 85-115.

Lee, Kyu-Yong. 2009. "Comparison of Employment Policies: 1997 Asian Financial Crisis vs. Recent Global Financial Crisis." *Monthly Labor Review* (2009.4): 3-16. Korea Labor Institute.

Lee, Sang-Ho. 2019. *Job Revolution in Germany*. Seoul: Academy of Social Critics.

Lee, Seung-Hyun. 2013. "German Agenda 2010." *International Labor Brief*. 11(4): 50-65, Korea Labor Institute.

Lehmbruch, Gerhard. 1979. "Liberal Corporatism and Party Government", in Philippe C. Schmitter and Gerhard Lehmbruch (eds) *Trends Toward Corporatist Intermediations*. London: SAGE. Pp. 147-83.

LGERI. 2010. *Best Practices for Creating Jobs for the Youth*. LG Economic Research Institute.

Milberg, W. and Ellen Houston. 2005. "The High Road and the Low Road to International Competitiveness: Extending the Neo-Schumpeterian Trade Model Beyond Technology, " *International Review of Applied Economics,* Vol. 19, No. 2, pp. 17-162.

Ministry of Finance and Economy. 1998. "The Promoting Direction of the First Step in Four Sectors' Reform" (1998.4). Seoul: Ministry of Finance and Economy.

Morel, Nathalie, Bruno Palier, and Joakim Palme. 2012. *Towards a Social Investment Welfare State? Ideas, Policies, and Challenges*. The Policy Press.

O'Connor and Olsen. 1998. *Power Resource Theory and the Welfare State: A Critical Approach*. University of Toronto Press.

O'Connor, J. 1973. *The Fiscal Crisis of the State* New York: St. Martin's Press.

Obinger H., Schmitt, C. and Starke, P. 2013. Policy Diffusion and Policy Transfer in Comparative Welfare State Research. *Social Policy & Administration* Vol. 47(1): 111& Admi.

OECD. 1994. *The OECD jobs study*. Paris.

OECD. 2004. Employment protection regulation and labour market performance. In *OECD employment outlook*. Pp. 61-126. Paris.

OECD. 2006. Employment Outlook. Paris.

OECD. 2006. *Employment Outlook*. Paris.

OECD. 2011. *Employment Outlook*. Paris.

OECD. 2012. Employment Outlook. Paris.

OECD. 2013. Coverage and Classification of OECD data for Public Expenditure and Participants in Labour Market Programmes.

OECD. 2015. Employment Outlook. Paris.

Park, Dong. 2006. *Changes in the Korean Labor System and the Politics of Social Pacts*. Seoul: Dongdowon.

Park, Gwi-Cheon. 2016. "Background and Significance of the Enactment of the German Minimum Wage Act." *Labor Law Studies* (40): 201-233.

Peacock, A., and Scott, A. 2000. "The curious attraction of Wagner's law." *Public Choice* 102: 1–17.

Pierson, P. 2000. "Increasing Returns, Path Dependence, and the Study of Politics." *American Political Science Review* Vol. 94(2): 251–267.

Pierson, P. 2011. *The Welfare State over the Very Long Run*. Bremen: Centre for Social Policy Research.

Ram, R. 1986. "Government size and economic growth: A new framework and some evidence from cross-section and time-series data." *American Economic Review* 76: 191–203.

Rinne, Ulf and Klaus F. Zimmermann. 2021. "Another economic miracle? The German labor market and the Great Recession." *IZA Journal of Labor Policy*. Institute for the Study of Labor (IZA). http://www.izajolp.com/content/1/1/3.

Rostow. 1956. "The Take-off Into Self Sustained Growth." *Economic Journal* 66: 25-48.

Rueda, David. 2007. *Social Democracy Inside Out. Partisanship and Labor Market Policy in Industrialized Democracies* Oxford, UK: Oxford University Press.

Scharpf, F. W. 1997. "Balancing sustainability and security in social policy." In OECD (Ed.), *Family, market, and community: Equity and efficiency in social policy* (Social Policy Studies, No.

21; pp. 211-22). Paris: OECD.

Scharpf, F. W. 2010. The asymmetry of European integration, or why the EU cannot be a 'social market economy.' *Socio-Economic Review* 8 (2): 211-250.

Schmid, G. 2008. "Main reforms and achievements in German employment policy." *International Labor Brief* 6(7): 20-30. Korea Labor Institute.

Schmidt, Manfred G. 1992. "Regierungen: Parteipolitische Zusammensetzung." In *Lexikon der Politik, Band 3. Die westlichen Länder,* edited by Manfred G. Schmidt, 393-400. München: C.H. Beck.

Schmitter, Philippe. 1979. "Still the Century of Corporatism?," in Philippe Schmitter and Gerhard Lehbruch (eds.) *Trends Towards Corporatist Intermediation.* NY: Sage.

Scruggs, Lyle, Detlef Jahn, and Kati Kuitto. 2014. "Comparative Welfare Entitlements Data Set 2, Version 2014-03. Codebook."

Seeleib-Kaiser, Martin, and Timo Fleckenstein. 2007. "Discourse, Learning, and Welfare State Change: The Case of German Labour Market Reforms," *Social Policy & Administration* 41, no. 5: 427–48.

Shahidi, F.V. 2015. Welfare Capitalism in Crisis: A Qualitative Comparative Analysis of Labor Market Policy Responses to the Great Recession. Journal of Social Policy (July 2015): 1–28.

Song, Ji-Won. 2015. "The Swedish government's youth unemployment measures included in the 2015 budget." International Labor Brief, August 2015., Korea Labor Institute.

Soskice, D. 1999. Divergent production regimes: Coordinated and uncoordinated market economies in the 1980s and 1990s. In H. Kitschelt, P. Lange, G. Marks, & J. Stephens (Eds.), *Continuity and Change in Contemporary Capitalism* (pp. 101-134). New York: Cambridge University Press.

Spero and Hart. 2003. *The Politics of International Economic Relations*. Thomson/Wadsworth.

Stephens, J. D. 1979. *The Transition from Capitalism to Socialism* London: Macmillan.

Streeck, W. 2011. "The crises of democratic capitalism," *New Left Review* 71: 5-29.

Summers, Larry. 2015. "Persistent jobless growth." In *Outlook on the Global Agenda 2015: Top 10 Trends of 2015*. World Economic Forum. http://reports.weforum.org/outlook-global-agenda-2015/top-10-trends-of-2015/2-persistent-jobless-growth/

Summers, Lawrence H., and Vinod Thomas. 1995. "Recent Lessons of Development." in *International Political Economy: Perspectives on Global Power and Wealth*, 3rd ed., Jeffry A. Frieden and David A. Lake eds. (423-433). New York: St. Martin's.

Swenson, Peter A. 2002. *Capitalists against Markets: The Making of Labor Markets and Welfare States in the United States and Sweden.* Oxford, UK: Oxford University Press.

Taylor-Gooby, P. 2013. *The Double Crisis of the Welfare State and What We Can Do About It.* NY: Palgrave Macmillan.

Taylor-Gooby, Peter. 2004. "New Risks and Social Change," in *New Risks, New Welfare?* ed. P. Taylor-Gooby. Oxford, UK: Oxford University Press.

Torfing, Jacob. 1999. "Workfare with Welfare: Recent Reforms of the Danish Welfare State," *Journal of European Social Policy* 9(1): 5–28.

van Berkel, Rik and Vando Borghi. 2008. Introduction: The Governance of Activation. *Social Policy and Society*, Volume 7(3): 331-340.

Van Ours, J.C. 2004. "The locking-in effect of subsidized jobs." *Journal of Comparative Economics* 32:37–52.

van Vliet, Olaf and Ferry Koster. 2011. Europeanisation and the Political Economy of Active Labour Market Policies *European Union Politics* Vol. 12(2):

van Vliet, Olaf. 2010. Divergence within convergence: Europeanization of social and labour market policies Journal of European Integration Vol. 32(3): 269-290.

Vis, B. 2009. "The importance of socio-economic and political losses and gains in welfare state reform," Journal of European Social Policy 19(5): 395–407.

Visser, Jelle. 2011. THE ICTWSS Database: Database on Institutional Characteristics of Trade Unions, Wage Setting, State Intervention and Social Pacts in 34 countries between 1960 and 2010; Version 3.0. Amsterdam: Amsterdam Institute for Advanced Labour Studies (AIAS).

Wade, Robert. 1992. "East Asia's Economic Success: Conflicting Perspectives, Partial Insights, Shaky Evidence." World Politics 44(2): 270-320.

Wagner, A. 1958. "Three extracts on public finance." In R. A. Musgrave, & A. T. Peacock (eds.), *Classics in the theory of public finance* (1–15). New York, NY: MacMillan.

Wright, E.O. and Joel Rogers. 2010. "High Road Capitalism (Ch.9)," *American Society: How It Really Works*. Norton: W. W. & Company, Inc.

Wu, Shih-Ying, Jenn-Hong Tang, and Eric S. Lin. 2010. "The impact of government expenditure on economic growth: How sensitive to the level of development?" *Journal of Policy Modeling* 32: 804–817.

Yin, R. K. 2008. *Case Study Research: Design and Methods*, California: Sage Publication Inc.

Yoo, Kil-Sang. 2011. *The Introduction and Development of Employment Insurance (EI) in Korea*. Korea Labor Institute.

Yoo, Kil-Sang. 2012. "Proposed Development Programs for the Employment Insurance System from the Perspective of the Transitional Labor Market." *Quarterly Journal of Labor Policy* 12(2): 131-164. Korea Labor Institute.

Yoo, Tae-Geun. 2017. "Job Creation in the Social Service Sector: Policy Issues and Tasks." *Health and Welfare Policy Forum* (2017.9). Korea Institute for Health and Social Affairs.

Zegelmeyer, S. 2010. "Company-level employment relations during the global financial crisis: five illustrative cases from Germany," Proceedings of The Industrial Relations Conference, IREC, Oslo, Norway.

Zimmermann H. 2002. *Money and Security*. Cambridge, UK: Cambridge Univ. Press.

INDEX

(A)

activation 32, 131
active labor market policies 26, 100, 148
Agenda 2010 174
Agreement 252
ALMP expenditures 68, 91, 256
ALMPs 26
analytic method 54
anti-discrimination 273
Anti-Discrimination Act 153
anti-immigration 109
apprenticeship program 135, 142
atypical labor 277
atypical labor rates 59
Ausbildung program 171, 172
autocorrelation 59

(B)

bailout 208
bargaining system 29, 41, 52
bi-polarization 207
bilateral relations 266
Bildt Cabinet 98, 108
Bonoli's typology 84
Bretton Woods system 103
by-polarization 268

(C)

cabinet composition 87, 257
cabinet composition (Schmidt-Index) 89

capital market opening 106
case study 50, 63
causal factors 49
center-right coalitions 106
central bargaining 102
central economic wage negotiations 103
central negotiations 104
central-right coalitions 106
Centre-right Alliance 108
child care 277
classification 29
Co-determination Act 168
collective agreement 273
collective bargaining 269
collective bargaining coverage 57, 58
collective bargaining system 42, 50
Committee for Modern Services in the Labor Market 175
community solidarity 273
Comparative Welfare States Data Set 60
Competition Act 106
competitiveness 73, 102, 267
Comprehensive Unemployment Measures 216
compromise 273
conservatism 61
conservatism market countries 51, 58
continental European market countries 41
convergence 45, 64
convertible part-time 118
coordinated market economies 41, 47, 52
coordinating mechanism 273

coordination of wage-setting　57
corporate tax　114
corporatist arrangements　51, 97
corporatist structure　41, 85
coverage rate　269
cross-sectional data　59
Customized One-Stop Employment Service Program　237

(D)

de-commodification　61, 62
decision-makers　46
decision-making shortcuts　43
democratization　263
dependent variable　86
deregulation　103, 266　273
deregulation measures　106
descriptive statistical analysis　256
descriptive statistics　50
determinant factors　55, 85
devaluation of currency　103
differences　274
digital service economies　53
digital transformation　80, 256
direct job creation　33, 55, 77, 82, 92, 241, 248, 254
direct job creation policy　200
disease allowance　101
Dismissal Protection Act　182, 183
Dispatch Worker Act　178
divergence　64
domestic politics　49
dual labor market　37, 95
dual labor market structure　207
dual vocational training system　189, 198
dummy variables　90

(E)

early childcare　30

Early retirement　164
East Germany　158
Economic and Social Development Tripartite Commission　251
economic crisis　25, 30, 256
economic governance　48
economic growth rate　110
economic ideology　43, 44, 48
Economic Labor Summit　201
economic openness　57, 58, 97
economic restructuring　212
economic situations　28
education contract system　135
employee council　168
employee retention　246, 270
employer organization of big companies　104
employment　25
Employment Adjustment Act　222
Employment Agency　147
employment assistance　34, 45, 81
employment flexibilization　177
employment incentives　33, 55, 73, 95, 150
employment indicators　254
employment insurance　212, 230
employment insurance benefits　178
employment insurance system　226, 251
Employment Office　177
employment probability　78
employment protections　58
employment rates　59
Employment Recovery Project　219
employment retention　251
employment security　125, 227
Employment Service Center　147
employment service delivery system　229
employment stabilization　229
Employment Success Package Program　238, 252
Employment Success Package Project　250
Employment support　131, 178

Employment Support Center   181
emulation   47
endogenous factors   47
equal treatment principles   273
Esping-Anderson   29
EU   48
European Commissio   44
European Employment Strategy   26
European Recovery Program   156
exogenous factors   47
expenditures   28, 48
explanatory variables   57
export-oriented economic structure   97
export-oriented economy   29
external quantitative flexibility   272
Extra Job   147

(F)

family allowance   101, 102
Fast Track   145
Feb·6 Social Pacts   222
Federal Employment Service   163
Federal Labor Administration   164, 165
Federal Labor Agency   181, 200
Federal Labor Service   166
Federal Vocational Training and Training Institute   191
Financial Market Stabilization Act   162
fiscal expansion policy   113
fiscal policy   112
fiscal stimulus measures   112
fixed-effects model   60
flexibility   73, 108
flexibility policy   168
flexibilization   202
flexible working system   165
4th industrial revolution   255
framework agreement   266
frictional unemployment   148

full employment   99
full employment policy   103
functional flexibility   154

(G)

German Trade Union Confederation   202
German unification   157
Germany   29, 63, 92, 155
gig jobs   28
global economic governance   44, 53, 58
globalization   25, 44
government party   50, 58
government subsidies   113
Great Depression   25
Great Recession   25

(H)

Hartz Committee   175
Hartz I Act   177
Hartz II Act   179
Hartz IV Act   185
Hartz labor reforms   166
Hartz Reforms   155, 168, 176, 192, 266, 267
Hausman test   59, 86
high education   30
high road   27, 28, 94
higher education   28, 54, 86, 277
Hope Work Project   233, 241
housing subsidy   101
human capital investment   55
human capital investment or up-skilling   81
human investment   172
hypotheses   51

(I)

idea-based approaches   43
idea-oriented approaches   37
IF Metall   125
IMF economic crisis   70, 205

IMF Agreement 212
immigrant unemployment 144
incentive reinforcement 34, 81
income inequality 59, 254, 276, 277
income tax 104, 114
independent variables 57, 58, 86
individual activation plan 251
individual job-seeking activity plan 238
industrial bargaining 104
industrial restructuring 99, 101
industrial structure 29, 57, 58, 86
industrialization 263
inefficiency hazard 254
inequality 207
inequality structure 206
information technology 48, 86
institutional factors 47
institutional variables 89
Institutionalist approaches 40
institutionalist approaches 37, 43
insurance system 185
Interest-based approaches 38
interest-based approaches 40
internal flexibility 168
internal functional flexibility 272

(J)

Job and Development Guarantee program 131
job creation 27, 255
Job creation measure 185
job creation policies 274
Job Guarantee for Youth 134
job insecurity 277
job instability 94
job matching 274
job matching services 86
job mismatches 189
Job placement 156
job placement assistance 251

job retention 166
job rotation 33
Job Security Council(JSC) 137
job sharing 33, 120, 246, 270
job training 78
Job-AQTIV Act 172
Job-AQTIV law 170
job-creation policy 54
job-matching 28
job-matching services 54, 73
job-sharing 247, 253
job-sharing measures 166
Job-to-Job-Placement Agency 163
joblessness growth 26
joint decision-making system 270
JUMP plus program 171, 170
JUMP program 171

(K)

Kim Dae-Jung administratio 205
knowledge service industry 80
knowledge-based economies 73, 86
Korea 29, 63, 92
Korean Tripartite Commission 212, 214

(L)

labor flexibility 125, 179
labor market education programs 143
labor market flexibility 155, 206, 246, 267
labor market flexibilization 215
labor market instability 254
labor market institutions 67
labor market policy 33, 44, 114
labor market programs 36
labor organizations 104
Labor Relations Act 212
labor unions 46
labor-management co-determination 202
labor-management compromise 169

labor-management relations system   127
Last-in & First-out Principle   141
left parties   52
left party   47, 51, 85, 94
left-wing government   52, 94
left-wing rule   91
leftist parties   88
liberal market countries   42, 51, 58
liberal market economies   41
liberalism   61
liberalization   103
liberalization of capital markets   105
life-long education   36, 54, 86
life-long training   277
livelihood support   251
low consumption   95
low productivity   95
low road   28, 94
low wages   95
low-wage job creation   94
low-interest housing   106
low-skilled labor   95
Low-skilled workers   35

(M)

macroeconomic stability   101
main puzzle   27
managerial dismissals   183
manufacturing-oriented vocational training   80
market openness   87, 89
market-oriented reform measures   106
Marshall Plan,   156
matching program   142
matching services   156
medical insurance   101, 102
Memorandum of Understanding   215
Merkel government   163
metal union (Industrifackct Metall, IF Metall)   104

midi jobs   179
Midi-job system   179
Mini-job system   179
mini-jobs   179
moral hazard   254

(N)

national tax   101
negotiation   47, 273
neo-liberal influence   91
neo-liberal policies   115
neo-liberal structural reform   270
neo-liberalism   45, 53, 58
neoliberal economic ideology   53, 94, 271
neoliberal ideology   90, 257, 258
neoliberal influence   48
neoliberal reform   154, 274
neoliberalism   53
new apprenticeship job model   145
New Employment Program   238
New Start Job   147
New Start Project   252
new start program   115
New-Start Jobs   131
90-day Guarantee for Youth Unemployed   135
non-regular employment   206
non-regular workers   276
Nordic countries   41
Nordic Europe   51
null hypothesis   60

(O)

occupation   34, 81
OECD   48
OECD datasets   50, 60
oil shocks   103
one-person enterprise   179
one-size-fits-all policy   52
open method of coordination   43

orporatist structure   52

(P)

panel data   59
parental leave   118
part-time job   247
part-time work   118, 120, 138
participation   277
Participatory Administration   234
partisan control   29, 47, 50, 52, 85
partisan government control   57
partisan politics   29
passive labor market policies   148
Paternalism   62
pension schemes   102
pension system   101
people's house   152
personal service agency   177
Plus Job   114
policy choices   37, 53
policy consultation   224
policy diffusion theory   37
policymaking   29
political actors   52
political coalitions   52, 85
political compromises   47
political exchange   222
political factors   85
political parties   28
politics of job creation   29, 31
pooled cross-sectional   50
pooled crossectional data   59
power resource theory   37, 38, 39
Preparatory Actions   131
price stability   99
pro-market measures   84
productivity   102
Promote and Demand   173
property tax   114

public and mandatory private spending   56
public childcare   118
public employment services   33, 55, 235, 271
public sector   105
public work   28, 73, 78, 274
public work programs   242
public work projects   252

(Q)

quantitative analysis   28
quantitative and qualitative analysis   49
quantitative flexibility   154

(R)

random-effects model   50, 59, 60
refugee settlement programs   145, 146
Regional Labor Office   193, 200
regression analysis   59, 90
rehabilitation   33
Rehn-Meidner model   39
relocation   248
representation   267
rescue package   164
research puzzle   259
Restructuring Planning Board   219
retirement allowance   33
right-wing coalitions   106
right-wing government   47, 85, 91, 115

(S)

Sabbatical year program   114
Saltsjöbaden Agreement   99, 116
Schröder government   159, 200
self-employment   143
seniority-based wage system   117
service economies   274
service industry   58
short time-based employment incentives   86
short-term work allowance   165

sick pay 102
similarities 274
small state 97
SME Fast-Track Program 221
Social actors 46
social actors' preferences 47
social agreements 126
Social Allowance 185
social bi-polarization 196, 206
social concertation model 276
social consensus model 273
social democracy 61, 273
social democratic countries 62
social democratic market countries 41, 51, 58
Social Democratic Party 101
social democratic system 276
social dialogue 99, 125, 266, 267
social fund system 101
social inclusion 32
social inequality 30, 94, 268
social insurance 273
social interest groups 28
social investment policies 277
social job project 245
social pacts 251, 269
social partnership 190, 266
social polarization 254
social protection 43
social safety net 164, 218, 254
social security 26
social security institutions 99
social security system 32, 202, 222
Social service jobs 246
social trus 154
social welfare system 101
social-democratic strategy 32
social-democratic welfare regime 39
solidarity 106
solidarity wage policy 32, 98, 99, 100, 116
Special Measures for Disabled 131

start-up spending 80
startup incentives 33, 80
STATA statistics program 60
state institutions 47
strategic behavior 47
structural reform 213, 267
subprime mortgage 209
subsidized employment 73, 95
subsidy-type employment policy 153
sustainability 78
sustainable growth 255
Sweden 29, 63, 92, 97
Swedish Confederation of Trade Unions(LO) 145
Swedish economic model 115
Swedish Employers Association(SAF) 101
Swedish Employment Agency 136
Swedish Establishment Reform 146
Swedish model 39, 97, 102
Swedish Social Democratic Party 103
Swedish Trade Union Confederation(LO) 101
Sätchevaden convention 152

(T)

target groups 45
tax system 101
TFD(Teamarbeit für Deutschland) program 170
the 2008 economic crisis 26
the 32-Member Economic and Labor Summit 164
the 4th Industrial Revolution 92
the cabinet composition (Schmidt-Index) 88
the minimum period of unemployment insurance coverage 182
the New Start Job Program 114
the Short-term and Fixed-term Work Act 184
the third way 103
The third-way policy 105
training consultation 251

training spending 71
transitional part-time 119
trend 258
tripartite agreement 224
Tripartite Committee 221
tripartite social pact 125
tripartite social partnership 202
two-stage bargaining model 125

(U)

unemployment 25
unemployment benefit 33, 114, 137, 178, 185, 228
unemployment benefit I 185
unemployment Benefit II 185
unemployment benefit system 182
unemployment crisis 112
unemployment insurance 153
unemployment insurance system 124, 136, 188
unemployment measures 244
unemployment rate 59, 105, 107, 110
union density 29, 90
union density rate 47, 50, 57, 58, 85, 94, 257
union organization rate 87, 89
union participation in management 271
unionism 105
up-skilling 34, 40, 53

(V)

Varieties of Capitalism 41
vocational education 137
Vocational Skills Development Account System 250
vocational training 36, 91, 95, 150, 156, 172, 233, 250, 251, 271
Vocational Training Agreement 171
Vocational Training Bonus Program 191
vocational training program 32, 108, 153
vocational training system 92, 230

vocational training voucher system 178
Volkswagen 169

(W)

wage adjustment 247
wage flexibility 125
wage restraint 101
wage-setting 57
wage-setting coordination 50, 87, 89
wage-setting coordination system 85, 90, 94, 257
welfare regimes 27, 54
welfare state regime types 58
welfare system 80
Welfare to Work 174, 201
Work Experience 133
Work Hours Act 184
work-life balance 118
workers counci 167
workfare 32
working hour account 169
working hour account system 166, 168
working hours 120

(Y)

Youth Employment 235
Youth Employment Service 237
Youth Employment Service Program 239
Youth Guarantee 128, 142, 188
Youth Guarantee Policy 133, 153
Youth Guarantee program 171
Youth Internship 244, 268
youth internship program 235, 242
Youth Program 132
youth unemployment 170, 234
youth unemployment rate 140